STUDIES IN ENGLISH LITERATURES

Herausgegeben von Koray Melikoğlu

Wei H. Kao

The Formation of an Irish Literary Canon in the Mid-Twentieth Century

STUDIES IN ENGLISH LITERATURES

Herausgegeben von Koray Melikoğlu

ISSN 1614-4651

1   *Özden Sözalan*
      The Staged Encounter
      Contemporary Feminism and Women's Drama
      ISBN 3-89821-367-6

2   *Paul Fox (ed.)*
      Decadences
      Morality and Aesthetics in British Literature
      ISBN 3-89821-573-3

3   *Daniel M. Shea*
      James Joyce and the Mythology of Modernism
      ISBN 3-89821-574-1

4   *Paul Fox and Koray Melikoğlu (eds.)*
      Formal Investigations
      Aesthetic Style in Late-Victorian and Edwardian Detective Fiction
      ISBN 978-3-89821-593-0

5   *David Ellis*
      Writing Home
      Black Writing in Britain Since the War
      ISBN 978-3-89821-591-6

6   *Wei H. Kao*
      The Formation of an Irish Literary Canon in the Mid-Twentieth Century
      ISBN 978-3-89821-545-9

FORTHCOMING (MANUSCRIPT WORKING TITLES)

Lance Weldy
Seeking a Felicitous Space
The Dialectics of Women and Frontier Space in *Giants in the Earth*, *Little House on the Prairie*, and *My Antonia*
ISBN 3-89821-535-0

Paola Baseotto
Spenserian Views of Death
ISBN 3-89821-567-9

Melanie Ann Hanson
Decapitation and Disgorgement
The Female Body as Text in Early Modern Drama and Poetry
ISBN 3-89821-605-5

Kevin Cole
Levity's Rainbow
Menippean Poetics in Swift, Fielding, and Sterne
ISBN 3-89821-654-3

Shafquat Towheed
New Readings in the Literature of British India
ISBN 3-89821-673-X

Wei H. Kao

THE FORMATION OF AN IRISH LITERARY CANON IN THE MID-TWENTIETH CENTURY

ibidem-Verlag
Stuttgart

Bibliografische Information der Deutschen Nationalbibliothek
Die Deutsche Nationalbibliothek verzeichnet diese Publikation in der Deutschen Nationalbibliografie; detaillierte bibliografische Daten sind im Internet über http://dnb.d-nb.de abrufbar.

Bibliographic information published by the Deutsche Nationalbibliothek
Die Deutsche Nationalbibliothek lists this publication in the Deutsche Nationalbibliografie; detailed bibliographic data are available in the Internet at http://dnb.d-nb.de.

Cover illustration (River Liffey, Dublin) by the author.

∞

Gedruckt auf alterungsbeständigem, säurefreien Papier
Printed on acid-free paper

ISSN: 1614-4651

ISBN-10: 3-89821-545-8
ISBN-13: 978-3-89821-545-9

© *ibidem*-Verlag
Stuttgart 2007

Alle Rechte vorbehalten

Das Werk einschließlich aller seiner Teile ist urheberrechtlich geschützt. Jede Verwertung außerhalb der engen Grenzen des Urheberrechtsgesetzes ist ohne Zustimmung des Verlages unzulässig und strafbar. Dies gilt insbesondere für Vervielfältigungen, Übersetzungen, Mikroverfilmungen und elektronische Speicherformen sowie die Einspeicherung und Verarbeitung in elektronischen Systemen.

All rights reserved. No part of this publication may be reproduced, stored in or introduced into a retrieval system, or transmitted, in any form, or by any means (electronical, mechanical, photocopying, recording or otherwise) without the prior written permission of the publisher. Any person who does any unauthorized act in relation to this publication may be liable to criminal prosecution and civil claims for damages.

Printed in Germany

Table of Contents

Acknowledgements	ix
Introduction	1
1. The Decolonisation of a "Murder Machine": Education and the Catholic Church in Post-Treaty Ireland	15
1.1. Two Failed Educational Ambitions: The English National System versus St Enda's Revivalism	19
1.2. Catholic Education in Ireland and the Influences of European Teaching Orders	28
1.3. Catholic-Ruled Education in Post-Treaty Ireland: The Reproduction of the English Educational Machinery	34
2. Education and the Formation of the Irish Canon in the Mid-Twentieth Century: Curriculum and Textbooks for Primary and Secondary Schools	47
2.1. The Formation of the Literary Canon and the Making of Irish National Curricula	50
2.2. Inclusions and Exclusions in English and History Syllabi	58
2.3. Formation of a National Literary Canon and Pedagogies for State Examinations	68
2.4. Irish Textbooks in Progress and the Remaking of Anglo-Irishness	76
3. Politics, Literary Canon and Historiography at Dublin's Universities: The Examination Papers of TCD and UCD in the 1930s as Models	85
3.1. Some Common Features in the Departmental Administrations of TCD and UCD	88
3.2. De-Anglicisation within Trinity College Dublin	94
3.3. Moves Towards Decolonisation within University College Dublin	101
3.4. (De)Colonising Examination Papers: Trinity College Dublin	107
3.5. (De)Colonising Examination Papers: University College Dublin	117
4. Practices of the Theory of Canon: Irish Anthologies Revisited	129
4.1. Some Consequences of Canon Formation in Ireland	129

4.2. Inventing Irish Anthologies	137
4.3. Short Story Anthologies in Irish Literary Politics	143

5. Historiography and the Motif of the Rising in Some Irish Short Stories and Novels — 157

5.1. Varying Sentiments in Historical Representations	161
5.2. Fictional History: The Decentralisation of Historical Narratives in Some Short Stories	166
5.3. The Lockup Strike and James Plunkett's *Strumpet City* (1969)	169
5.4. The Easter Rising and Iris Murdoch's *The Red and the Green* (1965)	173
5.5. The Anglo-Irish War and J.G. Farrell's *Troubles* (1970)	177

6. The Awakening of Irish Private Conscience: Mary Lavin, Her Texts, and the Canon — 185

6.1. Repositioning Mary Lavin	189
6.2. Stories in Perspective	196
6.3. Class and Patriarchy in *The House in Clewe Street* (1945)	204

7. Divinity and Humanity: The Heterodox Writings of Kate O'Brien — 213

7.1. *The Land of Spices* (1941): Irish Nationalism, Homosexuality, and Private Conscience	215
7.2. *Mary Lavelle* (1936): Forbidden Desires versus Catholic Teaching	223
7.3. *As Music and Splendour* (1958): Leading towards Lesbian Liberation	227
7.4. *Pray for the Wanderer* (1938): An Irish Artist's Protest	232
7.5. Kate O'Brien: A Cultural and Literary Critic ahead of Her Time	238

Conclusion	247
Bibliography	253
Textbooks and Anthologies	262
Examination Papers of Trinity College, Dublin	264
Examination Papers of University College, Dublin	264

Acknowledgements

I would like to express my most profound thanks to my supervisor, Professor Lyn Innes, for the amount of time, patience, and care she has devoted to me – far more than she should. I am hugely in debt to her not only because of the insightful advice she has generously shared with me, but her extraordinary tolerance at different stages of this book. I am also grateful for her kindness in writing many letters of recommendation to enable me to go on research trips to Ireland – with scholarships from various institutes. The institutes which have provided generous funding include the W.B. Yeats Society in Sligo, the James Joyce Summer School in Dublin, the Kent Institute for Advanced Studies in the Humanities (KIASH), and the School of English Research Committee at the University of Kent in Canterbury. In addition, there are a great number of unnamable librarians to whom I am obliged for their kind assistance in finding first-hand materials from their archives. These librarians were from the British Library, the National Library of Ireland, the libraries of Trinity College Dublin and University College Dublin, the Templeman Library, the Johns Hopkins University Library in Baltimore, and the Purdue University Library at West Lafayette.

I also appreciate the comments and encouragement I have had from other research fellows and colleagues who shared similar interests in Irish studies. They were Prof. Declan Kiberd, Prof. Norman Vance, Dr. Janet Montefiore, Dr. Caroline Rooney, Dr. Eugene McNulty, Dr. Jennifer Ballantine Perera, Dr. Elodie Rousselot, Dr. Christian Li-Ju Tsai, and Dr. Graham Mallaghan, amongst many others. They cheered me up in different ways and on different occasions, "rescuing" me from occasional frustrations with their heartfelt concern and fun time during the four years' research. Other teachers and friends who have given constant support during my overseas stay in Canterbury were Prof. Cecilia Liu and Dr. Belen Sy from Fu-Jen University in Taiwan, Agnes Cheung, and Lu Zou. I am particularly in debt to Andrew and Caroline Way from St Mary Berdin Church for being my "guardian angels" who helped me out on many occasions and invited me to join their family activities. Also thanks to Sherry Lee and Sam Liu in London, and Dr. Stephanie Newell and Basil (the lovely cat!) from Trinity College Dublin, who kindly accommodated and entertained me during my research trips there. I thank John Welford, Koray Melikoğlu, Denise Jackson, Ben Grant, and Danny Flecknoe for their efforts in proofreading the book and giving me valuable comments. John Welford should be acknowledged in particular for his very helpful remarks on my work!

Last but not least, I owe my greatest thanks to my parents and siblings, Chin-roa Kao and Hsin-hwa Hwang, Hui-chuan, and Wei-tzun, who have been most supportive and encouraging to me for as long as I can remember. My parents, in particular, always put aside their own interests for the sake of their children during both the difficult and good times for our family. My special gratitude is extended to Ji-Wen Wu for the most heartfelt friendship I am privileged with. The love, care and friendship I received from all of you during my ups-and-downs seem to me a testimonial of W.B. Yeats' great saying:

> Think where man's glory most begins and ends
> And say my glory was I had such friends.

Introduction

A stranger comes to the city and is immediately impressed with its orderliness and efficiency. He is told that the good order of the municipality has much to do with the firing of a cannon from the castle walls at precisely one o'clock every day. He goes to see the cannon and asks the soldier how he can be sure that it is always precisely one o'clock when he fires. 'Ah', says the soldier, 'each day as I come up here to fire the cannon I pass the jeweller's shop. In the window is a chronometer and beside the chronometer is a sign which says, 'This is the most accurate chronometer in the world.' I set my watch by it and then proceed up here to the walls.' The stranger is impressed, and as he walks back down towards the city he passes the jeweller's shop. Sure enough, there are the chronometer and the sign. 'How', he asks the jeweller, 'can you be sure that your chronometer is the most accurate in the world? 'Well', says the jeweller, 'every day a cannon is fired from the walls of the castle at precisely one o'clock. I check my chronometer against it and it is always right.' So it is with the canon of literature.[1]

The sharp satire in this simple parable shows that a so-called classic canon, as a product of sophistry, can be vulnerable, yet secure at the same time. Its vulnerability lies in the fact that the interdependence between the jeweller and the soldier relies greatly on tacit but somehow fragile human trust. If one of them misses checking the time, chaos may arise. People might wonder what would happen if a war broke out, and one of them, or both, were killed: I assume that the jeweller's descendants would continue his job, and the lord of the city would assign new soldiers to keep his city in order. Time can be reset either by firing the cannon again, or by adjusting the chronometer. However, it should be noted that the jeweller's and the lord's unscientific measures set the daily schedule of people who have no choice but to acknowledge the "agreed" accuracy of the clock.

---

[1] Fintan O'Toole 24. I include O'Toole's comment on this parable, as, although it is not part of the parable, its cynicism is instructive enough: "A piece of literature is great because it is in the canon of great works. It is in the canon of great works because it is great." The sophistry could have no end since the definition of "great" can be vague, so that the classics last without being questioned, particularly in an ideology-bound but unquestioning cultural environment.

Irish Literary Canon

The lord who resides in the castle with the authority of resetting the clock, presumably functioning to maintain social order, may signify here the operator of a literary canon whose formation is inevitably subject to various determinants: aesthetics, politics, economics, education, and so forth. These determinants have varying degrees of impact upon the canon through which the public receives an orthodox impression of society in the past and at present. Although the lord's leading position over the national/social mechanism can be verified through the demonstration of military power, an effective method of showing its authority might be through the promotion of a supporting literary canon. That is, the public, or the ruled, by reading, teaching, and studying the approved canon, might hence internalise the sentiments and perspectives sanctioned by the ruler.

However, canons are not unalterable. A major political upheaval might diversify, or reformulate, a literary canon which was popularised by the former political authority. As John Guillory points out, canons are "the repositories of cultural values." In his view, the canonical values can be decanted, "ritually qualified, subverted, or rejected," alongside the changes of political powers.[2] Bill Readings also claims that canon does not necessarily "contain truth; it makes a demand of exegesis and application, by virtue of its very closure."[3] The "closure" he refers to, on the one hand, defines the canonicity of selected literary texts. On the other hand, it might exclude those texts not readily available for political uses at present. Take "The Irish Mode," for instance, was proposed by Thomas MacDonagh, a 1916 Easter Rising participant, as literature "from, by, of, to and for the Irish people."[4] He proposed it largely to differentiate "Irish literature in English" from British literature with nationalistic sentiments. Although "The Irish Mode" covered widely the literary works written or translated by both Anglo-Irish and Irish writers, only those presenting "the ways of life and the ways of thought of the Irish people" were privileged. Put another way, the "Mode" MacDonagh proposed excluded those Irish-born writers who already had a wide readership overseas but who wrote on topics that were not directly concerned with the affairs of Ireland, such as George Bernard Shaw and Oscar Wilde.[5] The

---

[2] Guillory 488.
[3] Readings 168.
[4] MacDonagh xiv.
[5] Although George Bernard Shaw dealt with the Irish problem and the issue of Home Rule in his *John Bull's Other Island* (1904), most of his plays were set in Britain and primarily for English-speaking audiences. Similarly, that Oscar Wilde produced little apprecia-

Introduction

emergence of "The Irish Mode," though not fully satisfactory to those nationalists who expected an "Irish-Irish" patriotic canon, was still set against the English Classic canon. (The Classic canon had been introduced to Irish pupils via different approaches, such as the English national school system in Ireland.) In general, Ireland in the early twentieth century, owing to political upheaval, had prompted a reformulation not only of a new national identity but also of a literary canon: the former reinforced the making of the latter which served as the supporting discourse for the former. This study will explore how a variety of political, religious and social determinants counterbalanced each other to legitimise a new Irish canon. "Participants" in the making of the Irish canon included members of the Educational Board, university faculties, clerics, textbook editors and anthologists, historians, creative writers, literary critics, politicians, censors, and so on. The different traditions and perspectives they represent complicate the formulation of the canon through which many antagonistic ideologies give shape to the various versions of Irishness.

Arguably, the political turbulence that the Irish people experienced in the early twentieth century was due to the failed quests for a unified national identity, going back for centuries. Militant events, such as the 1916 Easter Rising and the 1919 Anglo-Irish War, reflected the growing impatience of extreme nationalists who expected to put their political aspirations into practice through radical means. The conflicts amongst Irish nationalists themselves, resulting in the Anglo-Irish War, may be seen as the conflicts between different concepts of Irishness. As the sentiments of Irish patriotism had been encouraged through propaganda since the mid-nineteenth century and before, it is understandable that the emergence of a patriotic Irish canon was in view long before the establishment of the Free State. To glorify Irish patriotism, many anthologies – which I will exemplify in this study – had been published in Ireland in increasing numbers since the end of the eighteenth century. In other words, works relating to the independence of Ireland were frequently discussed, reprinted, and anthologised, while other facets of Irish literature, such as romances, travelogues, or creative works written in an experimental method, received much less attention.

---

ble Irishness in his works might be the reason why MacDonagh did not include them in his "Irish Mode." As their works did not exactly feature qualities "from, by, of, to *and for* the Irish people," many Irish writers, like Shaw and Wilde, could hardly fit into MacDonagh's "Irish Mode." Wilde's homosexual behaviour was deemed morally wrong, which prompted him to be left out of both British and Irish canons for quite a long time.

Irish Literary Canon

The making of a new Irish canon with patriotic appeal was certainly not the only proposed literary solution to the Irish Question, given that many critics and writers with diverse political stances were keen to rebuild the (cultural) confidence of the Irish people, while at the same time proposing different kinds of Irishness. The versions of Irishness they formulated, though dissimilar to some extent and perhaps over-idealised, were designed to counteract an unfavourable stereotype conceived by the English towards the Irish. Irish people were either conceived by the English as a feminine race, as Matthew Arnold imputed in his *The Study of Celtic Literature* (1867), or more derogatively as "the missing link between the gorilla and the negro."[6] Some Anglo-Irish cultural nationalists, such as W.B. Yeats and Lady Gregory, taking upon themselves the responsibilities for redressing the misrepresentation of Irishness and revitalising Celtic culture, endeavoured to collect and rewrite Irish folklore. They and their followers also attempted to circulate a sense of heroism by dramatising mythic figures, such as Cú Chulainn and Cathleen Ni Houlihan. The movement of the Irish language revival – promoted by the Gaelic League – was also a key cultural activity in de-Anglicising Irish culture after 1893, although the movement was gradually politicised by the Leaguers who saw the Irish Revival as a necessary step towards political independence. (The politicisation of the Gaelic League prompted its President, Douglas Hyde, to resign in 1915). These conflicting expectations of Irishness on the one hand enriched the discourse of Irish nationalism, but on the other hand, testified to how cultural nationalists had, as Seamus Deane suggests, rendered Irishness "in the manner of Romantic aesthetics," particularly the Irishness proposed by those of "Yeats' Ascendancy."[7] It could be advised that those radical nationalists had their own romantic, or impossible, imagination of the Irish nation: a state free from English cultural influences. To realise their "dream," many of them opted for a militant approach, regardless of the opposition from other nationalists. Eoin MacNeill, a Gaelic Leaguer and the founder of the Irish Volunteers, had attempted to prevent a

---

[6] Quoted in Lebow 40. This study surveys the Irish-related caricatures and cartoons printed in *Punch*.

[7] Deane, *Celtic Revivals* 30. Deane suggests that Yeats' reconstruction of Irish history may not have been persuasive but was nevertheless fascinating, as he approached history "with the fortunes of the Imagination, and therefore, almost indistinguishable from aesthetics." Deane refers to William Black, Samuel Coleridge, Thomas Carlyle, William Morris, and Matthew Arnold, arguing that the Irishness which Yeats romanticised had components similar to the feminine version of Irishness that Arnold characterised in his *The Study of Celtic Literature* (1867).

Introduction

large-scale insurrection after the Easter Rising, for he thought not only that the Rising would not be successful due to the discovery of the German arms by the British, but also that military action would be "morally wrong" without the prospect of success: "to kill any person in carrying out such a course of action is murder."[8] His advice or warning, however, did not have much effect.

What should also be noted is that as the majority of the population in Southern Ireland were Catholics, the remaking of Irishness at the turn of the twentieth century was understandably embroiled with religious elements. The romantic Irishness, which "Yeats' Ascendancy" was keen to invigorate, was no more influential than "Catholic Irishness." The latter was presumably endorsed by the Irish Catholic Church and was promoted more efficiently, through schools operated by Catholic orders. The making of Catholic Irishness was exemplified by Patrick Pearse, who set up St Enda's School in Rathfarnham in 1908. It was a school known both for its Irish-Irish orientation and the strong Catholic ethos on campus. The short life of St Enda's, which was shut down in 1913 for financial reasons, had a strong influence, however, on the education of Post-Treaty Ireland, as its curriculum was written to inculcate "Catholic Irishness." Notably, the compulsory study of the Irish language at primary and secondary schools, and the special position granted to the Catholic Church in the new 1937 Constitution, illustrate how "Catholic Irishness" was promoted through government institutions. What can be criticised about the preference for Catholic Irishness is due to the fact that the "theme of identity saturates the discursive field, drowning out other social and cultural possibilities."[9] Nevertheless, this particular version of Irishness seemingly dominated Irish society after the Free State was founded. The educational and cultural policies were mostly formulated in line with Catholic moral guidance and for de-Anglicising purposes. One consequence in relation to the making of an Irish canon – to be studied by Irish pupils – was that only those works which were not anti-Catholic and which met with nationalistic expectations would be selected by textbook editors. Literary works which did not conform to public taste, religious constraints, and current political ideologies would be rejected by the editors for their lack of canonical elements. The intentional deselection of those works thus resulted in the negative reviews – mostly by traditionalist Catholic critics – of new writing by Mary

---

[8] Quoted in Boyce 164.
[9] Lloyd 3.

Lavin and Kate O'Brien. The unconventionalities of the two women writers and the social context which they criticised will be discussed later in this book.

To demonstrate how the formation of the Irish nation had impacts on the making of an Irish canon, this study will discuss relevant issues at institutional and textual levels. The institutional, as the first three chapters will elaborate, will focus on Irish education from primary to tertiary levels. These three chapters will reveal how the teaching of Irish literature might have significantly de-Anglicised Irish pupils, and how it sought to secure an Irish national identity. The discussion of Irish education will begin in Chapter One by comparing the English national school system with Pearse's St Enda's: the former was introduced to Ireland in 1831 in an attempt to make Irish pupils "happy English child[ren]"; the latter aimed to de-Anglicise pupils by permeating the campus with a strong Catholic ethos, making Irish its official language.[10] Both educational experiments were well supported by cultural discourses, but coming from opposing political viewpoints. What should be noted is that the antagonism between the two educational systems was somewhat mediated by foreign Catholic orders, a growing number of which came to Ireland from the end of the eighteenth century. Many of these foreign orders, particularly those with a French origin, catered for the educational interests of the middle class, while their contributions were rarely documented by Irish or English historians. These foreign orders to some extent maintained their non-Irish tradition at their schools, attracting middle-class parents to send their daughters and sons to them. They became more Gaelicised towards the end of the nineteenth century – under the pressure of local nationalist clerics. Some of the convent schools were even ahead of their time in providing job training for girls, and in encouraging them to pursue a higher level of study in university/college.[11] The existence of these foreign orders and their more liberal education significantly facilitated the liberation of Irishwomen. Chapter One will also discuss the potential reproduction of the English "murder machine" during the Free

---

[10] Quoted in Lyons, *Culture* 9. The idea of making every Irish pupil a "happy English Child" was propounded by the Protestant Archbishop Richard Whately (1787-1863), one of the earliest Commissioners at the English National Board.

[11] However, some foreign orders which catered for male students, such as the Jesuits from Italy and Marist Brothers from France, were deeply Gaelicised, or localised, educating pupils in a way similar to that used at school run by the Christian Brothers of Ireland. Foreign religious orders for Irish girls, on the contrary, were more reluctant to adopt nationalistic or Irish-orientated curricula. I will further elaborate on this point in Chapter One.

Introduction

State period, in that the educational freedom that Pearse pursued did not seem to be fully put into practice. More specifically, the freedom of teaching and study which Pearse endeavoured to rescue from the English "murder machine" did not seem to have outweighed the social expectation of the rapid stabilisation of the Free State. Students were prompted to prepare mechanically for the Leaving Certificate examination, and their parents were unable to question the authorities involved in the provision of a nationalistically inclined education.

Following discussion of the orientation of the Leaving Certificate examinations and a comparison of Irish education during and after the colonial era, Chapter Two will further examine the English and History curricula that the Department of Education approved for primary and secondary education during the mid-twentieth century. The state curriculum, which was introduced in 1938 by Eamon de Valera as the Minister of Education, was used for nearly three decades with only limited revisions. The curriculum, along with a set state exam and an emphasis on the acquisition of the Irish Language, successfully familiarised students with the Irish cultural heritage, but it was objected to for not encouraging pupils to study a second or third European language. This is a kind of curriculum which undoubtedly produced "Irish-Irish" pupils but probably disqualified them from being future participants in international matters. It is also worth noting that the impact of such a curriculum on the making of the Irish canon was that many of the selected authors were Irish patriots, even though their works included in textbooks were not necessarily on nationalistic themes. To name a few of these writers, textbooks edited by James Carey and H.L. Doak during the 1940s and 1950s included works by Theobald Wolfe Tone, Thomas Davis, John Mitchel, Thomas Francis Meagher, Sir William Francis Butler, Stephen Gwynn, and Joseph O'Neill.

On the other hand, the appreciable impact on the teaching of history was that English history, as my survey of the state-approved reading lists in Chapter Two will reveal, was intentionally put second to Irish *political* history. There were limited references to the history of other European countries alongside that of Ireland, while the strong emphasis on Irish history might have benefited the making of Irish-centred historiography, it may have encouraged pupils to adopt a narrow historical perspective, or become insular in their view of world affairs. The reduction of Irish nationalistic elements in the curriculum could only be achieved gradually rather than radically, since its makers had to conform to social expectations rather than personal interests.

To trace how the state curriculum underwent significant changes, and how those changes were effected in the editing of textbooks over the years, this chapter will look into a series of curricula and textbooks published from the 1940s to the 1960s. It was a period in which (southern) Ireland had found its feet and was about to be more open to the outside world.[12] The survey of relevant textbooks and curricula will reveal the changes of social ethos and how decolonial forces became weaker as time went on. This chapter will show that as the 1960s drew to a close, some editors started attempting to reintroduce the "international" tastes of English literature to pupils, regardless of its potential effects of cultural imperialism.

Chapter Three is a further investigation of the way in which the canons were revised in Irish higher education, when the current political authority was replacing the previous one. By reviewing the English and History examination papers used at two prominent Dublin universities in the 1930s – Trinity College Dublin (TCD) and University College Dublin (UCD) – this chapter will show that the process of remaking canons might be more arduous than the shifts of political power, in that the former was subject to a wider range of aesthetic, historical, religious and social factors, and could not simply be de-Anglicised as a result of a political uprising. More specifically, the exclusion of any literary work from the traditional canon could be objected to by certain members of the faculty, and they might endeavour to keep the English Classic canon intact or to subjugate the emerging Anglo-Irish canon to it. Conflicts amongst faculty members in relation to the reformulation of canons and related historiographies were revealed in the making of English and History syllabi, exam papers, and the selection of textbooks. My survey of these educational products in the 1930s will suggest that the research interests of the chairpersons mattered for the results of canon formation during their terms of office, whereas their successors, particularly those with reservation regarding the Anglo-Irish canon, might amend the syllabi to meet the interests of the traditionalist faculty.[13] These curricular amendments, and

---

[12] J. Hally, J.P. Dunleavy, P.J. Diggin, and James Carey were among the editors who had chaired the editing boards over these decades. I will survey the textbooks under their editorship in this chapter.

[13] For example, Robert Donovan, who was a friend of Roger Casement and the chairman of UCD's English department from 1929 to 1936, introduced quite a few nineteenth-century Anglo-Irish writers to students. These writers included Thomas Moore, George Darley, Aubrey de Vere, James Clarence Mangan, Samuel Ferguson, Thomas Davis, Denis MacCarthy, Percy Fitzgerald, William Allingham, Gerald Griffin, William Carleton, and John Mitchel. Arguably, the selection of these writers might be in accor-

Introduction

resistance to them, were common to the English and History departments of both TCD and UCD, as many of the faculty members had an Oxbridge background and, to varying degrees, came to have English perspectives and historiography. On the one hand, they learnt to adjust the curriculum to meet demands for (educational) de-Anglicisation, but, on the other hand, some insisted on teaching the English Classic canon for its assumed universal merits, managing to open the traditional canon up in a discreet manner. To more properly scrutinise whether or not Irish higher education was decolonised effectively, this chapter will also look into the English and History curricula used at Queen's University in Belfast, in order to see whether Irish literature and history were taught differently in Northern Ireland, which remained part of the United Kingdom.

Chapters One to Three might be read as a postcolonial observation of the emergence of an Irish canon at different levels of education. Chapters Four to Six, following the demonstration of the success and failure of educational de-Anglicisation, will draw attention to literary works *per se*, to see why certain choices of themes would be admitted to, or left out of, the canon, and under what circumstances. To address this issue, Chapter Four will start with a survey of a number of Irish anthologies published since the late eighteenth century. Some anthologies aimed to strengthen the patriotic ethos; some included works ridiculing Englishmen in opposition to "stage Irishmen"; some highlighted stories set in the west of Ireland with nostalgic themes, and some portrayed historical events, such as the Easter Rising and the Northern Troubles. This survey will illustrate the changes in the social ethos during the time when these anthologies were made, and how they contributed to the formulation of Ireland as a nation. It could be contended that these Irish-themed anthologies were also made to deconstruct the authority of the English Classic canon, and to secure an Irish-centred cultural discourse. To give proper shape to the favoured cultural discourse, some works were deselected, and some stories were either cut short or amended by the editors, perhaps without the consent of the authors. These approaches

---

dance with (cultural) nationalistic concerns, as they either translated Gaelic poems into English or presented the misery of Irish peasantry; some rewrote Irish myths, and so on. The study of these writers might have benefited the making of an Irish cultural and national identity. There were no Irish women writers introduced on the syllabi he approved. What is noteworthy is that the subsequent chairperson, Jeremiah Hogan, perhaps due to his strong commitment to the traditional English canon, left these Anglo-Irish writers out of the syllabi during his term of office. For more information, see Chapter Three.

to the making of Irish anthologies, and their consequences, will be illuminated in this chapter, along with an investigation of those published in the US by an Irish American, Edward O'Brien, during the 1920s to 1930s. It was a period when the Irish Free State government was finding its feet, but British cultural imperialism was still strong throughout much of the world. Any minor modification in this series of Irish anthologies made overseas might suggest, arguably, how the "keepers" of the English canon learnt to deal with growing decolonial forces and recognise the values of other regional literatures in English.

It might be worth clarifying the reason why the second part of the study focuses on Irish fiction, rather than other genres. It is not because drama and poetry are free from disputable issues relating to canon formation, but because prose writings – which can also produce the same unsettling effects – did not always attract enough attention from readers and critics due to the lack of reprints or wide circulation in Ireland. Some were confiscated by customs officers, if published overseas, before they were dispatched to bookstores. Furthermore, although Irish prose often "represent[s] [. . .] highly diverse and uncooperative" opinions and was considered "to be in a [more] aggressively healthy state," poetry and drama lend themselves better to producing a direct impact on readers and audiences because of the effects of a compact language and form – for being recitable or ideally suitable for political propaganda.[14] In addition, the number of prose writings to be reprinted from editorials, columns, speeches, and letters was always smaller than that of poems, in that the latter could be collected in anthologies and textbooks, and nationalistic drama could be restaged from one theatre to another.[15] The most comprehensive collection of these prose writings might be the *Field Day Anthology*, which was published in 1991, when the twentieth century was almost drawing to its end.

The last two chapters, on Mary Lavin and Kate O'Brien, will demonstrate the way in which Irish women writers were ignored by their male critics, regardless of whether they wrote *seemingly* in support of middle-class values or put the fundamental Catholic teaching into question. Both writers started their writing career in the 1930s, while their works were mostly published outside Ireland and had few reprints in Ireland before the end of the twentieth century. Mary Lavin, whose writing tech-

---

[14] Quoted in Cronin 14-16.

[15] O'Leary, *The Prose Literature of the Gaelic Revival, 1881-1921*. With this book, Philip O'Leary attempted to remedy the current deficiency of Irish literary history in which the named types of prose writing were more neglected than attended to by critics.

Introduction

niques were often criticised for not being as innovative and experimental as those of her Irish male compeers, was in fact a master of literary realism, depicting how Irish women of different social classes strove to survive their patriarchal and hierarchical suppression. She did not write as a feminist but, with a thorough observation of puritanical Ireland, remarked with sympathy upon the weaknesses of both males and females. Her realistic portraits of Irish women's life – observed with feminine sensitivity – should have turned over a new leaf of Irish literary history, but her works were not studied critically in Ireland until the 1970s. Kate O'Brien, whose works were more critical of Irish parochial life, was censored in Ireland for her delineations of homosexual relations. Different from Lavin, she protested more unrelentingly against the insularity of Irish culture, criticising explicitly the cultural policy of the Free State government, as well as the Catholic Church, which had over-dominated Irish society. Writing as a literary critic, she also raised challenging questions relating to the under-representation of women writers in traditional canons, calling for a more serious study of women diarists.

In general, being women writers, Lavin and O'Brien both showed a great concern for the predicaments of Irishwomen in a society strictly dominated by Catholic doctrines. Their attempts to voice the concerns of women in neglected and peripheral communities, such as unmarried mothers, low-paid maids, lesbians, and Irish governesses overseas, understandably contradicted the ideal image that the Church put in place for Irishwomen. What is noteworthy is that Lavin and O'Brien were not necessarily anti-Catholic, but were introducing a more sympathetic and liberal understanding of Catholic teachings. The significance of their intensive portraits of the lives of Irishwomen from the lower to middle classes lies, on the one hand, in their revelation of the hypocrisy of the Irish bourgeois. On the other hand, their works document the facets of women's lives which their male critics might have failed to understand. These reasons directly and indirectly resulted in their being ignored in the traditional male-dominated Irish canon.

Last but not least, I shall admit that, partially owing to limitations of space, I have not been able to elaborate on some factors that have significantly given shape to the Irish canon. One of the factors which should be discussed is media censorship, which was rigorously enacted from 1929 until the 1960s. It was a censorship carried out in line with puritanical Catholic values, deeply influencing the public and private lives of most Irish people. The limited discussion on censorship in this study, however, is not because the author does not recognise its unhealthy effects on Irish society, but because, when compared with education at different levels, censorship was less important owing to the dichotomy it promoted as a literary standard. That is, in the view of the censors, only two kinds of literature were discernable: decent and indecent, moral and immoral. Education, on the contrary, due to its involvement with parents (of different social classes), examining boards, textbook editors, and faculties of various religious persuasions and political interests, produced more sophisticated effects on the making of canons. Consequently, I have chosen to elaborate more on educational factors than on censorship. The last chapter, on Kate O'Brien, will demonstrate the negative consequences borne by Irish readers – referring to her *Pray for the Wanderer* and *The Land of Spices* in particular; the latter was banned for its homosexual subplot.

It should also be pointed out that some of the novels and short stories which are to be studied in the second half of this study were not published in the first few decades of the twentieth century, although this is the period which the first three chapters cover. By reading those novels published after the 1940s, one might be able to observe how the changes of social ethos could affect writers' choices of perspectives in dealing with Irish historical events. James Plunkett's *Strumpet City*, Iris Murdoch's *The Red and the Green*, and J.G. Farrell's *Troubles* are examples which suggest that how history is perceived by readers does not necessarily lie in events *per se*, but in the ways in which writers, including historians, approach them. The works of Lavin and O'Brien examined in this study will illustrate how they experienced the lingering effects of a nationalistic canon formulated under the supervision of the Free State government and the Catholic Church. More specifically, themes which were not in line with the sentiments of Catholic Irishness would hardly be regarded as politically and morally acceptable, regardless of the time when they were dealt with in post-Treaty Ireland. During their lifetime, Lavin and O'Brien, whose writing careers spanned the mid-twentieth century, bore the consequences of Irish canon formation – largely dominated by male critics, nationalists, and the Church.

Through analyses of selected literary texts and their accompanying social contexts, this study intends to dissect how literary canons have been formulated when political and religious ideologies were more influential than other factors. The achievement of writers was therefore judged by standards that were religious and political rather than aesthetic. Although the establishment of the Free State did contribute to the emergence of an Anglo-Irish canon, the fact that Irish culture was an ethnic, denominational and political medley potentially disqualifies any Irish canon for being unrepre-

Introduction

sentative. That is to say, as there is no simple version of Irishness that is able to cover the different aspects of multi-cultural Ireland, it is possible that diverse canons would be formulated to give a voice for specific interested social groups, alongside different political and religious anticipations. Having said this, to seek a "neutral and natural" canon might not be impossible, as there are always exclusions and inclusions of literary works in support of a favoured canon. This study will aim to demonstrate how canon formation is a "battlefield" where, to borrow Gayatri Spivak's words, all sorts of sources of "epistemic violence" are exercising their power.[16]

---

[16] Spivak 154.

1. The Decolonisation of a "Murder Machine": Education and the Catholic Church in Post-Treaty Ireland[17]

In his preface to *After Colonialism: Imperial Histories and Postcolonial Displacements*, Gyan Prakash writes that modern colonialism has operated more subtly, through intellectual activities involving native élites educated in western academies, rather than by military means. These élites formed a dominant class as they restructured the postcolonial state. Prakash also observes that their contribution, if any, was the reinstitution of "enduring hierarchies of [colonial] subjects and knowledges"; they came up with limited innovations with regard to the decolonisation of the new-born state.[18] They, to a relative extent, inherited a colonial mindset with which they learnt to conceive the world as "the Occidental and the Oriental, the civilised and the primitive, the scientific and the superstitious, the developed and the undeveloped."[19] With this colonial mindset, the élites were inclined to privilege themselves as the new, more "civilised" authority over the native people. Interestingly, Frantz Fanon describes the re-adoption of the colonial mindset in similar terms in his *The Wretched of the Earth*. He contends: "In its willful narcissism, the national middle class is easily convinced that it can advantageously replace the middle class of the mother country."[20] For both Prakash and Fanon, the new dominant class became another oppressor who did little to liberate the colonised and instead justified his own superior position in relation to those less educated and advantaged indigenous peoples. The members of the new dominant class endeavoured to claim a singular, national consciousness by introducing new constitutions, rules and programmes, while to some extent they mimicked – with a few novel experiments – the administrative, bureaucratic system that the former coloniser had formulated. Their leading position and own interests were strengthened in the process of national formation, but the concerns of po-

---

[17] The post-Treaty period is taken here and throughout this study to cover the 1920s to 1940s, during which Ireland gained its political independence in 1921 with the signing of the Anglo-Irish Treaty. The Treaty created an Irish Free State of twenty-six counties, and was defined by its Constitution as a dominion of the British Commonwealth. The political affiliation with the former coloniser ended in December, 1948, when J.A. Costello, the former Prime Minister, declared Ireland to be a Republic and to be leaving the Commonwealth.
[18] Prakash 3.
[19] Prakash 3.
[20] Fanon, *Wretched* 120.

litical dissenters and religious minorities, which had existed long before Ireland became independent, were not resolved. Post-Treaty Ireland, in my opinion, illustrates the problems that Prakash and Fanon have addressed. Take, for instance, the predicament of Unionist senators in the Free State. Although their number was sixteen out of thirty in the new Senate, they were often given "a special position [. . .] to watch the work of the dominant Dáil from close quarters."[21] The Dáil was "deliberately intended to be dominant" not only over the Senate but also over the executive government upon which many Protestant Unionists, including W.B. Yeats, as a senator who was concerned about his Anglo-Irish heritage, could have limited influence.[22] The union of the nationalistic government and the Catholic Church turned into a powerful body that constrained dissenting voices through a variety of measures. National education – which this chapter will dwell upon – was one of the methods that attempted to blur those religious, ethnic, political, and cultural divides, or to assimilate them into the mainstream Catholic ethos.

However, Ireland, as the only colony of the British Empire in western Europe, was rather different from other colonies in pursuit of decolonisation. The complexity of the Irish Question lay in the fact that, firstly, Ireland and England, primarily due to their close geographical distance, had shared a long partnership in commerce and agriculture since 1800 under the Act of Union. Secondly, Ireland had been, by the end of the nineteenth century, transformed in many ways into an Anglicised state under the influences of Victorian England. According to F.S.L. Lyons, not only had the economic interests of industrial England flown across the Irish Sea but also "English Fashions in dress and speech, English journalism and advertising, English books and plays, English music-hall, English concert programmes and concert artists, English painting, English sports and pastimes [. . .] grew and flourished in an Ireland which, in the second half of the century especially, seemed little more than a province in the empire of Victorian taste."[23] Moreover, although Irish was still spoken by many Irishmen, English was the common language amongst the majority of the urban Irish and with English people. Thirdly, in politics, there was a severe split amongst Irish parliamentarians at Westminster arguing for or against Home Rule after the fall of Charles Parnell.[24] The fall of Parnell, in one way or another, incurred deep suspicions

---

[21] Lyons, *Ireland* 474.
[22] Lyons, *Ireland* 474.
[23] Lyons, *Culture* 7.
[24] Charles Stewart Parnell was an Irish nationalist parliamentarian at Westminster. He was

1. Education and the Catholic Church in Post-Treaty Ireland

between Irish Catholics and Protestants, and between revolutionary nationalists and home rulers. These factors all directly and indirectly confounded the solution to the Irish Question. Nevertheless, before any political agreement was made to solve the Irish Question, militant Irish nationalists, mainly Irish Volunteers and the Irish Citizen Army, had triggered the Easter Rising in 1916, facilitating the establishment of the Irish Free State in 1922. "[T]he tragic interplay of two emotional forces: nationalism and faith," according to one historian, therefore empowered the new government and the Catholic Church to direct the construction of the Free State in the way they wished.[25] What is noteworthy is that the politicians who were involved with the making of the Free State by and large were members of the élite receiving their education at colonial institutes, or former parliamentarians (at Westminster), or both. They learnt a great deal about English codes and regulations, redefining them in line with their patriotic and Catholic ideals, ignoring the fact that Ireland was a state with a mixture of cultures, denominations, languages, and races. They, to some extent, reproduced a mindset similar to that of the former coloniser in discouraging non-nationalistic interests. Many of the Protestant minority had therefore criticised the imposition of Catholic values upon them through various governmental policies.[26]

It is true to say that the establishment of the Irish Free State in 1922 came with the emergence of a privileged ruling class which could decide by themselves how the country should be (re-)built, according to their nationalistic aspirations. Although Unionists, whether Catholic, Protestant, or Anglo-Irish, could express their opinions in the Senate and other public meetings, they could not always have a decisive impact on the matters that concerned them due to their being a minority in the Executive Council (of the Free State). These native élites, mostly Catholic nationalists, hence contributed to "the only integral Catholic State in the world," legitimising the joint rule of the Church and the government.[27] On the one hand, the élite – who stood by Irish nationalism – reconstructed what Fanon called the "hierarchy of cultures": to

---

elected leader of the Irish Parliamentary Party whose object was Home Rule and the establishment of a separate Irish parliament in Dublin. In 1890, the party split as a result of Parnell's scandal with Katie O'Shea, the wife of Captain William O'Shea who was one of Parnell's party aides.

[25] Blanshard 14.

[26] Johnson 6. The media censorship, for instance, was severely criticised by some Catholic intellectuals and Protestants, but it was not less rigorously enacted until the 1960s.

[27] Quoted in Blanshard 4. It was contended by Dr. James Devane, one of Dublin's noted champions of the Church.

maintain not only the security of the nation but their leading position.[28] On the other hand, they reversed the order of the hierarchy by placing the Gaelic culture, which used to be under the suppression of the English coloniser, at a more dominant level. The strong preference for "Irish Irishness" can be seen from the insistence of the Ministry of Education, though not without criticism, on making the learning of the Gaelic language an obligatory course in primary and secondary education; and the revision of textbooks on literature, history and geography to include more lessons about Ireland or Irish authors.

Although Fanon's concept of a "hierarchy of cultures" initially referred to the *white* coloniser's attempt at making the indigenous culture inferior, it could be argued that Irish cultural nationalists in the ruling class possessed a similar attitude in privileging "Irish Irish" rather than the English version. Nevertheless, the project of re-Gaelicising Ireland could not be deemed entirely successful, as the consequences of Anglicisation had been very far-reaching and could hardly be removed. Specifically, by the 1970s, "[o]utside school, English was [still] the language [students] heard and spoke; it was the language their parents spoke; and the language of newspapers, books and radio."[29] Although the Ministry of Education did try to re-Gaelicise Ireland through education by similar means to those that the English had used to impose Anglicisation, the results were not always as satisfactory as patriotic educationalists expected, in that there were always non-educational factors that hindered "the decolonisation of the mind" – a phrase coined by Ngũgĩ wa Thiong'o.[30] The movement of de-Anglicising Ireland, as this chapter will discuss, cannot be claimed as a definite success.

This chapter will focus on the ways in which education was used as a method to promote privileged cultural and political ideologies before and after the establishment of the Free State. What was similar between the English colonisers and the Irish nationalistic educationalists was that they both thought highly of schooling and its influences on future generations; both structured national education systematically and introduced a common curriculum. The marked difference, however, was the extent to

---

[28] Fanon, "Algeria Unveiled" 41.
[29] Durcan 157.
[30] In Ngũgĩ wa Thiong'o's opinion, the complete decolonisation of the mind is unlikely to happen, as children for centuries have been imbued with Eurocentric perspectives by the coloniser, which makes the decolonising process at the mental level difficult. For details, see his *Decolonising the Mind*.

1. Education and the Catholic Church in Post-Treaty Ireland

which denominational schools were encouraged by the colonial and nationalistic governments; the former provided very limited public funds to them, while the latter were more generous. I will examine in particular the Catholic convent schools run by foreign teaching orders, some of which managed to maintain a non-Irish-nationalistic and non-Anglican education for pupils from the middle class, and were not as deeply Gaelicised as those run by the Irish Christian Brothers. The contributions of these foreign orders to Irish education have often been ignored. I will also compare St Enda's School, which was founded by Patrick Pearse, with the schools under the English national school system and the Catholic system before and after Irish independence. In addition, I will discuss how the Intermediate and Leaving Certificate examinations affected the ways in which knowledge was taught and received, and their contribution to the joint rule of the Church and the government over the Free State. In short, how education was conducted significantly underpinned the formation of a nationalistic canon, since such a canon might incorporate various social and political interests, including aesthetic ones.

1.1. Two Failed Educational Ambitions: the English National School System versus St Enda's Revivalism

Education has always remained an important and effective channel for any political authority to promote favoured ideologies, based on the widely received premise that it is easier to influence young pupils' ideas than adults who have already formed their opinions. Education could also be a method to assimilate those whose religious, political, and cultural backgrounds remained heterodox, as a method to keep the colonial sovereignty integrated. It could be argued that the education that the English colonisers promoted in Ireland since the eighteenth century involved two purposes at least – to resolve the Irish Question and to assimilate the Irish-speaking population. As the passing of the Union of Act in 1800 had legalised English rights over Ireland, education became an essential means to promote a culturally, religiously, and linguistically unified British Empire. Nevertheless, the English national school system, introduced in 1831, never fully succeed in assimilating the Irish-speaking public.

Before this chapter moves on to discuss how post-Treaty education would serve as an instrument in Gaelicising pupils, it is first necessary to understand the political agenda behind the English national school system, and how this system was received in both Ireland and England. This consideration will underpin my later elaboration of the reasons why Irish education in the post-colonial period would be, on the one hand, anti-colonial, while on the other hand it would be as authoritarian as in the colonial era.

It may be observed that the political agenda behind the introduction of the national school system was mainly to have Ireland Anglicised, although this intention was under the guise of bringing culture and civilisation to people of lower classes and in remote regions. One of the noticeable traits of colonial education was that English was the only language to be allowed in classrooms, "even in predominantly Irish-speaking areas."[31] The curriculum taught no Gaelic and had little focus on Irish history and culture. However, for colonial educationalists, it was an education expected to benefit "a fully integrated nation" and "prepare children loyal to the Sovereign, to be obedient to the laws," as an inspector commented in an 1855 report.[32] This underlying intention of Anglicising Ireland through education was more apparent in the fact that educational reports – written by teachers, commissioners, and administrators – were all in English, despite a large percentage of the authors being native Irish. Specifically, they represented the Irish and the English mostly as "us" or "the same," while it could be assumed that not all Irish teachers were Unionists; some might have sympathy for nationalistic causes to some degree.[33] These discordant voices were largely silenced in these official reports – reviewed not only by educational commissioners in England but also by readers (mostly) in the teaching profession in Ireland. Hence, it can be argued that different levels of the national school system, from the making of curriculum to the writing of educational reports, have aimed to address a similar purpose of Anglicisation. In other words, the promotion of the English national school system was to cultivate every Irish pupil into "a happy English child," as the Protestant Archbishop Richard Whately (1787-1863), one of the earliest Commissioners at the National Board, contended.[34]

Although the Anglicisation of Ireland was not solely effected through education but was achieved in various ways, the function of the English national education in Ireland was pivotal, on the grounds that the English government had invested a great deal of money – "long before public money was spent on English education." According to J.M. Goldstrom, it was to keep the colonisers from "los[ing] their purse

---

[31] Coleman, "Representations" 47.
[32] Quoted in Coleman, "Representations" 42. This was included in the report written by the inspector, Patrick J. Keenan.
[33] Coleman, "Representations" 37.
[34] Quoted in Lyons, *Culture* 9.

1. Education and the Catholic Church in Post-Treaty Ireland

strings" of the "hostile population and alien religion" in Ireland.[35] Within two years after 1831, there were almost 800 schools established or brought within the state system with over 100,000 pupils. By 1900, the government had set up 8,674 national schools, admitting 700,000 pupils across Ireland, according to the report of the National Education Board of Ireland.[36] Although government funds did subsidise schools outside the national school system, they were largely for those adopting non-denominational curricula approved by the state. The amount of subsidies, moreover, varied from school to school, and teachers' salaries differed from individual to individual, based upon students' examination results and other criteria. The subsidies were "fairly" distributed according to the number of "passed" students, and how teachers performed their duties under "The Rules and Programme for Secondary Schools," a handbook published annually by the Ministry of Education.[37] If the number of "passed" students was comparatively less than that of other schools, or in the case of teachers being found teaching subjects other than those regulated in these Rules, then such individuals would risk reducing their own salary as well as the school subsidies. On the one hand, this system of fee allocation might ensure the quality of national education, and create competition among schools. On the other hand, it compelled teachers not only to consider materialistic profits but also to encourage students to prepare well for examinations. This tended to stifle creativity in the domains of teaching and learning. However, not only were there many Irish educationalists opposed to such a method of education, but some English scholars had reservations about the way in which the state's education was being run. E.G.A. Holmes, an English educationalist, detailed the consequences of a standardised, national education in 1912 as follows, arguing that it would turn teachers and students into "slaves" of teaching and learning:

> The State, in prescribing a syllabus which was to be followed [. . .] by all the schools in the country [. . .] told [the teacher] in precise detail what he was to do each year in each 'standard', how he was to handle each subject, and how far he was to go in it; what width of ground he was to cover; what amount of knowledge, what degree of accuracy was required for a 'pass.'

---

[35] Goldstrom 52.
[36] Coleman, "Representations" 36.
[37] The scheme of distributing secondary school subsidies according to examination fees was justified under the Intermediate Act of Education, passed in 1878.

[. . .] The teacher who, in response to the deadly pressure of a cast-iron system, has become a creature of habit and routine, cannot carry out his instructions except by making his pupils as helpless and as puppet-like as himself.[38]

Holmes' view of the negative consequences of national education can be applied to the educational *status quo* in both England and Ireland, on the grounds that teachers and pupils in both areas had to conform to teaching manuals produced by the Board of National Education on every subject. The Board also drew up regulations concerning the distribution of subsidies and teaching grants. Under such circumstances, teachers had virtually no freedom in deciding how and what to teach, but were obliged to follow the standard instructions given by the Board, so as to help students passed the Intermediate Examination.[39] The preparation for examinations disciplined both students and teachers to work with "mechanical obedience," and diminished their confidence in questioning authority.[40]

The national school curricula also served to prompt the Irish to identify with the values and perspectives of the English upper class. As E.J.R. Eaglesham observed, the curricula for both Irish and English pupils reflected values "not from Leeds or West Ham but from Eton and Winchester."[41] It would be justifiable to say that the promotion of the culture and interests of the English dominant class since the mid-nineteenth century served to reinforce the imperialistic hierarchy, so that pupils within the British Empire could learn to justify the superiority of colonial values, and serve the ruling class in the future. Only in 1908 did the subject of Irish history become a separate discipline within the curriculum due to increasing demands from Irish nationalists. Prior to this date, "Irish children learned little Irish history, unless individual teachers risked teaching it."[42] It could therefore be assumed that the introduction of the national school system to Ireland represented an act of promoting the values and culture of the English upper-classes. Its success was also consolidated

---

[38] Holmes 103-04.
[39] According to the 1904 Regulations for Secondary Schools, the courses for examination as defined by Sir Robert Morant at the Board of Education, included English Language and Literature, Geography, History, Mathematics, Science, and Housewifery for girls. See Coodson ix.
[40] Holmes 103
[41] Eaglesham 59.
[42] Coleman, "Representations" 45.

1. Education and the Catholic Church in Post-Treaty Ireland

by the intensive interactions in commerce, politics, arts, and journalism between Ireland and England during the course of the nineteenth century.

Some might argue that the English national school system was not necessarily detrimental to Ireland, as it ensured pupils of all denominations were taught at improved, state-funded schools. Although many Catholic traditionalists did express their concern about an insufficient level of religious practices at national schools, the English government still efficiently promoted a non-denominational education with financial advantages, mostly derived from industrial English society at the end of the nineteenth century. It can be therefore deduced that the colonial government, under the influences of the Industrial Revolution, regarded a national school system as an effective method of modernising Ireland. Nevertheless, this agenda along with standardised programmes and rules might work to efface the cultural and ethnic identity of the Irish; in other words, to assimilate the non-English-speaking population within the Empire in the name of modernisation.

The consequences of the Great Irish Famine (1845-1848) also facilitated the promotion of the national school system in Ireland. On the one hand, as the finances of the Irish Catholic Church had not been able to receive adequate support as before from the local merchant class, the Church experienced difficulties in maintaining its network of primary education under such economic recession. On the other hand, as the English government did enhance the facilities of national schools with its ample financial resources, many Irish parents felt prompted to send their children there for better education. Nevertheless, even though the Irish economic situation was deteriorating, the determination of Irish Catholic educationalists to maintain a distinct, denominational education did not diminish. Feeling unsettled about the "Godless" state education, they cooperated with many European teaching orders to provide education exclusively for the Catholic pupils, particularly during Paul Cullen's period of office as archbishop of Dublin (1851–1878).[43] The religious atmosphere at these Catholic schools was presumably more intense than that at national schools, where religious images and instructions were banned, except during the limited times set aside for each denomination.

It is fair to assume that the consistent maintenance of denominational schools in Ireland, even during a period of deteriorating economic circumstances, suggests that

---

[43] I will later name those teaching orders from the European mainland and the years they arrived in Ireland.

Ireland's ethnic, cultural, and political diversities were not easily erasable. It should be also noted that the maintenance of Catholic schools involved more than religious concerns. A sentiment of Irish nationalism always underpinned Catholic educationalists' belief in the necessity of having a separate, religious schooling for Irish pupils. Partially due to nationalistic motives, the demand for a separate education for Irish children's religious, educational, and linguistic interests became more insistent at the turn of the twentieth century, as fundamental nationalists found such education essential in counteracting the ongoing Anglicising influences. Patrick Pearse, for example, founded St Enda's School, or Sgoil Éanna, as an institute that was "distinctively Irish in complexion, bilingual in method, and of a high modern type generally, for Irish Catholic boys," as its 1909 prospectus declared.[44] The significance of St Enda's lies in its aim to meet a marked social expectation for this type of Irish-Irish school to counter English-oriented schools, notwithstanding the support of many unpaid but loyal staff who, at times, were needed to rescue it from financial crises. Notably, its curricular paradigm had lasting effects on education in post-Treaty Ireland.

Pearse was a leading revolutionary, Catholic educationalist, an active member of the Gaelic League, and editor for *An Claidheamh Soluis*, a weekly paper of the League. He established St Enda's to countervail "the examination fetish[ism]" prevalent at schools that adopted the state-approved syllabus on the one hand, as well as to fulfil the goal of the Irish Revival, which was being advocated by Gaelic Leaguers with enthusiasm.[45] St Enda's was fundamentally different from English-dominated schools. For instance, students entering the campus would immediately encounter a nationalist fresco with the motto: "I care not though I were to live but one day and one night, if only my fame and my deeds live after me."[46] This is a statement attributed to Cú Chulainn, a hero of Irish sagas who sacrificed his life out of loyalty to Conchubor, King of Ulster. The teaching of the Gaelic language also had a primary emphasis: "Irish is established as the official language [. . .] and is, as far as possible, the ordinary medium of communication between teachers and pupils."[47] Most subjects were taught bilingually. Irish history, geography, literature, and legends formed an important part of the curriculum and were meant "to instill into the minds of the pupils an intimate and lively love of their fatherland," according to the school pro-

---

[44] Pearse, "Prospectus" 317.
[45] Lyons, *Ireland* 332.
[46] Quoted in Lyons, *Ireland* 332.
[47] Pearse, "Prospectus" 318.

1. Education and the Catholic Church in Post-Treaty Ireland

spectus.[48] These highlighted subjects made St Enda's significantly different from English-orientated schools where Irish pupils were examined and trained to acquaint themselves with English culture and values, not least of which were its historiography and classical literature.

Religious training constituted an essential element of the St Enda's curriculum. As Pearse stressed in 1913 in *An Craobh Ruadh*, a publication for the Belfast Gaelic League, "St Enda's is a Catholic school," and parents were assured that their children would receive proper Catholic and moral training.[49] As a result, pupils were not only required to attend daily mass and receive half an hour of instruction each day for catechism, but the school also opened and closed with formal prayers. This deep-seated and permanent religious atmosphere as developed by Pearse aimed to lead students "towards the awakening of a spirit of patriotism."[50] It also had the intention of making St Enda's "worthy of our fame as the most Irish of Irish schools."[51] It is therefore fair to say that St Enda's, with its explicit emphases placed on Irish language, culture, Catholicism, and patriotism, served as an example for Pearse's successors as nationalistic educationalists. That is to say, most schools in the Irish Free State adopted a similar model of curriculum and textbooks to those Pearse introduced. Details on the textbooks selected and used during post-Treaty Ireland will be further elaborated in the following chapter.

The foundation of St Enda's as an Irish-Irish school realised Pearse's educational aims in redressing the repressive effects of English-orientated schools on Irish pupils. He addressed relevant issues with regard to the suppressive English education in *The Murder Machine*. In this work, he compared the (English) national school system in Ireland to the system of slave education, in that both taught students "to be sleek, to be obsequious, to be dexterous," and "not to be strong and proud and valiant," turning them into "not slaves merely, but very eunuchs, with the smoothness and softness of eunuchs."[52] In particular, he denounced the Intermediate Examination programmes and educational boards, for in his view they "chained the English-Irish educational donkey" to a machine-like system in which "specialists 'grind' them for the English

---

[48] Pearse, "Prospectus" 319.
[49] Pearse, "St Enda's" 345.
[50] Pearse, "Prospectus" 318.
[51] Pearse, "By Way of Comment" 324. This article appeared in *An Macaomh*, which was the school journal of St Enda's.
[52] Pearse, *Murder* 4.

Civil Service and the so-called liberal professions [. . .]."[53] To him, the most beneficial education for Irish pupils should be developed "in God's way, [not] in the Board's way," and cultivate students' "heroic spirit."[54] Nevertheless, in reality this ambitious Irish-Irish educational goal could only be practised in part, since in its later years St Enda's did open courses preparing students for the "machinery" examination, following parents' demand. Faced with the difficulties of finding fully competent teachers to conduct subjects in Gaelic, together with criticisms (principally from Unionists) about the suspiciously over-patriotic agenda of the school, Pearse became more reserved about the result of his bilingual experimentation. In an article for *An Macaomh*, St Enda's school journal, he admitted that a purely Gaelic-speaking school did not really suit the contemporary needs of Ireland, even though he had formerly expected Gaelic to be its official language: "I do not think that a purely Irish-speaking school is a thing to be desired; at all events, a purely Irish speaking secondary or higher school is a thing that is no longer possible."[55]

I would argue that this statement was made with some degree of frustration stemming from Pearse's forced compromise between his ideals and the pressure exerted by parents, who expected St Enda's to open review courses for students to prepare for the Intermediate Examinations, on the grounds that an Intermediate Exam certificate would be an effective means to help to open doors to suitable jobs. In other words, since parents were the major fee-payers to non-state-supported St Enda's, it is likely that Pearse had to respect their opinions and meet their expectations in one way or another. St Enda's bilingualism probably is the result of a compromise which Pearse had been obliged to make long before the school was set up. That is, his idealistic "Gaelic-speaking" school had to be capable of catering for the pragmatic needs of prospective Irish pupils in a society in which English was always the dominant language.

What is also worth noting about the operation of St Enda's was its "modern" curriculum which was built upon the foundation of "the high tradition of Cú Chulainn."[56]

---

[53] Pearse, *Murder* 18. He specified four educational boards which he supposed put Irish pupils in servitude: the Commissioners of National Education, the Commissioners of Intermediate Education, the Commissioners of Education for certain Endowed Schools, and the Department of Agriculture and Technical Instruction.

[54] Pearse, *Murder* 13, 16.

[55] Pearse, "By Way" 324.

[56] Pearse, "By Way" 324.

1. Education and the Catholic Church in Post-Treaty Ireland

The two pursuits of education, however, were contradictory, as there was hardly any common ground on which to accommodate modernisation and tradition at the same time. In the St Enda's prospectus, the school was introduced as "a high modern type," while Pearse had denounced the defects of modern education elsewhere.[57] For instance, in *The Murder Machine*, he argued that modern education would impair students rather than benefit them, as "[i]t should be obvious that the more "modern" an education is the less "sound," for in education "modernism" is as much a heresy as in religion."[58] Although the modern education that Pearse targeted was more likely that being practised in the state's schools, the curriculum of St Enda's was not much different from theirs in reality. The subjects taught at St Enda's were almost the same as those in English-orientated schools, except for the particular subject of "Christian Doctrine." More specifically, common subjects to be taught at St Enda's and English national schools included: history, geography, nature-study, experimental science (chemistry and physics), mathematics (arithmetic, algebra, euclid, and trigonometry), handwriting, drawing, manual instruction, hygiene and first aid, book-keeping, shorthand, typewriting, elocution, vocal and instrumental music, dancing and physical drill.[59] Although the teaching of history, geography, and music was essentially Irish-orientated, pupils could in fact acquire relevant British historiography and relevant knowledge in review courses for exam purposes. It was a curriculum able to match the needs of students who wanted to sit for the Intermediate Examinations for entry to a university first degree programme, or who intended to enter employment following graduation from a university.[60] As the "modern" curriculum stands, it could be argued that St Enda's would have been one of the modern schools that Pearse would have criticised, had he not been its principal. It also seems justified to observe that the formation of St Enda's as a "high modern type" was likely the result of parents' requests, since they, as tuition-fee payers, might not have expected their children to be educated in a provincial manner, but rather under the auspices of a

---

[57] Pearse, "Prospectus" 317.
[58] Pearse, *Murder* 8.
[59] Pearse, "Prospectus" 319.
[60] Under the 1878 Intermediate Education Act there were junior, middle and senior grade Intermediate examinations for secondary-school students. The senior grade certificate would be the most valuable, designed for those who wished to study for a Bachelor's degree, followed by employment in positions that granted access to the higher social ranks. I am grateful to Prof. Norman Vance for this information.

Irish Literary Canon

modern school; the ability to speak Gaelic was as important as serving an English-speaking society. The ideal that Pearse pursued might therefore be understood differently in the eyes of those parents who sent their children to St Enda's.

Although St Enda's only survived for five years, from 1908 to 1913, it had far-reaching effects for the history of Irish education in post-Treaty Ireland, where Catholic nationalists were active in restructuring the nation and its educational apparatus. In the following section of this chapter, I will explain how the Catholic Church produced another educational framework, and in what way and to what degree post-Treaty education was based upon Pearse's educational aspirations. Last but not least, I will discuss how foreign teaching orders subscribed to different pedagogical views with regard to the teaching of pupils from the middle classes and I therefore will compare their schools with those emphasising the Irish-Irish tradition. I will further analyse how "modern" concepts of education were absorbed and practised at different levels of education, particularly for women, through a process that had unsettling effects.

1.2. Catholic Education in Ireland and the Influences of European Teaching Orders

Long before the National School System was introduced to Ireland in 1831, Catholics had developed a strong tradition of running their own schools catering for Catholic children. This tradition became more spirited, particularly after 1782 when the English Penal Laws and an act of the Dublin Parliament annulled the proscription of Catholic teachers. Not only did foreign orders in Europe arrive in Ireland to set up branches in increasing numbers, but some native middle-class Catholics were able to conduct their own charity services. The foundation of the Christian Brothers of Ireland, which later became the principle Catholic teaching order with influences on many aspects of Irish education, was therefore laid in the social context of early nineteenth-century Ireland.[61]

---

[61] In 1802, Edmund Ignatius Rice, a Catholic merchant in Waterford, founded a primary school there and attracted a number of religious brothers to assist. In 1803, a local monastery was built and more people joined it. Soon Waterford became renowned for its Catholic education with an increasing number of voluntary teachers. Similar organisations and schools with support from the Archbishop of Dublin, the Most Rev. Dr. Murray, were later set up in Cork in 1811 and in Dublin in 1812. These organisations, with numerous branches throughout Ireland, contributed to the Christian Brothers of

1. Education and the Catholic Church in Post-Treaty Ireland

It is fair to maintain that the growth of the Christian Brothers in the nineteenth century was a result of Catholic Emancipation during the 1830s and 1840s, as a result of which Catholics could be admitted to Parliament and military offices under a Relief Act in 1782. Although the English government during the same period had invested a great deal of money in setting up non-denominational schools against Catholic ones, the Christian Brothers, with support from the Vatican, still spread through major Irish towns and also to Liverpool and London, and established schools and orphanages in other large population centres in England. In the second half of the nineteenth century, the Christian Brothers became known for missions to Gilbraltar, Africa, India, Australia, New Zealand and the Far East, promoting not only Catholicism but also the standard of monastic education.[62] What is noteworthy is that, apart from the expansion of the Christian Brothers from Ireland to foreign lands in the nineteenth century, there had been a group of male and female European congregations arriving in Ireland during the nineteenth century, setting up monasteries and convents with different traditions from that of the native Christian Brothers. Amongst these foreign congregations, French religious orders in particular pioneered the introduction of a more liberal curriculum and foreign culture to Irish middle-class pupils, shadowing a series of changes at different levels of Irish women's education later at the turn of the twentieth century.

Before this section further discusses the impact that these French religious orders produced on Irish women's education, it is necessary to note that the roles that Irish women were actively encouraged to adopt, under the traditional Christian doctrine, were largely domestic. Education for Irish women, whether under the National or the Catholic school system, diverged distinctly from that for men, in that women were supposed to take a different direction of life from that of males. Notably, in the Catholic Church, as a woman one was strongly admonished not "to parade [one]self before the public gaze in a character so unworthy as a Child of Mary," as Edward

---

Ireland. In 1820, the Christian Brothers became the first Irish male order approved by a charter from Rome. See Slattery.

[62] Nevertheless, it could be argued that the development of the Christian Brothers was not all due to the consequences of Catholic Emancipation but in part to the toleration of the English coloniser, who, in one way or another, might have deemed Catholic congregations useful in cultivating the indigene in the newly-expanded Imperial territories. The Christian Brothers was therefore able to enjoy a prosperity that Irish Catholics in the eighteenth century could hardly have expected under the Penal Law.

McCabe, Archbishop of Dublin, put it in his condemnation of the suffragettes in 1881.[63] John William Burgon, a High Church Anglican priest, was firmly opposed to the idea of equal education for girls and boys: "to educate young women, like young men, [is] a thing inexpedient and immodest."[64] These comments suggest that, before the turn of the twentieth century, both the Anglican and Irish Catholic Churches were satisfied with only teaching "young women to be wise, to love their husbands, to love their children; to be discreet, chaste, sober, having a care of the house, gentle, obedient to their husbands."[65] There were few public careers that were considered suitable for girls by fundamentalist Catholics and Anglicans.

The views held by fundamentalist Anglicans and Irish Catholics towards women's education revealed distinct patriarchal sentiments, while European teaching orders in Ireland were more liberal in the way they educated pupils from the middle class. These orders arrived in Ireland mostly during the mid-nineteenth century, such as the Sacred Heart (1842), the Faithful Companions of Jesus (1844), Sisters of Charity of St Louis (1859), Sisters of St Joseph of Cluny (1860), and the Marists (1873). They joined three other teaching orders that already resided in Ireland: the Dominicans (1644), the Ursulines (1771), and the Loreto (1822).[66] What is worth noting is that, amongst these orders, the Ursulines, the Sacred Heart, and the Faithful Companions of Jesus (FCJ), by the end of the nineteenth century, had "displayed the greatest degree of French influence."[67] The curriculum used at these schools had a somewhat metropolitan outlook. According to Anne V. O'Connor, classes for senior pupils were almost entirely conducted in French, and upon graduation these pupils were virtually bilingual. Their parents, presumably, were most supportive of the European-orientated schooling, since their daughters could have "an advantage for which they would otherwise have had to go abroad."[68]

---

[63] McCabe 263. The open letter appeared first in *Freeman's Journal*, 12 March 1881. McCabe was Archbishop of Dublin from 1879 to 1885.

[64] Quoted in Walsh 76.

[65] Quoted in A.V. O'Connor 36. The next chapter will exemplify how these gender stereotypes were passed on to pupils year after year through school textbooks, and their consequences on the literary canon.

[66] A.V. O'Connor 38. The dates given in brackets show when these European orders arrived in Ireland. The Dominicans and the Marists ran schools for both boys and girls; the native-born Christian Brothers order taught only boys.

[67] A.V. O'Connor 38.

[68] A.V. O'Connor 38. Nevertheless, there were French orders which catered particularly for

1. Education and the Catholic Church in Post-Treaty Ireland

As foreign orders were traditionally not subject to local authorities, these French-orientated convent schools enjoyed greater pedagogical freedom with respect to the construction of the curriculum, unlike those run by the Christian Brothers or the English at national schools. Although these "foreign" convent schools did share similar Christian doctrine with other Catholic schools in Ireland, the former were better able to maintain their own approach to women's education: not leaning towards either a conservative or progressive attitude. More specifically, these European-orientated convent schools disciplined pupils basically in line with Catholic values, but the curriculum for them had an emphasis on vocational skills. This was different from the curriculum commonly used at national schools, which highlighted the skills of "knitting, weaving, and patchwork" for girls.[69]

It could be conjectured that the introduction of vocational training was, on the one hand, due to the French nuns' understanding of the consequences of the Industrial Revolution in mainland Europe; or, on the other hand, to the support of middle-class parents who had benefited from the advance of industrial England. As the Irish Catholic middle class was forming its economic and political power during the period 1880-1890, parents from this social rank then expected their daughters to be more highly educated: not just for domestic roles but for socially profitable purposes. They consequently expected the schools where they sent their daughters to make those subjects, such as Book-keeping, Shorthand, and Typewriting, as available as they were to boys. In addition, since a few Protestant schools in Dublin, Belfast, and Cork had provided practical training for girls, girls' schools unavoidably had to modify their curricula to comply with the needs of middle-class Catholic families. Those convent schools with a French origin were, as a result, able to "insist on the new departures in the face of Episcopal disapproval."[70]

The influence of the Industrial Revolution was also reflected in the way in which girls were educated in French-orientated convent schools. At these schools, pupils

---

the education of the poor, such as the Brigidines, the Presentation Sisters, the Holy Faith order, and so on. They set up day-pension or "pay" schools, in contrast to boarding convent schools for children of the well-to-do. This chapter mainly discusses middle-class Irish women's education run by the French, in that the middle class had greater influences on the changes in education at different levels at the turn of the twentieth century.

[69] Knitting, weaving, and patchwork were three main subjects in reading books for girls, both at Catholic and English national schools.

[70] Cullen 3.

were encouraged to compete for prizes: whether for essay writing, elocution, term examinations, or good conduct, even though this philosophy jarred the nerves of Irish Catholic fundamentalists, for "public opinion in Ireland was originally opposed to examinations for girls."[71] Nevertheless, it could be contended that the modification of the curriculum for Catholic girls in the late nineteenth century was also desirable due to the passage of the Intermediate Act of 1878. Under this Act, the (English) Board of Educational Commissioners distributed financial grants for both girls' and boys' schools on an examination results basis, despite their denominational differences. This Act therefore facilitated some fundamental changes in women's education in Ireland, enabling both girls' and boys' schools to compete on a controversial, but equal, "fees" basis. This Act also provided some basis on which some European convent schools had a different standing from other "Irish-Irish" Catholic schools in late nineteenth century Ireland. That is, by preparing pupils for the Intermediate Exam, some of these convent schools were oriented towards exam results. These European convent schools were, to some extent, tinged with Irish and English characteristics but did not necessarily become an organ for the Celtic Revival. The teaching of French, for instance, was still a highlight of their curricula. It is true to say that some schools, perhaps under pressure from local communities and Irish clerics, indeed offered courses in the Irish language at the turn of the twentieth century, but these courses were often optional rather than compulsory.[72] Pupils could still opt for the acquisition of other European languages.

    These convent schools with a European tradition also played an important role in providing tertiary education for Irish Catholic women, because some of the pupils who passed the Intermediate Examinations then expected to go to a college run by Catholics. Without having a choice, before the Royal University of Ireland was set up in 1879 and admitted girls, some of these pupils had to go on to colleges operated by

---

[71] Luddy 91.

[72] The final chapter on Kate O'Brien will introduce Laurel Hill School in Limerick, as a French-run convent school attended by O'Brien herself during her childhood and adolescence. The Mother Superior for this school, as O'Brien recalled, understood the causes of Irish nationalism but did not deem it was appropriate to have local nationalistic clerics Gaelicise her school, on the grounds that her foreign order was not supposed to be involved with local politics. She grudgingly allowed Irish nuns at her convent to teach the Irish language to pupils, admitting that it was not the mission of her order to open such courses. The teaching of the Irish language was only an optional course at her convent school.

1. Education and the Catholic Church in Post-Treaty Ireland

Protestants, such as the Ladies' Collegiate School in Belfast, the Queen's Institute and Alexandra College in Dublin. Sympathetic towards those who had to attend Protestant colleges, nuns with a foreign origin were active in pleading for the establishment of separate colleges for Irish women students. As Anne V. O'Connor recorded, one of the most active orders in this respect was the Dominican Sisters, which set up the first girls' colleges in Dublin in 1883. The Dominican nuns, however, were not satisfied with their own achievement but kept writing to Dr. William Walsh, the new Catholic archbishop of Dublin appointed in 1885, urging him to set up more colleges for intelligent Catholic Irishwomen.[73]

Foreign teaching orders, such as the Dominicans, did instigate a new phase for Irish women's education, providing a different choice of culture for the middle-class Irish. However, to some extent these orders had to rely on English rules and programmes to differentiate themselves from those schools run by local Catholic orders. Their endeavour in preparing girls for the Intermediate Examination can be seen as an example of this reliance, even though it was deemed to be against the traditional teaching of Irish Catholicism. What is worth noting is that the English rules and programmes with which these foreign orders complied, can be regarded, in the view of Irish nationalists, as suspicious devices that the coloniser created to Anglicise the Irish. In particular, the scheme relating to grant distribution based upon examination results was probably, as mentioned earlier, a promotion of the values of Eton and Winchester, for instance, where the English upper middle class expected to educate their children. To maintain the Catholic ethos that fundamentally distinguished Irish pupils from those at English national schools, nuns at these European-orientated convent schools still managed to place an emphasis on Catholic practices in their curricula. That is, pupils not only studied for the purpose of passing examinations but were also cultivated in a Catholic ethos. It might therefore be appropriate to judge that this was how these foreign orders found a balance between traditional Catholic teachings and the call from the Irish middle class for an improved curriculum for girls.

During the colonial era, these foreign teaching orders were still able to maintain some relative degree of independence in the making of their own curricula, while their independence was largely diminished after Ireland entered the post-Treaty period. These orders, under the joint rule of the Irish Catholic Church and the govern-

---

[73] A.V. O'Connor, 45-46.

ment, had to adopt a common curriculum that was distinctly "Irish Irish" with patriotic sentiments. Few of them were able to maintain a curriculum with a European outlook or conduct classes in languages other than English or Irish. School teaching during the post-Treaty period was almost completely led by examination, which standardised what pupils should learn and how teachers should teach. The next section of this chapter will illustrate how the educational authorities adopted a similar mindset to that of the former coloniser in recreating a Gaelicised "murder machine" for national education.

1.3. Catholic-Ruled Education in Post-Treaty Ireland: The Reproduction of the English Educational Machinery

The partition of Ireland in 1922 was a significant watershed in Irish history. Many Catholic nationalists, though by no means all, had to accept that it was the *faute de mieux* solution to the Irish Question. As for education, it was a "territory" over which Catholic nationalists were keen to reclaim their sovereignty. As education had been known to be an essential device with regard to the creation of national consciousness, the Department of Education, with Eoin MacNeill as its minister (he was also the founder of the Gaelic League), soon took over the functions of the (English) Commissioners of National Education in Ireland (C.N.E.I.). What was passed on from the C.N.E.I to the new Department of Education, however, was not simply a directorship for national education, but an educational system, programmes and rules that the former coloniser had made ready and practised for years in Ireland. Specifically, the ready-made system and programmes were accompanied by a domineering attitude with which the state assumed itself responsible for the decolonisation of education nationwide. Very few pupils could be spared the study of the Irish language, even though they and their parents had been protesting against this language imposition for decades.

Although the new educational board did make a number of slight modifications to the inherited educational system to comply with the movement of Gaelicisation, the system *per se* was problematic, as it was originally that with which the former coloniser used to assimilate the Irish, namely the system of upper-class cultural values. One of the notable examples of the inherent problems inherited by the post-Treaty educational authorities was the emphasis on patriotic and Irish-Irish sentiments in the revision of history textbooks; the idea of unionism was little acknowledged, even though it had been formerly proposed as a solution to the Irish Question. The making

1. Education and the Catholic Church in Post-Treaty Ireland

of the curriculum also acknowledged a few opinions from "parents and other potential educational interest groups" but the government acted mainly on the advice of the Christian Brothers between 1922 and 1962.[74] It is true to say that the whole educational apparatus of the Free State was mainly controlled by the nationalistic government and Catholic Church with the common aim of producing a unified, national(istic) consciousness against "foreign influences." Most importantly, the union of the Catholic Church and the government underpinned the way in which the literary canon should be conceived. This section will explore how these two powerful bodies paved the way for this unified, national consciousness built on the foundation of the educational legacy left by the former coloniser.

That the passage of educational authority and policies from the C.N.E.I. to the Department of Education could proceed smoothly should be attributed to the fact that the values inherent in many of the C.N.E.I. programmes had actually been acknowledged by the Irish middle or upper middle classes before Ireland became a Free State. As the Irish middle class had been the major economic force in society, it is understandable that their desire for a more stable society would be recognised by the new government, on the grounds that no party could benefit from a troubled country. On the one hand, as the Easter Rising of 1916 and the Anglo-Irish War had produced tremendous disturbances in Ireland, it is reasonable that the public also expected that social order would soon be restored. On the other hand, since the former coloniser had already introduced many effective and systematic programmes and rules that did comply with the interests of the middle class, the new government did not therefore bother to remake them but adopted what had been made already. Education, which was one of the infrastructures that the English government had maintained with consistent programmes, was soon taken over by the Department of Education as the new authority. Nevertheless, as the national education system in Ireland had formerly been aiming to make every pupil "a happy English child" at an elementary level of education, along with an examination programme for secondary-school students – which Patrick Pearse denounced as a "murder machine" – it is possible that a similar educational hierarchy was produced in its stead that provided the educational institutions with a powerful authority by which to imbue pupils with nationalistic sentiments.[75]

---

[74] O'Donoghue 2.
[75] Quoted in Lyons, *Culture* 9.

It might be appropriate to say that the smooth transference of Irish educational authorities from the C.N.E.I. to the Department of Education should also be attributed to the hierarchal nature of Christianity with regard to "Apostolic Succession."[76] For Irish Catholicism, as its doctrine and clerical system contained distinct hierarchical elements, the joint rule of the Catholic Church and the Free State government would therefore act on those elements to direct how government policies should be made. As for education, since the Catholic Church claims to be the sole body through which the salvation of souls could become possible, and was highly experienced in Catholic schooling for centuries, the Free State soon recognised it as the most appropriate establishment for de-Anglicising Irish education. The Irish Catholic Church was therefore authorised to take a leading role in national education not only for decolonising purposes but also for religious aims. With endorsement from the government, and *vice versa*, the Church became an almost insuperable voice in directing the course of many Irish domestic affairs.

In the matter of education, the Church, as an establishment responsible for the salvation of souls and the decolonisation of Ireland with governmental endorsement, would consequently assume itself accountable for the (re-)making of educational policies, and the revision of a national curriculum and textbooks. For fundamentalist Catholic nationalists, the newly-retrieved responsibility was almost like a "second coming" for the Irish Catholic Church, in that many Catholics had regarded themselves as suppressed by the Protestants in the previous colonial era – in one way or another. As the majority of the Irish in the Free State were Catholics, it was entirely justifiable for the Church to view itself as the representative of its people, no matter whether it was granted a "special position" in the 1937 Constitution.[77]

Although the Catholic clergy did not have any official position in the government, its influence was significant. The Christian Brothers, for instance, were "consulted

---

[76] The doctrine of "Apostolic Succession" legitimises the authority that the Catholic Church exercises over its followers. Through the "Apostolic Succession," Peter, traditionally the first Pope, was given authority, through Jesus, from God. He was to pass God's instructions down to the bishops, who were then authorised to do the same for the clergy, and then down to the people. That is also how hierarchy implies authority.

[77] The "special position" of the Roman Catholic Church was formally recognised in the new Constitution of 1937. However, the influence of the Catholic Church had been strong since the establishment of the Free State in 1922. The recognition of its special position was now likely to double, confirming its legitimacy in directing domestic affairs. Not until 1972 was this article removed.

1. Education and the Catholic Church in Post-Treaty Ireland

directly by the Irish Department of Education" and given the task of revising textbooks for Irish Catholics.[78] It became the most influential educational body supervising the way in which knowledge was passed on to pupils. Notwithstanding this, a large percentage of schools were put under Catholic management during the Free State period. Compared with Irish parents during the colonial era – who could choose *not* to send children to Catholic schools but to English non-denominational national schools instead – parents in post-Treaty Ireland could only send their children to Catholic ones.[79] Deliberately sending children to non-Catholic schools, no matter whether "primary or secondary or continuation or university," was, according to Dr. John Charles McQuaid, Archbishop of Dublin from 1940 to 1972, a "mortal sin," and parents would be "unworthy to receive the sacraments."[80]

That the Church could maintain its strong position in educational matters was also due to the state's generous financial support, of which the former colonial government had never given enough. According to Thomas A. O'Donoghue, who compared Catholic education in Ireland and other countries in the mid-twentieth century, Ireland was one of the very few countries in the world in which its government devoted a large amount of funds to church schools; in the Soviet Union, no religious orders were allowed to operate schools; in the United States and many other countries, church schools received no direct aid from the government and maintained their financial independence.[81] Despite the fact that state funds were also made available to non-Catholic schools, it could not be denied that Catholic schools were the major recipients due to their overwhelming number in Ireland. By the 1930s, "the Church's hold over the control of the schools was secure."[82] Arguably, the Irish Catholic Church was never so privileged in manipulating the state's education.

The teaching order which received the largest financial benefit from the state was, understandably, the Christian Brothers, which had been an organ for Irish nationalism and "virtually synonymous with the Gaelic Ireland ideal" since the colonial era.[83]

---

[78] O'Donoghue 3.
[79] According to a survey in 1984, of the 3,500 national schools in the Republic of Ireland, 3,400 were under Catholic management. The remaining 100 were managed by the Protestant Churches, including Church of Ireland, Presbyterian, and Methodist. See Inglis 59.
[80] Quoted in Whyte 306.
[81] O'Donoghue 2.
[82] O'Donoghue 43.
[83] O'Donoghue 116.

With the state grants, the Christian Brothers in the Free State period developed to its full potential by setting up more primary and secondary schools, and teacher training colleges, in Ireland. However, some of the training colleges operated by foreign orders, such as Mary Immaculate College in Limerick, run by the French Oblates of Mary Immaculate (O.M.I.), and St. Patrick's Teacher Training College at Carysfort, run by the Presentation Sisters, were shut down in 1943 due to lack of funding.[84]

The dominant position of the Catholic Church in educational matters could also be seen from its rejection of the proposal from lay teachers of joint responsibility for schools between laity and clergy. To hold public schools securely under the Church's control was "the only format ever acceptable by either the secular clergy or by members of religious orders or congregations."[85] What is more noteworthy is that lay teachers at Catholic schools, unlike people in other professions, could expect to receive a salary but not a pension.[86] This discouraged lay teachers from entering the teaching profession thus enabling the clergy to remain dominant in school administration and teaching practices in classrooms, as monks and nuns need neither salaries nor pensions. The number of lay teachers was also reduced through several other measures endorsed by the government and the Church. For instance, lay women teachers were obliged to retire at marriage, as the Church expected them to be mothers and wives fully devoted to their families, rather than working women. In 1934, the state even decided that only those graduating from state-recognised training colleges within the Free State could be qualified to teach; those with teaching certificates from training colleges in the United Kingdom, including Northern Ireland, could no longer be hired by schools in the Free State. Those who wanted to be teachers could only choose training colleges run by either the Christian Brothers or the De La Salle Brothers – both were recognised and funded by the state.[87] That is to say, the training of teachers, at this point, was strictly under the joint supervision of the Catholic Church and the state. It might be appropriate to say that the restriction put on teachers from non-Catholic training colleges was to prevent them from instilling unorthodox influences into the minds of pupils.

In the early part of this section it was mentioned that the Irish educational authorities shared a similar domineering attitude with that of the former coloniser in direct-

---

[84] O'Donoghue 133.
[85] Titley 5.
[86] Titley 115.
[87] O'Donoghue 133.

1. Education and the Catholic Church in Post-Treaty Ireland

ing national education, and to a large extent relied on the programmes and rules that the English had exercised in Ireland. This point could be further explored by scrutinising the school system, national curricula, and the state examination system during the Free State period, as they were major channels through which Catholic nationalists promoted selected political and religious sentiments. After the establishment of the Free State, schools originally under the English national school system mostly came under the management of diocesan Catholic authorities, except for those run by Anglicans, Presbyterians, and Methodists. There were a few non-denominational schools, but they were strictly under the supervision of the Catholic Church. In general, Irish primary and secondary education was not just to de-Anglicise pupils, but more importantly, to "recruit candidates for the religious life."[88] The success in enticing pupils to join the religious ranks can be seen from the satisfaction that the clergy explicitly expressed with regard to the increasing number of postulants. In an address given by the Reverend Aubrey Gwynn, S.J., to St. Joseph's Young Priests' Society in Dublin in 1937, there was "an amazing harvest of vocations in Ireland. Young boys [were] clamouring for an opportunity to become priests."[89] In 1940, Bishop O'Brien of Kerry also attributed the large number of vocations in his diocese to the "God-fearing [lay]men and women teachers."[90] All this suggests that pupils – having the lowest rank within the hierarchy of church schools – would learn to be submissive to religious authorities: not only within seminaries but also in life outside school. The maintenance of the religious ethos and the reproduction of the clerical hierarchy on campus would therefore, in the view of the Church, reinforce the loyalty of the Catholic laity in the future, even if pupils did not choose a religious career.

The strong influences of the joint rule of the government and the Catholic Church on education can also be seen in the promotion of a national curriculum between 1934 and 1971. Within this period, nearly all primary and secondary schools, "great and small, urban and rural," followed a common curriculum designed by the Department of Education (with advice from the Christian Brothers).[91] There were very few schools able to maintain a European-tinged curriculum, similar to that operated by foreign teaching orders in Ireland before the establishment of the Free State. The

---

[88] Titley 145.

[89] Quoted in Titley 145.

[90] Quoted in Titley 145. From the transcribed sermon of Bishop O'Brien of Kerry at Killarney in 1940.

[91] Coolahan, *Irish Education* 43.

promotion of a common curriculum was, on the one hand, to enable pupils to have a standard guideline when preparing for Intermediate and Leaving Certificate examinations. On the other hand, it was also to facilitate the movement of Gaelicisation on a national scale, as cultural nationalists wished. In this national curriculum, not only was the study of the Irish language made compulsory but there was also a distinct Irish emphasis in the teaching of history, music, and geography. As for the obligatory study of Irish, it incurred a certain amount of criticism from both students and parents who did not feel it worthwhile to study a dying language in a society whose dominant language is English; it would help them little in future business dealings with the outside world. For British Protestants who resided in Ireland and regarded themselves as members of religious minorities, the compulsory study of Irish was seen as "a discriminatory measure" against them.[92] Nevertheless, the educational authorities never loosened their grip over this issue, despite their awareness that there was an insufficient number of teachers competent in the language.[93]

It is true to say that the ideology behind the obligatory learning of Irish lies in the strong nationalistic sentiments lingering from the colonial period into post-Treaty Ireland. Thomas Derrig, Minister of Education from 1932 to 1939, claimed that to enable pupils to speak Irish was to "foster a patriotic and Gaelic outlook."[94] In the name of patriotism few Irish pupils were therefore spared studying the language. What is necessary to note is that the cultural nationalists' ambition of Gaelicising Ireland was indeed expedited under the joint rule of the Catholic Church and the state, and substantially affected the operation of foreign teaching orders in Ireland. Take, for example, the French teaching order, the Oblates of Mary Immaculate (O.M.I.), which came to Ireland in 1856. Perhaps to maintain a mutual relationship with and receive support from the local authorities, it became a firm instrument in echoing the Irish nationalists' call for the revival of the Irish language and the promotion of related activities. This French order, under the supervision of the Department of Educa-

---

[92] Quoted in Coolahan, *Irish Education* 76. For details, see *Irish Times*, 8 Nov. 1926; *Times Educational Supplement*, 27 Nov. 1927.

[93] Coolahan, *Irish Education* 76. In the 1920s and the 1930s, as the number of qualified teachers was not enough to meet the high demand of schools to teach Irish as a compulsory subject, the government arranged summer courses every year to improve current teachers' competence in both written and spoken Irish. From 1926 an examination in oral Irish became a requirement for being a secondary teacher.

[94] Quoted in Coolahan, *Irish Education* 42.

1. Education and the Catholic Church in Post-Treaty Ireland

tion, did publish a significant number of manuals for the teaching of Irish with Irish patriotic sentiments. Father D.A. Collier, O.M.I., the author of one of the manuals, *Irish Without Worry for Everyone*, was a strong advocate of making Irish a widely spoken language for patriotic reasons. What is striking is that he actually represented an order with a French tradition. He contended in the preface to *Irish Without Worry for Everyone* that "To ask the Irish nation to take a referendum as to whether we should allow the language to live or to die is akin to asking the nation to commit national suicide. As the soul gives life and vigour to the body, so does the language give life and self-respect to the nation."[95]

It might be appropriate to conjecture that Father D.A. Collier was one of the Irish clergy of the O.M.I., and his statement above shows that this French order did have difficulties in counteracting the dominant influence of the Irish Catholic Church and the nationalistic government. Against the background of the increasing number of the Irish clergy in foreign orders like the O.M.I., and given the objective to facilitate their missions in Ireland, it is understandable that the clergy of the O.M.I. would involve themselves with the local, secular campaign for Gaelicising Ireland, so as to make the order vernacular, rather than "foreign." Notably, the O.M.I., amongst other foreign orders in Ireland, was no less fervent than the native Christian Brothers in the "important crusade" of promoting the Irish language, because it would "knit the people together as a nation" and "serve as a practical stronghold against outside influences," as Father Collier stated in his manual.[96] It could hence be claimed that this French order had allied itself to Irish patriots in the matter of de-Anglicising Ireland, and was deeply involved in secular politics.

The other controversy about the national curriculum, apart from the patriotic agenda of Gaelicisation, concerned its distinct Victorian characteristics that were dominant in English national schools in the first half of the twentieth century and were copied in Irish schools from the Free State period until the early 1980s. It was the kind of curriculum that the English revised in the 1940s to suit the needs of the modern welfare state. According to John Devitt, the curriculum – which was masterminded by Eamon de Valera in 1939 as Minister of Education and used for three decades – was "a monument to an essentially Victorian sensibility."[97] D.H. Akenson made a similar comment, contending that De Valera's curriculum was "quintessen-

---

[95] Collier vii.
[96] Collier vii.
[97] Devitt 106.

tially Victorian" and "resembl[ed] that of the English public schools of the mid-Victorian period," in that it highlighted "hyper-academic" subjects: not just English and Irish but also Latin and Greek.[98] What is worth attending to is that the curriculum, as introduced by De Valera, "focus[ed] on theoretical lessons rather than practical or experimental experiences."[99] The "theoretical lessons," in fact, referred to the study of Classical subjects that were the highlights of Victorian education. It is therefore justifiable to contend that the national curriculum was a creation devised by the Irish élite who thought in line with the traditional values of the "mother country," even though in politics nationalists had created a radical divide between themselves and their coloniser. This Victorian-orientated curriculum – which was implemented during those crucial decades when many western European countries were transforming and modernising – did not lead the Irish to a less parochial state, but showed that the authorities were concerned about the possible materialistic effects on pupils in modern education.

However, although the re-making of a curriculum with Victorian elements might have illustrated that its proponent, De Valera, was a product "of his own Classical secondary education" and a "prisoner to his own teaching experience," it was actually an artefact favoured by the Catholic Church.[100] This was largely because the Victorian-style curriculum, which put more emphasis on Classical subjects than on practical/vocational training, corresponded to the ideal of education justified by fundamentalist Catholics. For them, vocational training might incur "deviat[ion] from the central moral aims of schooling."[101] Moreover, since the Catholic Church had traditionally seen schools as a medium for recruiting postulants, as I have discussed earlier, a curriculum which highlighted its practicability might have seemed to them a breeding ground for materialistic attitudes. Such attitudes would possibly divert pupils' attention away from the vocation, and in the long run, the Church might lose its control over the future dominant class. The Church's strong concern with the way in which pupils were educated can be seen from a statement from a Jesuit priest, quoted by E.B. Titley, about appropriate education for Irish pupils: "[a] suitable and thorough education for this body manifestly lies at the very bedrock of Ireland's moral, intellectual

---

[98] Harman Akenson 1, 76.
[99] O'Donoghue 93.
[100] O'Donoghue 93.
[101] O'Donoghue 100.

1. Education and the Catholic Church in Post-Treaty Ireland

and material well-being. If they are sound, the country is safe."[102] I would argue that here the term "material well-being" refers to, in the view of a priest, not the enrichment of materialistic life, but the attainment of basic human needs for laymen. Besides, to keep pupils in line with religious morality was always the essential end of Catholic schooling, as the priest's statement suggests.

The English programme that was reintroduced to the Free State, as well as the Victorian-orientated curriculum, including the examination system, was of little benefit to pupils, on the grounds that they had to learn largely by rote in order to pass the Intermediate and Leaving Certificates examinations.[103] Although the notorious scheme for paying teachers according to examination results, along with the State Examination system, was abolished in 1922 by Eoin MacNeill, a founding member of the Gaelic League and Minister of Education, the exam pressure on pupils was never taken away but increased to its full during the Free State period. From the early 1920s to the 1960s, Irish secondary schools single-mindedly aimed to prepare students for the two state exams, because the Certificates guaranteed access to secure employment such as in banks, the civil service, county council offices or insurance firms.[104] Students with high marks would be granted scholarships to universities where they could look forward to a promising future as doctors, dentists, lawyers, engineers, and so on. In other words, passing these exams with good marks would make it easier for students and their families, particularly those from the lower levels of the social hierarchy, to rise to higher, more financially secure, positions. However, as the curriculum that every school had to follow was Victorian in nature, with an emphasis on Classical studies, and pupils had to study by rote for many subjects, they did not learn to develop their creativity, or other more sophisticated cognitive skills.

I would argue that the examination system which dominated the way Irish pupils acquired knowledge was in fact akin to the English "murder machine" – described by Pearse when referring to the defects of colonial education – on the grounds that

---

[102] Titley 153.

[103] The Leaving Certificate Examination, established in 1924, is the final examination in the Irish secondary school system, to be taken by students in the seventeen to nineteen age bracket. It was the former senior grade of the Intermediate Examinations. The (Junior) Intermediate Examination was replaced by the Junior Certificate Examination in 1992, and to be taken in a secondary school student's third year and not before age fourteen. Those who want/ed to pursue a college or university degree were/are required to study for the Leaving Certificate two to three years after completion of the Junior Certificate.

[104] O'Donoghue 87.

learning and teaching were very much standardised and pupils were given little freedom to develop their own independent consciousness. Although the examination system was, in one way or another, tinted with some degree of Irishness – with an increasing number of topics on Irish history and geography – the system did not actually come up fully to Pearse's ideal of Irish education. What resulted from the device of examinations, in my observation, was perhaps the compelling of pupils to learn the Irish language attentively, while studying other subjects by rote, thus greatly depriving the system of the freedom that Pearse had pleaded for as follows:

> The first thing I plead for [. . .] is freedom: freedom for each school to shape its own programme [. . .] freedom again for the individual teacher to impart something of his own personality to his work, to bring his own peculiar gifts to the service of his pupils, to be, in short, a teacher, a master, one having an intimate and permanent relationship with his pupils, and not a mere part of the educational machine.[105]

Obviously, neither schools nor individual teachers had "freedom" in choosing what and how to teach. Teachers became merely "transmitters of knowledge," but hardly mentors, counsellors, or guides for young students. What is more noteworthy is that religious training at schools – of which the Catholic Church always thought highly – did not really moderate the pressure on pupils who had no choice but to manage to survive in this educational "murder machine" akin to the system of the former coloniser. The teaching of Catholic doctrine was mainly through catechism. In the 1960s, the Church even spent a great deal of money and time on devising books and tapes for catechism at schools. Pupils were required to pray at the routine times and occasions the clergy specified: the beginning of each day, lessons, sodalities, missions, retreats and so on.[106] They were disciplined at school under the supervision of the state and the Church, in that religion was stipulated as "the most important [. . .] of all the parts of a school curriculum," as the Rule for National Schools stated.[107] There was little freedom for them to acquire latitudinarian ideas, as liberal Catholics in other European countries might do.

---

[105] Pearse, *Murder* 15.
[106] Inglis 58.
[107] Quoted in Murphy 155.

1. Education and the Catholic Church in Post-Treaty Ireland

In conclusion, I would contend that due to the rigorous control of education by the overpowering union of the Irish Catholic Church and the government, many Irish people did not learn to question authority but were presented with a fixed set of religious and secular instructions. It is also true to say that Irish educationists during the Free State period did not really contribute to the decolonisation of the country but, to a relevant extent, reinforced the inviolable directorship that the former coloniser had transmitted into their rules and programmes. However, the adoption of these ready-made programmes might have benefited most those members of the élites who had identified their inherent values and perspectives, for it was this privileged group that orchestrated that movement lower down the social scale in which rank amongst the political and economic hierarchy was decided. That is to say, they formed a new class of rulers with the same attitudes or prejudices as the former coloniser. Philip G. Altbach has made a similar observation on postcolonial education, as it was often built "on the ruins of traditional colonial empire" and implied "a new, subtler, but perhaps equally influential, kind of [neo-]colonialism."[108]

The advantage to the reintroduction of the coloniser's programmes, rules, and mindset that could not be denied was that it at least helped to stabilise a once turbulent society and rebuild it systematically on an already formed foundation, although in education it was at the expense of teachers' autonomy and pupils' creativity and talents. In order to see how the English and Irish "murder machines" were run and resisted, and to determine their influences on Irish literary canons, the next chapters will compare and analyse textbooks used at primary and secondary levels before and after the establishment of the Free State, as well as examination papers used in university classrooms, as a method for exploring how political ideologies and religious sentiments confronted or cooperated with each other in the making of literary canons.

---

[108] Altbach 452.

2. Education and the Formation of the Irish Canon in the Mid-Twentieth Century: Curricula and Textbooks for Primary and Secondary Schools

The establishment of the Irish Free State in 1922 was a watershed in Irish history, as it led to profound changes in various aspects of the Irish nation in the following decades. One of the major consequences in politics was that the Free State, with the support of Roman Catholics, who constituted most of its population, became "the only integral Catholic state in the world," as James Devane, one of Dublin's noted champions of the Church, acclaimed it in 1952.[109] Prior to the time that Devane made this statement, the Irish Catholic Church and the secular government had formed a privileged, church-state alliance – legitimised in the 1937 Irish Constitution. It was a Constitution that not only granted the Roman Catholic Church a "special position" in domestic matters in Ireland, but also secured for it a favoured discourse in the creation of an independent nation.[110] Moreover, as the Free State government was fundamentally a nationalistic entity, aiming to de-Anglicise Ireland, the government's efforts in creating a distinctive national identity – different from that given by the former coloniser – were widely supported. The establishment of Irish as the first official language of the state, for instance, was one of the approaches through which the nationalistic government attempted to formulate a separate national discourse against that of its English-speaking neighbour, in spite of the fact that English had been, and still was, a virtually dominant language in Ireland. As the Free State was by and large created to fulfil Catholic nationalists' aspirations for what they imagined would be an ideal Ireland, the birth of the Irish Free State was hence a result of political confron-

---

[109] Quoted in Blanshard 4. James Devane's comment appeared in the *Irish Rosary*, Dec. 1952. A survey which was done in 1971 shows that over 90 per cent of the population in Southern Ireland were Catholic. It can be assumed that when James Devane made his comments in 1952, the percentage of Catholic population was not less than this figure. See O'Donoghue 2.

[110] Media censorship, for instance, can be seen as a product of this church-state alliance, endorsed by the Constitution. Article Forty of the Constitution provided the grounds for censors to prohibit "the radio, the press, the cinema" from "criticis[ing] Government policy" and "undermin[ing] public order or morality or the authority of the State." The text and relevant amendments of the Constitution are available on the official website of the Irish government: <http://www.taoiseach.gov.ie/upload/publications/297.htm>, 4 Apr. 2004.

tation with Britain, and mixed with cultural, social and religious appeals, in the hope of decolonising and liberating Ireland from the influences of Britain/England.

For Irish cultural nationalists, the decolonisation of Ireland could only move towards complete facilitation when Irish culture, arts, literature and language were revived on a national scale. They endeavoured to call people's attention to the decline of the Irish language and customs, arguing that the foundation of "a separate nationality" for "the world's recognition" was laid on the Irish cultural heritage, as Douglas Hyde had stated in "The Necessity for De-Anglicising Ireland" in 1892.[111] Headed by Hyde himself, a group of cultural nationalists, including Eoin MacNeill, Patrick Hogan and Thomas O'Neill Russell, established the Gaelic League in Dublin in 1893 as a non-sectarian and non-political body, to promote the Irish language and relevant cultural activities. Although in 1915 Hyde resigned from his post as President for being unable to maintain the League as a broad cultural movement free from political involvement, most Leaguers still identified with his petition for reviving the Irish language through education. Its branches – more than six hundred in number – continued to offer Irish-language classes and social gatherings where Irish dancing and music were encouraged. What is worth attention is that the educational policy of the new state was deeply influenced by Gaelic League ideas; curricula and textbooks were remade to include distinctive Irish components, as a method of ensuring the de-Anglicisation of Ireland from the primary to the higher levels of education.

It could be argued that the emphasis on education as the means for creating an Irish (cultural) identity suggests that such an identity – which nationalists endeavoured to recreate – was not something given, and could be acquired through repetitive learning in schools. Irish nationalists might not have considered that the identity that they strove to *re*-create might have never existed as a fixed ideal, since the Irish population *per se* was a mixture of peoples arriving at the Emerald Isle from the Continent at different times. Some were from the Mediterranean, some from northern Europe, some from the Iberian peninsula, and some from Scotland and England. (In recent years, some have come from Eastern Europe and Africa as refugees.) The cultures they brought to Ireland were always in progress towards further integration. That Irish people acquainted themselves with English manners and language might testify to the inevitability of cultural coalescence, and not necessarily have been an act of "imitation," as Hyde generalised in his speech on the consequences of Anglici-

---

[111] Hyde 527.

2. Curricula and Textbooks for Primary and Secondary Schools

sation.¹¹² My point is that, by suggesting the influences of the Gaelic League on post-Treaty Ireland, Irish nationalists might have over-emphasised education as the agent for the creation of an exclusive national and cultural identity, which actually circumscribed Irish culture, preventing it from absorbing metropolitan elements from the mainland. They might have ignored the fact that one's attempt to learn the best of English or European culture could be one's personal choice and did not mean that one ceased to be Irish. However, as the Department of Education of the Free State had largely taken in the ideology of the Gaelic League, requiring all pupils in the regime to learn Irish but not necessarily a second European language, the movement towards inter-culturalism slowed down in the Free State period; there was no personal choice as to join the campaign for Irish language revival or not. It could therefore be argued that as pupils had to sit for relevant tests in Irish to pass the Leaving Certificate examinations, the sense of Irishness they "retrieved" was constructed more through paper examinations or in the classroom, than given in an Irish-speaking environment. (English was/is still the dominant language in Irish society.) In other words, the state examination aimed to "standardise" the sense of Irishness that the nationalistic authorities expected, but failed to help diversify Irish culture within a broader European framework.

This chapter will draw attention to the making of national curricula and textbooks used during those formative years in which the Irish Free State attempted to de-Anglicise itself, following on from the discussion of the similarities and differences between the English national school system and Pearse's experimentation at St Enda's in the preceding chapter. My interest in primary and secondary education stems from the fact that it served as a platform on which various social forces collaborated or competed against each other in seeking to interpret what Irishness was/is. By studying the choices of lessons in textbooks and the amendments in curricula, this chapter will explore how the notion of Irishness changed over the years and how it was a gendered product under the influences of Catholic teaching. I will attempt, apart from specifying those texts/textbooks illustrating Irishness, to examine related

---

¹¹² In his article, Hyde observed that Irish people had maintained themselves in an "illogical position" by which "they hate the country which at every hand's turn they rush to imitate" (527). However, Hyde might not have realised that it was the British misrule of Ireland that irritated some Irish people, rather than English culture *per se*. That Irish people chose to "adopt English habits" might be because they recognised their merits and did not all hasten to judge their English neighbour from nationalistic points of view.

Irish Literary Canon

educational factors that contributed to the formation of the literary canon(s), as well as the relevant pedagogy by which teachers imbued pupils with a standardised perception of their new Irish nation. I will also compare the history and literature curricula used at primary and secondary schools in Southern Ireland with those used in the North under the English educational system, to demonstrate how education could be bound to different ideologies and sentiments.[113] This chapter will, by examining examples of textbooks with strong patriotic and religious elements, illuminate how Irish post-Treaty education carried a more rigid cultural and social ideology, and did not free the Irish psyche from political determinants.

2.1. The Formation of the Literary Canon and the Making of Irish National Curricula

Before this section discusses how Irish curricula underpinned the formulation of literary canons, it is important to note that a curriculum can be seen as a package of selected subjects that "organise our comprehension of the world around us," as Kenneth Milne defined in his article "A Curriculum for Irish Education" in 1970.[114] It was also a package of selected moral, cultural, and political values that pupils had to familiarise themselves with before they left school and started their working lives. For curriculum makers, curricula were not only designed to prepare pupils for life, but to enable them to appreciate society's "cultural, technical and artistic achievement" by "transmitting knowledge and skills from generation to generation."[115] For the Irish educational and religious authorities, a state-approved curriculum, to some extent, was intended to standardise the way in which pupils saw themselves as social and religious beings, in case of "a deterioration in the quality of life, [. . .] or a falling away from the Christian standard of conduct between citizens."[116] It is hence safe to say that the duty of curriculum makers was seen to provide not only relevant knowledge

---

[113] In Chapter One, I have mentioned that the curricula – approved by Eamon de Valera as Minister of Education in 1939 and used until the 1970s – had been criticised for their outdated Victorian characteristics and sentiments. It was the curricula that justified the grounds on which traditionalist educators emphasised the study of classical subjects, rather than science.

[114] Milne 33.

[115] Milne 36.

[116] Milne 37.

2. Curricula and Textbooks for Primary and Secondary Schools

and training for future members of society, but identical moral and cultural groundings on which the security of a nation could be maintained.

Milne's elaboration of the meaning of the curriculum and its related functions, interestingly, was akin to the definitions of canon that many critics had presented and argued for in the 1980s. According to John Guillory, canons are like "the repositories of cultural values, [. . .] the selection of texts is [therefore] the selection of values."[117] Charles Altieri also defines "canon" similarly as "ideological constructs."[118] The "repositories," in Guillory's view, functioned to accommodate elements that appeared to be socially acceptable, including existing aesthetic and ethical standards. Those critics who defend the existence of a traditional canon believe that the canon "incarnates transcendental values or truths" and secures "a collective identity" of a people.[119] However, for the assailants of the traditional canon, such as Douwe Fokkeman, it is no more than "an arbitrary solution to a social coordination problem where there is more than one possible equilibrium."[120] Critics who accept Fokkeman's point would therefore be reluctant to identify a canon which "serves as an adequate basis for a common (literary) culture."[121] Those who hold more radical views than Fokkeman would be even less likely to acknowledge the value of any canons, not only because of their incomplete portrayal of a diversified society, but because aesthetically, "literary values" seem to them "an illusion or an arbitrary construction."[122] In other words, a traditional canon, in the eyes of these critics, is likely to re-inscribe idealised, aesthetic criteria which are illusionary *per se*, even though they are widely accepted by the mainstream public.

I do not intend to argue for, or against, any of these standpoints regarding the value of canons, because any judgements might be, to different degrees, influenced by one's biases. For instance, an Irish nationalistic critic might be disinclined to acknowledge the intrinsic excellence of the classic English canon, preferring the formulation of an "Irish-Irish" canon in which the voices of Irish people could be brought to light. Traditionalist English critics might be more reserved in acknowledging the strengths of other regional literatures in English; say those produced by

---

[117] Guillory 488.
[118] Quoted in Readings 151.
[119] Readings 149.
[120] Quoted in Livingston 146.
[121] Livingston 146.
[122] Livingston 147.

writers of an Irish, Australian, Indian, Canadian, or Nigerian origin. It could hence be contended that any decision made in support of the canonisation of certain texts, or the highlighting of particular subjects in curricula, is likely to be dominated by current ideologies. The ideologies – which are usually endorsed by religious and political authorities and internalised by the people – would therefore legitimatise canons, or curricula, for assumed cultural interests. That is to say, the decisions which were made to ratify or revise a canon are in fact subject to a number of extrinsic factors, such as ethnocentrism, whether or not critics or readers were aware of their own prejudices. Having said this, I do argue with Paisley Livingston that no canon is clear of subjective human decisions, as "none [. . .] is ever rational."[123] Canons should therefore not be relied upon to solve either "basic literary problems that we face" or more profound ones in politics.[124]

Some critics who have held more liberal attitudes towards the remaking of canons have suggested that the coexistence of canons – which cater for differently interested groups – should be encouraged, as few canons can fully satisfy readers with various backgrounds. More specifically, as "a canon is context-bounded," these critics would be unlikely to oppose "a canon of a reading-club, a canon of a literary magazine, an academic canon or a school canon," believing that different social groups or literary circuits deserve a canon addressing their particular interests.[125] Differently from those who are sceptical of the values of any canon, these liberal critics more quickly accept the pluralisation of canons which "leads to a specification as well as to a broadening of the canon concept."[126] Their generosity in acknowledging the merits of different canons, on the one hand, shows that canonisation is subject to a series of acts of exclusion and inclusion. Take the canon of a juvenile reading club for instance. What is often excluded is the material that adults identify as unsuitable or too sophisticated for the underaged, while the former might underestimate the intelligence of the latter. What is included therefore are those items with homogeneous elements – sanctioned by parents, teachers, and "juvenile specialists." On the other hand, the recognition of a variety of canons – within one broader social context – suggests that a canon does not necessarily present an absolute truth but a selection of knowledge and opinions favoured by a specific group of people. What is notable is that the mak-

---

[123] Livingston, 149.
[124] Livingston 149.
[125] Jozien Moerbeek, "Canons in Context" 187.
[126] Moerbeek 187.

2. Curricula and Textbooks for Primary and Secondary Schools

ing of a canon, even that of juvenile or children's literature, can be subject to overpowering political and religious factors in an attempt to produce either "a happy English child" or a devoted Irish Catholic pupil.[127] Textbooks were consequently made to meet these political and religious appeals; the state examination was set to confirm whether pupils had acquired knowledge and opinions that reached the accepted "standards."

This elaboration on the different shades of opinion regarding the formulation of canons may serve as the theoretical foundation on which the following investigation of Irish national curricula can develop. The association between a canon and a national curriculum stems from the fact that a more effective method than state education to circulate a favoured canon and its relevant values is unlikely to exist. In other words, there was no better medium than the state education structure through which social élites could promote their preferred ideologies and deconstruct those they identified as unfit for Catholic Ireland. The study of a series of national curricula should provide a clearer picture of how Irish canons are restructured along with significant social changes.

In the case of mid-twentieth century Ireland, according to the survey carried out in 1969 by the Organisation for Economic Cooperation and Development (OECD), an international consultant body to which the Irish government resorted for advice on the improvement of its national education, Irish pupils had spent far too much time on the learning of the Irish language and classical subjects, and religious practices.[128] The foreign surveyors then speculated that this educational deficiency, directly and indirectly, thwarted Ireland's economic growth in general, compared to other European countries. By examining the average weekly timetable at Irish primary schools from the 1940s to the 1970s, the surveyors more specifically pointed out that pupils spent 10 hours weekly in acquiring languages (Irish and English), and 2.5 hours in religious practices, out of 22.5 hours of their total school time.[129] Nevertheless, before these investigators published their figures, John MacNamara, an Irish educational psychologist, had demonstrated a similar point in 1966 in his *Bilingualism and Pri-*

---

[127] Quoted in Lyons, *Culture* 9.

[128] This educational deficiency was in fact pointed out by some Irish educationalists, long before the foreign OECD conducted this survey. For more information, see *Reviews of National Policies for Education: Ireland* in the textbooks and anthologies section of the bibliography.

[129] *Reviews* 35. There were 5 hours for mathematics, and another 5 hours for other subjects.

mary Education. According to his estimate, 42% of pupils' school time in the 1970s was devoted to the study of the Irish language, 22% to English, and 24% to arithmetic, not regarding 2.5 hours allowed for religious instruction every week.[130] The two surveys seem to suggest that if Irish pupils could have spent more time on science subjects – as at those English schools whose curricula I will discuss later – Ireland by the 1980s might have been established as more than a country mainly dependent on agriculture, and have acquired more advanced industries.

It could be argued that the value of the Irish language and religious practices in schools was to reconstruct and circulate a sense of Catholic Irishness amongst Irish pupils, as Catholic nationalists expected; the required study of Irish might be seen as a backlash against the former colonial education system. The primary school curriculum, according to the OECD's report, was modified to a large extent from 1932 onwards for use in British and Northern Irish schools, whereas the Department of Education of the Free State had adopted it in the 1920s without making significant changes and used it until the 1970s. More specifically, as pupils in Northern Ireland were spared from the required study of Irish and time devoted to religious practices, their curricula were more flexible in accommodating a greater number of optional courses: from handwork, nature study, elementary science, algebra, geometry, horticulture, French, Irish and Latin, to physical science (including light and magnetism). Apparently, Irish was only one of the optional courses (for pupils in the fifth grade) amongst these subjects.[131] However, curricula for Southern Irish pupils, although also classical to some degree, were dominated by compulsory subjects: religion, Irish, English, arithmetic, history, geography, music and (for girls) needlework. In general, Southern Irish pupils, compared with those in the North, had fewer opportunities to learn science subjects and were confined to *rural* science or nature study, even until the 1970s. Other science subjects were either unavailable or were non-compulsory. Thomas Joseph Durcan, who had surveyed primary school curricula used in southern and Northern Ireland between the early 1930s and the 1970s, therefore claimed that those circulated in the North did "show clearly the important place given to practical subjects."[132] What is noteworthy is that the Free State allowed women teachers not to teach algebra and geometry, so that girl pupils – taught mostly by women at convent

---

[130] MacNamara 132.

[131] A more detailed discussion on the curricula for primary school pupils in Northern Ireland since 1932 can be found in Durcan 175-89.

[132] Durcan 180.

2. Curricula and Textbooks for Primary and Secondary Schools

schools – could presumably have more time for the acquirement of cookery, laundry work, and/or domestic economy.[133] Notably, the curricula distributed in the Free State were distinctly more Irish-orientated and gendered, compared to those applied in the North, where pupils did not have to study Irish and boys could be taught needlework, according to the new programme coming into force in 1932 for British primary schools.[134]

The promotion of the acquisition of Irish and the insufficient teaching of science subjects were also features of the curricula for secondary schools in the Free State. The emphasis on the study of Irish, rather than other continental languages, was specified by the OECD's advisors as a hindrance for Ireland on her way to becoming a more active participant in the European Economic Community.[135] Irish pupils' incompetence in European languages was revealed through the Leaving Certificate examinations. For instance, amongst 24,556 pupils who sat for the Leaving Certificate exam in 1963, only 165 boys were awarded honours for French, 16 for Spanish, 6 for German and 1 for Italian, but 88.3% of boy students sat for the examination in Latin, despite Irish being an obligatory subject.[136] Although the lack of qualified teachers might be the cause of a limited number of pupils studying a second European language, the fact that pupils had spent so much time learning Irish and that they might not be encouraged to learn more languages should be noted. Pupils' incompetence in continental languages, consequently, resulted in the insularity of Irish culture in the mid-twentieth century. It could be pointed out that, as pupils learnt to conceive the world largely through English, Irish and/or Latin, they could not freely absorb viewpoints through other European languages. As English remains the major language in Irish society, Irish people were, to a large extent, still subject to English-centred perspectives which were not necessarily more accommodating to cultures other than Irish ones.

---

[133] *Reviews* 35.
[134] Durcan 181.
[135] *Reviews* 41.
[136] *Reviews* 41, 49, 55. The reason why the majority of Irish pupils would sit for the examination in Latin was largely that it was the language taught and used frequently during their daily religious practices at school. In addition, the Mass was always said in Latin in the days before Vatican II. It was the language Irish pupils were most familiar with, aside from Irish and English.

The lack of balance between traditional humanities and science subjects in Irish secondary education was noted not only by foreign advisors from the OECD but also by local educationalists in the 1970s, when the Irish economy had remained stagnant in comparison with other European countries. The report, *Investment in Ireland*, written by Irish surveyors appointed by the Minister of Education in 1965, indicated that secondary school pupils devoted less than 10% of their school time to physics and biology, whereas about half their time was assigned to traditional subjects.[137] Some students could pass the Intermediate Certificate examination with a high mark without studying much science at school. What is notable is that Irish pupils in the 1970s, unlike those in post-industrial English society who might opt for subjects of study out of vocational considerations, whatever their sex, were still confined to society's gender expectations. That is, there was a greater number of both boy and girl students taking examinations in geography (boys 80.9%; girls 89.1%), History (boys 64.3%; girls 73.1%), and Latin (boys 88.3%; girls 38.3%); while the number of pupils taking science examinations was contrastingly low: Physiology and Hygiene (boys 1.0%; girls 41.8%), Physics (boys 28.8%; girls 2%), Chemistry (boys 31.7%; girls 4.8%), physics and science (boys 7.2%; girls 4.7%).[138]

It could be argued that the number of female pupils taking science was low not because they were not interested in, or capable of, scientific studies, but because Irish society traditionally expected girls to be more serviceable in the domestic sphere, rather than at workplaces. More specifically, as Catholic/Christian teaching used to encourage Irish women to model themselves after "Our Lady" as a virgin and devoted mother, girls' future roles were confined to the family context.[139] They were not particularly encouraged to compete for "professional" careers but to behave as "angels in the house." It is true to say that this patriarchal ethos was strongly maintained through the 1938 Irish Constitution masterminded by Eamon de Valera, who was not only a "product of his own Classical secondary education under the Intermediate Education system" but a fundamentalist Catholic. To quote from the Constitution he introduced: "The State shall [. . .] ensure that mothers shall not be obliged by economic necessity to engage in labour to the neglect of their duties in the home."[140]

---

[137] *Investment in Education* 276. See the textbooks and anthologies section of the bibliography

[138] *Investment* 276.

[139] A.V. O'Connor 36.

[140] Constitution of Ireland, <http://www.taoiseach.gov.ie/upload/publications/297.htm>, 4

2. Curricula and Textbooks for Primary and Secondary Schools

Girls were consequently channelled to a domestic arena, instead of a more competitive world where more vocational knowledge and skills were required. In addition, as post-Treaty education had acquired many Victorian characteristics lingering from the nineteenth century through the English national school system, as demonstrated in Chapter One, the Victorian ideal of women's service and devotion to men remained in force, restricting women from having a wider range of job choices.[141] These factors might have been the cause of the low number of Irish boys taking physiology and hygiene, since the two subjects seemed more suited for girls.

My discussion of Irish boys' and girls' different leanings in their choices of school subjects suggests that women in Ireland had been encouraged to take up more domestic roles through education, whereas men were expected to be breadwinners in a society not only dominated by fundamental Catholic doctrines but stricken by the effects of the economic recession because of World War One. In addition, the state textbooks – which I will investigate later in this chapter – did not feature women pursuing vocational opportunities but the achievements of male politicians and historical figures. Notably, that the Irish canon was largely dominated by male writers was probably the consequence of the unequal gender status between Irishmen and women. Only a very limited number of women were able to develop careers as writers. As to the emphasis on Irish but not other European languages, it had contributed to the formulation of a national/nationalistic canon in which Irish women writers were

---

April, 2004.

[141] During the English national school period, girls were given different materials to cultivate their motherhood. For example, in the *Reading Book for the Use of Female Schools*, published by the Commissioners of National Education in 1854, many lessons were devoted to the care of children, cooking, housekeeping, knitting, and nursing, such as "A Visit to an Infants' School," "On Attending the Sick," "Duties of a Housemaid," "Female Benevolence," "A Mother's Experiment," "On Cleanliness," "The Manufacture of Pins and Needles," and so on. There were some literary materials, but they were largely confined to motherly subjects. Titles of poems selected for study included "Mother, What is Death?," "Power of Maternal Piety," "To My Mother," "What is That, Mother?," "To My Child at Play," "A Mother's Grief," "To a Butterfly," "The Orphan," "A Mother's Love," "To an Infant," and so forth. The number of lessons in history, geography, literature, mathematics and science, compared to the male-equivalent textbooks, was small, while the textbooks for girls served as manuals for domestic management. My argument is that Irish education in the Free State was not freed from the Victorian gender stereotype of women, which restrained them from studying science as a non-domestic-related subject.

rarely included. It could be argued that although an Irish-centred perspective might have been constructed successfully through the intensive teaching of the language, it was in fact a male-led perspective rather than one catering for non-nationalistic or domestic women. The next two sections will also be observing whether Irish texts (in English) were actually subsidiary to the canon of English literature – as shown in syllabi – and how the nationalistic canon survived constant challenges from the 1930s to the early 1970s. The more detailed investigation into the teaching materials in literature and history for secondary school pupils will aim to reveal how the foundation of the Irish canon and national formations were strengthened through compulsory education.

2.2. Inclusions and Exclusions in English and History Syllabi

The early part of this chapter has referred to John Guillory's definition of canon as "the repositor[y] of cultural values."[142] It is the kind of repository that can, under some circumstances, be decanted or refilled in accord with the interests of relevant authorities, although some degree of intellectual independence would be maintained by individuals (against the authorities). Charles Altieri gave a similar description of canon as "a repository of human ideals," arguing that it "functions negatively rather than positively and works to make us struggle against rather than to confirm our smugness."[143] In the case of Ireland, nevertheless, the refilling of the "repository" of literature, as I will probe later, was not necessarily subject to the changes of government in the early twentieth century. The literary standard and tastes that the former coloniser had promoted in Ireland through national education and other means were, to some extent, endorsed by Irish syllabus makers and textbook editors. More specifically, most English syllabi approved by the Dublin Examining Board (for the Leaving Certificate examination) in the 1930s were not particularly de-Anglicised; the number of Irish texts remained limited and could hardly counterbalance the English ones. What is notable is that the teaching of traditional English literature was not less emphasised even after Ireland became a Republic in 1948. Some syllabi which I have surveyed, and will analyse later, show that Irish texts (in English) were not always included after Ireland claimed to be an independent nation no longer under the English crown. The reason why the traditional English literary canon could still re-

---

[142] Guillory 488.
[143] Quoted in Readings 151.

2. Curricula and Textbooks for Primary and Secondary Schools

main in force in Irish classrooms could be conjectured as the difficulty of cultural decolonisation; however, it is possible that Irish people had become more confident in their own national identity constructed through the compulsory study of the Irish language. In other words, Ireland, particularly in the second half of the twentieth century, had been "Gaelicised" to a relevant extent, so that syllabus makers would not necessarily assume themselves to be required to de-Anglicise Ireland, but could treat English literature as a separate subject alongside others on the syllabi.

Take, for example, the reading list that the Dublin Examining Board made in 1936 for secondary school students preparing for the Leaving Certificate examination in English. The list was made when the Irish government was about to reinforce its independent status with a new constitution to be introduced the following year. The list significantly itemised a number of Irish-themed books written or edited by celebrated nationalists and Gaelic scholars. Two of the four Irish-related titles on the list were: Douglas Hyde's *The Story of Early Gaelic Literature* (1895), and Eleanor Hull's *A Text-book of Irish Literature* (1906).[144] Nevertheless, a reading list which appears more "patriotic" was the one designed for final-year students, comprising titles exclusively on nationalism, such as Alice S. Green's *Irish Nationality* (1911), and John Drinkwater's *Patriotism in Literature* (1924).[145] Although the number of Irish-themed books on the two lists, compared with lists that focused on English literature and composition, was small, the inclusion of these Irish titles with a political nature shows that the educational authorities at the time were keen to create an Irish-centred, patriotic ambience in English syllabi.[146] On these grounds, it should be appropriate to judge that the teaching of Irish literature might be an "act of expediency" with which pupils were "Gaelicised" for patriotic purposes. That is to say, the

---

[144] *Helps for Students* n. pag., see the textbooks and anthologies section of the bibliography. Hyde was President of Ireland from 1938 to 1945; Hull was renowned for her English translation of a great number of Gaelic verses. Apart from Hyde's and Hull's books, the other two Irish-themed anthologies to be studied were *Ireland in Prose and Poetry: Senior Book* (1930), and *The Voice of Ireland Calling Men and Women of Tomorrow* (1933).

[145] *Helps* n. pag. The other two Irish-themed books were: J.M Flood's *Ierne – A Selection of Prose and Poetry relating to Ireland* (1929) and Eleanor Hull's *A Text-book of Irish Literature* (1930).

[146] There were fifty-five books in total on the two reading lists for the Leaving Certificate examination in English, while there were only eight titles relating to Ireland or Irish literature. Other titles were on either English literature or writing skills in English.

Irish-themed books on the lists mostly aimed to develop a sense of patriotic Irishness amongst pupils. Unlike those on English literature, none of these Irish titles were unbiased or systematic studies of literature. Some of the English textbooks included were actually monographs on particular subject matters: W.P. Ker's *Medieval English Literature* (1912), G.K. Chesterton's *The Victorian Age in Literature* (1913), H.N. Brailsford's *Shelley, Godwin and their Circle* (1913), J.M. Robertson's *Elizabethan Literature* (1914), and John Bailey's *Milton* (1915).[147] None of these books were overtly political but more resembled in-depth commentary on specific interests than those textbooks assigned for the study of Irish literature. What is also notable is that the number of titles for the improvement of students' English writing skills was also greater than that of Irish-themed books.[148] It might therefore be true to say that the emphasis on English writing, on the one hand, was to prepare Irish pupils answering essay questions in English for Leaving Certificate purposes. On the other hand, it discloses the fact that the inclusion of Irish-themed books was to meet the demand of nationalists who had the upper hand in politics. The inclusion of *The Story of Early Gaelic Literature* by Douglas Hyde, President of Ireland from 1938 to 1945, might signify how syllabus makers might submit to current political forces.

However, although syllabus makers might be subject to political forces, their ideal syllabus might vary due to the changing social ethos. That is to say, nationalistic syllabi might only be fashionable in a particular social context. Experiencing the decreasing nationalistic ambience as Ireland grew politically self-confident, syllabus makers were gradually less keen on reproducing reading lists featuring Irish patriotism. They tended to justify the teaching of English canonical literature on account of its aesthetic merits, but at the same time maintained vernacular characteristics to some extent to reflect the interests of Irish pupils. To demonstrate the changing face of the syllabus in English, one can compare the reading list, or syllabus, used in the 1930s, as described above, with that used in the 1960s. The comparison should bring to light how the making of a syllabus might be determined by factors other than political ones.

---

[147] *Helps* n. pag.

[148] These books on English writing included F.H. Pritchard's *Essays of To-day: An Anthology* (1923), J.C. Nesfield's *Idiom, Grammar, and Synthesis for High Schools* (1924), W. Murison's *English Composition* (1926), W.J. Maguire's *Aids to General Knowledge and Essay Writing* (1932), etc.

2. Curricula and Textbooks for Primary and Secondary Schools

It could be advised that the making of a state syllabus is akin to the formulation of a national canon, as both have to come up to the expectations of the public: teachers, parents, pupils, and readers in general. It is therefore necessary for syllabus makers to modify their "products," according to the changing attitudes of the public. As Southern Ireland had gradually solidified its independent status through various means since the 1930s, it is understandable that the social ethos was less dominated by revolutionary fervency, even though the nation remained distinctively Catholic. That is to say, the majority of Irish people were Catholic by upbringing, perceiving the secular world largely from Catholic viewpoints. The 1966 syllabus in English for the Leaving Certificate examination, for example, was divided into four sections: English composition, drama, prose, and poetry. The prose section had very few works devoted to Irish patriotism, consisting mainly of texts by canonical eighteenth- and nineteenth-century English writers.[149] No Irish playwrights were included; indeed, William Shakespeare was the only dramatist on the syllabus. In comparison with the 1936 English syllabus as discussed earlier, the absence of Irish/Gaelic and patriotic material on this 1966 syllabus might suggest that the social ethos of the 1930s and of the 1960s were quite different. What is notable is that the Irish syllabus makers in 1966 still attempted to "indigenise" the syllabus by including three essays from John Henry Newman's collection of lectures, *The Idea of a University* (1873). The reason for including Newman's work, in my view, might be because it not only defends the proposal for a Catholic university but also illuminates the Catholics' ideal of higher education.[150] In other words, by reading Newman's essays, pupils might be reminded of how Irish Catholics had been denied admission to university, and learnt how Newman conceived of a modern higher education that accommodated Catholic viewpoints. As Newman's ideas had been well received in both Ireland and England by the time Irish pupils studied his essays, pupils might have learnt to attribute the

---

[149] Madaus and Macnamara 25. The English prose writers and their texts to be studied were: Joseph Addison's "Sir Roger de Coverley at Home," Charles Lamb's "The Two Races of Men" and "Old China," William Hazlitt's "Hamlet," William Thackeray's "Life of Goldsmith," John Ruskin's "The Throne," Robert Stevenson's "An Apology for Idlers," Augustine Birrell's "Book-Buying," and Edith Sitwell's "A Note on Charles Dickens." Amongst these authors, Robert Stevenson, author of *Treasure Ireland* (1883), was Scottish. Sitwell was a twentieth-century woman writer. The other work by an Anglo-Irish writer was Oliver Goldsmith's "Adventures of a Strolling Player."

[150] It has long been accepted as a piece of fine English prose, which is another reason for studying it.

modernisation of university administration to Newman as a Catholic. However, his "modern" ideas about dividing universities into various schools for arts, sciences, and professional subjects, and the selection by students of their own programmes of study, were not exclusively Irish or Catholic *per se*. His views were shared by many educationalists at his time. The inclusion of this particular text but not those by Irish prose writers seems to demonstrate Newman's contribution as a renowned Catholic educationalist, alongside the purpose of encouraging pupils to go to university.

As for poetry, this syllabus did include both English and Irish poets, although the number of the latter was small, compared to the greater number of Classic and Romantic English poets. There were only four Irish poets selected: Oliver Goldsmith, W.B. Yeats, James Mangan, and Seumas O'Sullivan.[151] They were placed after the canonical English poets on the syllabus, such as William Shakespeare, Henry Vaughan, William Blake, William Wordsworth, Lord Byron, P. B. Shelley, John Keats, Robert Browning, and G. M. Hopkins. The preference for Romantic poetry can be seen in one of the textbooks which was made according to the state syllabus: *Leaving Certificate Poetry: Interim Anthology*, edited by James Carey in 1968. Only a very limited number of the "Irish poems" which the editor included had a nationalistic theme. As for Yeats, most of his poems which were selected were thematically nostalgic, mystical, or romantic, such as "No Second Troy," "The Fisherman," "Sailing to Byzantium," "Among School Children," and "The Circus Animals' Desertion"; only "September 1913" was nationalistic.[152] As for the preference for James Mangan and Seumas O'Sullivan, their being included might be due to their contribution of English translations of Gaelic poetry. However, as Yeats, Mangan, and O'Sullivan were placed second to those English poets on the state syllabus, it could be conjectured that, apart from itemising selected poets in a chronological order, the syllabus makers were less concerned about nationalistic or de-Anglicising issues. They became more open-minded in acknowledging the shared aesthetic characteristics of Anglo-Irish and English poetry. The secondary position in which Irish poets were placed on the syllabus did not necessarily suggest the failure of cultural decolonisation but a

---

[151] It could be argued that Oliver Goldsmith was taught as an English writer. He was born in Ireland but moved away in his early 20s and did virtually all his writing in England. There is not much "Irishness" in his literary works. He is therefore in a different class of "Anglo-Irishness" from those writers of British ancestry who lived and wrote in Ireland.

[152] In particular, Yeats' "The Circus Animals' Desertion" has several references to Irish folklore.

2. Curricula and Textbooks for Primary and Secondary Schools

changing social ethos. That is, Irish society in the late 1960s had become more tolerant of the *Other* culture in Ireland; people might have been more confidently seeing themselves as Irish, recognising their cultural link to Britain with less antagonistic sentiments.

The changes made to state syllabi in English, from being patriotic to moderately nationalistic, as the 1936 and 1966 syllabi show, might again testify to Guillory's and Altieri's definitions of the canon as a "repository" of values. Since the making of syllabi was, to a certain degree, subject to variations in the social ethos, the formulation of canons/syllabi was rarely static but always in a state of flux according to a variety of external forces. The changes which were effected during this process might therefore have led to some positive consequences brought about by readers. One of these positive consequences might be that readers, particularly those of a new generation, could acquire different interests in (regional) literatures, broadening their horizons and not being confined to the "smugness," in Altieri's words, of traditional canons. Their constant intention of counteracting the existing canons with a revised one would facilitate the development of the literary canon *per se* and the diversification of society.

To discuss more fully how the formulation of a canon might be subject to social ethos, it is necessary to observe whether the teaching of Irish history is always being modified to meet the expectations of the public, as it could more directly touch upon political issues than the teaching of literary texts. In other words, how pupils were taught to conceive the history of *their* nation could more directly affect the movements of Anglicisation, Gaelicisation, or internationalism. Historians, or syllabus makers in history, were therefore tasked by the "current" authorities to channel Irish pupils to the "correct" readings of history. The historiography they formulated, or strengthened, through the making of history syllabi and textbooks, on the one hand benefited the construction of a national identity; on the other hand, it unified the ways in which people justified their cultural heritage, such as a literary canon. What should be noted is that the formulation of any historiography is often subject to the (educational) authority in power which suggests the inclusions and exclusions of certain perspectives. Ireland, as a state under partition, can testify to how different historiographies, under the supervision of two antagonistic political authorities, could be passed on to pupils out of dissimilar interests. Compared to the teaching of Irish and English literature – which might share transcendental values to some degree – the formulation of a historiography can be more radical, producing significant effects on the next generation.

To observe how an Irish-centred historiography was constructed, modified, and promoted through education, the making of history syllabi for the state exams and the accompanying pedagogy should be attended to, in that schools are likely to form the best platform from which the authorities can imbue pupils with particular political perspectives. Due to the immense pressure that the Leaving Certificate examination put on pupils, there was little political debate allowed in classrooms. The traditional pedagogy therefore ensured that "correct," or favourable, historical perspectives would be passed on to the younger generation. A case in point is the list for history made by the Dublin Examining Board in 1936. As the country was about to issue a new Constitution, what appeared "correct" to members of the Board was to de-emphasise the teaching of British history and prioritise Irish and European history. This can be seen from the following list of school textbooks, where only the last title relates to Britain, although presumably the language used to teach Irish and European history was English – the tongue of the former coloniser:

(1) *A Concise History of Ireland* (P.W. Joyce). New and Revised Edition. Educational Co.

(2) *An Economic History of Ireland* (D.A. Chart). Educational Co.

(3) *A Class-Book of European History* (A.D. Innes). Rivingtons.

(4) *European History* (H. Webster) - Modern Times. Part 3. Browne & Nolan.

(5) *Students' Notes on European History: 1789-1918* (J.G. Altham). G. Bell & Sons.

(6) *The French Revolution* (Louis Madelin). William Heinemann.

(7) *Historical Atlas of Europe* (J.H. Fudge). George Gill & Sons.

(8) *Oxford and Cambridge British History* (R. Mongan). Ditto.[153]

It could be assumed that the marginalisation of British history was an act of educational de-Anglicisation in progress. It was endorsed by the Department of Education, which supervised the Dublin Examining Board in making guidelines, rules and reading lists for the Intermediate and Leaving Certificate examinations. As the Irish Education Department was headed by Thomas Derrig, a former Irish Volunteer and par-

---

[153] *Helps* n.pag.

ticipant in the 1916 Easter Rising, it is understandable that the above reading list approved during his term of office aimed to draw pupils' attention to Irish rather than British history. The placing of European history second to that of Ireland might indicate, on the one hand, that Irish-centred historiography was being solidified. On the other hand, Irish history was taught either as an independent subject or under a European framework, or both. More specifically, the Dublin Examining Board, endorsed by the nationalistic government, was expected to liberate the teaching of Irish history from the colonial framework and reinforce pupils' sense of Irishness. Compared with Northern Irish schools under the British educational system, whose curriculum will be further explored in the next chapter, history teaching in the south was more distinctively Irish-orientated. In brief, since Northern Ireland was politically linked with Great Britain, it appeared reasonable to consolidate – through education – the historical, religious, and political significance of Northern Ireland's relationship to Britain, while in the South the objective of history teaching was to stress Ireland's independence from Britain. It would hence be appropriate to say that the different interests of political leaderships do affect the way in which history is taught and conceived, even on the same Emerald Isle.

Although the teaching of history and literature conform to similar linguistic and cultural norms, it proved to be technically easier to de-Anglicise history teaching by de-emphasising English history on the syllabi. The intentional de-emphasis of English history, according to my survey, was ongoing even many decades after the establishment of the Free State, whereas the teaching of literature was becoming less and less patriotically determined. The emerging differences between the teaching of literature and history might have originated because cultural decolonisation was evidently more difficult to achieve through radical means than political independence. To maintain an unambiguous political identity, the teaching of history was justified as a more effective channel through which pupils' perspectives of Irish history could be standardised. Ireland's separate political identity, unlike its rather indefinable cultural or literary one, would be more and more stable when Irish people gradually came to feel secure about their nation as an independent state. The continuous de-emphasis of English history can be seen in a 1957 textbook: *Intermediate History Notes: Irish and European*, published two decades after the above reading list. This textbook entirely dismissed English history.

It could be suggested that this textbook was primarily designed for preparation for the Intermediate Certificate examination, for it had no coherent and linear narrative but was a group of historical facts itemised "point by point" – probably intended for quick review or memorisation. What is also notable is that little English history was introduced amongst the fifty-one lessons in the two parts of the textbook. More specifically, in part one there were twenty-eight lessons in total devoted to Irish national history from the twelfth century to the Easter Rising; and there were twenty-three lessons in part two dealing with European history from the feudalism of the ninth century to the First World War. Those "Irish lessons" in part one included "The 1641 Rebellion," "Jacobite Wars," "Grattan's Parliament," "The United Irishmen," "Struggle for Emancipation," "Daniel O'Connell," "Young Ireland," "The Fenians," "The Land War: Parnell," "The Home Rule Struggle," "Rise of Sinn Fein," and "The Easter Rising."[154] As for the "European lessons" in part two, none of them related explicitly to Britain, although the country was rarely outside major military, political, and religious conflicts on the European mainland. The intentional dismissal of British history can be seen more clearly from the following list of lessons in part two:

Feudalism; 2. The Crusades; 3. Medieval Life; 4. The Great Schism; 5 The Renaissance; 6. The Reformation; 7. The Counter-Reformation; 8. Thirty Years' War; 9. Richelieu; 10. Louis XIV; 11. War of the Grand Alliance; 12. War of the Spanish Succession; 13. Rise of Russia; 14. Rise of Prussia; 15. War of the Austrian Succession; 16. Seven Years' War; 17. French Revolution; 18. Napoleon; 19. Peninsular War; 20. Unification of Italy; 21. Unification of Germany; 22. Franco-Prussian War; 23. The Great War.[155]

It could be argued that as these European-related lessons provided insufficient information about Britain, the "historical picture" that pupils received about European history could not be complete. In other words, as these lessons did not particularly address British interests in the named conflicts or present British perspectives, pupils might not gain full knowledge of the pivotal role that Britain had played in these events. With reference to the sole emphasis on Irish political and military history in part one of the textbook, it should be justifiable to say that Irish historians, textbook editors and syllabus makers had been collaborating in not just formulating but fortifying Irish-centred perspectives. In addition to this, since this textbook aimed to "help [pupils] in revision work" and the material was organised largely "point by point," it

---

[154] *Intermediate History Notes: Irish and European* 1.
[155] *Intermediate History Notes* 2.

2. Curricula and Textbooks for Primary and Secondary Schools

is possible that pupils would acquire over-simplistic or imprecise views about Ireland and its relations with other countries.[156] Ironically, this was a problem foreseen by its editor himself, E.J. Hally, who pointed out in the introduction that if pupils misused or over-relied on this exam-orientated history textbook, they would probably "miss the wood for the trees" and "remember details whilst forgetting their place and significance."[157] Perhaps being alert to the problems of introducing history "note by note" but unable to disappoint pupils' and teachers' expectations for such a textbook, Hally maintained a proviso in the introduction that this book "w[ould] not teach history," if not properly used.[158] His proviso suggests that historians, in Hally's time, were largely subject to the political and educational realities in writing history textbooks. Notably, they were expected not only to simplify the study of history when "helping" students to prepare for examinations, but also to submit to a nationalistic historiography that de-emphasised British history.

Nonetheless, it was not until the late 1960s that Hally could revise history textbooks so that they showed "new emphases on social, economic, and cultural history," and were not confined to political or military history.[159] In one of the textbooks he edited in 1969, *Intermediate Irish History*, there was a clearer account of Ireland through a detailed narrative from the prehistoric period to its entry to the United Nations in 1955 – with relevant photos in support of the historical events introduced. The addition of visual materials, in my view, was a significant step in the remaking of (Irish) historiography, in that history was being reconstructed through a "three-dimensional space," rather than a combination of words. In other words, Hally and his colleagues might have been seeking a more experimental historiography in opposition to the traditional, text-bound one.

By comparing and analysing relevant changes made in the secondary school syllabi in literature and history during and after the Free State period, the above discussion should have provided an understanding of how Irish national and canonical formations were reinforced through education. To sum up, syllabus makers as well as textbook editors were often tasked to facilitate the political and cultural decolonisation of Ireland, despite the fact that the "new" literary and historical perspectives they maintained could be untenable to a degree. The next section will further explore how

---

[156] *Intermediate History Notes* 1.
[157] *Intermediate History Notes* 1.
[158] *Intermediate History Notes* 1.
[159] *Intermediate Irish History* v.

Leaving Certificate examinations and related pedagogies might have functioned more decisively in standardising pupils' tastes and perspectives in literature and Irish history. A national canon was therefore acquired under examination pressure and could not be formulated so securely.

2.3. Formation of a National Literary Canon and Pedagogies for State Examinations

It could be claimed that the syllabi and textbooks which this chapter discussed earlier formed the framework under which pupils gained knowledge under the state's supervision. To ensure that knowledge was absorbed "correctly" by pupils, they were required to take a state examination before they left school and pursued either a job or went on to a higher level of education. One of the merits of the state examination, presumably, was that it ensured that every pupil received the same quality of education, which underpinned the future progress of the state. However, the intensive preparation for the examinations – in which pupils had to demonstrate as much "textbook knowledge" as they could – would restrain them from freely and creatively developing their own intellects. As students were expected to abide by the approved viewpoints and sentiments presented in the textbooks, they might gradually learn not to question the relevant authorities who sanctioned the textbooks, in order to receive satisfactory marks in exams. In addition, since many exams, such as those for Leaving Certificate, matriculation, and scholarships, had a major influence on whether pupils would have a more promising future and/or financial assistance, students had to make their answers conform to the textbooks as much as they could. They might not want to risk their admission (to university) by giving creative but inappropriate answers in relevant exams.

It could be argued that conforming to the knowledge in the textbooks created standardised and submissive pupils who could not challenge authority effectively. More precisely, who they were submissive to might not only be members of the Examining Board who approved the circulation of "textbook knowledge," but the state that had been supervising intellectual activities on and off campus. In the mid-twentieth century, Ireland as a new state was in the process of decolonisation and in need of political stabilisation. State examinations were widely recognised as a channel through which people could compete, based upon agreed standards, despite differences in class, race, religion, and gender. To prepare pupils for reaching the standards, Irish secondary education in the post-Treaty period had been known for

2. Curricula and Textbooks for Primary and Secondary Schools

being exam-orientated and was often criticised for this. A great number of Irish people, after they entered adulthood, recollected that the way in which they approached knowledge at secondary schools was by rote and repetitive "trial examinations." John McGahern, in *The Dark*, provided the following description of pupils who were bound by the result of examinations through financial pressure, which largely deprived pupils of personal interest in studying:

> The house exam was held at Christmas, as a trial run before the summer. It would decide who'd leave off to concentrate on passing, and passing was no good to you. You had to get high in the honours to stand a chance in the cut-throat competition for the scholarships or ESB [Electricity Supply Board] or Training College or anything. Passing was only good if you had your own money to go to the university and few at school had that. Most came from small farms in the country on their bicycles, stacked downstairs where they ate their lunches out of paper bags or horse played on wet days. They knew too it was get honours or go to England. The air was tense with fear through the exam.[160]

The study pressure that McGahern depicted might have significantly contributed to the stabilisation of the new nation, in that pupils' attention was successfully directed to the impending examinations. Unlike the older generation, which had experienced major political turbulence, the exam pressure had kept these pupils from posing arguments or questions, leading them to accept the textbook knowledge approved by the authorities. All secondary school students were required to take state examinations for either Intermediate or Leaving Certificates, or both, before leaving school. What is more notable is that, as Southern Ireland had been a highly nationalistic state since 1922, the exam pressure which was put on pupils might have, in one way or another, contributed to the nation's formation, particularly through the exams in literature and history. It is therefore worthwhile to investigate the pedagogies applied to

---

[160] McGahern 87-88. It could be surmised that this description was also based on McGahern's observation of students before the time he published the novel in 1965, apart from the fact that he survived the exam pressure and was thus able to study at St Patrick's Training College and UCD. He was a teacher under the system described. *The Dark* was banned under the Censorship Act for its homosexual subplot which was thought to be in opposition to the celibacy of the clergy, and McGahern was dismissed from his teaching post.

the two subjects, as they might have effectively secured the way in which the younger generation conceived their national and cultural identity.

Before this section explores the issues relating to the pedagogies and the nation's formation, it is necessary to keep in mind that a satisfactory score in the Leaving Certificate examination was commonly seen in Ireland as a substantial step towards university, teacher training, the civil service, and numerous other careers. To ensure good results for pupils in the examination, most teachers would abide by the pedagogies that could effectively raise pupils' scores. To help teachers to prepare pupils for exams, the Department of Education also approved a series of teachers' handbooks which prescribed teaching objectives and the scope of study in each subject. As these state examinations weighed significantly in pupils' futures, pressure from parents and teachers for them to achieve high marks would inevitably compel (some) pupils to learn by rote. Some people might argue that exam preparation might not necessarily be unhealthy or detrimental for Irish pupils, for they had religious practices at schools which might have enriched their spirituality. Nevertheless, as the union of the Catholic Church and the state was so firm in Southern Ireland – the former operated most Irish schools with subsidy from the state – pupils and teachers could hardly challenge the authorities they constantly copied through the educational mechanism. It should also be true to say that as pupils could not choose what to learn at their will, the Church and the state could benefit each other by establishing Southern Ireland as "the most Catholic country in the world."[161] Thomas O'Donoghue, who researched the Church's intervention in the making of the Secondary School Curriculum, had observed that the state examinations did minimise "potential intellectual challenges to the institutional Church [. . .] by the need to present knowledge as certainty, by the undermining of originality, and by the discouragement of liberal and innovative thinking."[162] Under these circumstances, that pupils and teachers would be greatly disabled from questioning the authorities year after year seemed an unavoidable consequence.

The early part of this chapter has mentioned that the curricula approved by De Valera in 1939 as Minister of Education were often the cause of complaint for their being parochial and lacking in "practical" and "experimental experiences."[163] As the

---

[161] Quoted in Blanshard 4. It was James Devane's comment on the nature of the Republic of Ireland.
[162] O'Donoghue 95.
[163] Quoted in O'Donoghue 94.

2. Curricula and Textbooks for Primary and Secondary Schools

curricula that the Department of Education approved were the set framework within which syllabi and textbooks were written, there was limited flexibility with which teachers could choose teaching material, and they had to teach the texts selected by the educational authorities. Take the study of drama for the English literature exam as an example. The three plays which were most often taught and rotated in textbooks for nearly thirty years were *Hamlet, Macbeth*, and *Julius Caesar*.[164] As the state examination did not test on drama other than these three plays, nor did it ask for pupils' critical opinions of assigned works, it was possible for teachers to teach literature "successfully by concentrating on only certain aspects of [a work]."[165] The use of this type of pedagogy for exam purposes was verified by George Madaus, who examined actual exam papers, on which pupils wrote their answers, before the 1970s. He found that "even if every student in a class answered [. . .] exactly the same," it was common that markers would award "high marks to the well prepared stock answers" they gave.[166] It is hence assumable that many teachers would urge pupils to memorise "potted answers" to directly benefit their exam scores; they did not have to cultivate the students' sense of literary history but asked them to drill on set texts. Hard-working students – after two years of study for the Leaving Certificate – could easily familiarise themselves with the three plays, or a selection of poems and articles collected in textbooks. The pedagogy for the examination in English was also to equip pupils with relevant skills in composition with which pupils presented their ideas in a formula-type, non-creative approach. A series for this purpose, *Composition Groundwork*, edited by H.L. Doak in the 1940s and 1950s, was often on the study list for English. (Doak was also the editor of many textbooks of literature. I will examine the textbooks he edited in the next section of this chapter as an example.)

This pedagogy in English was in fact constantly under criticism, since pupils did not, and could not, maintain their own private reading of texts, but worked solely on standard background information on authors, the storyline in texts, and the use of literary terms, and so on. Augustine Martin, a renowned Irish critic with teaching experiences both at high schools and Dublin universities, had made clear his severe criticism against this pedagogy when Irish education was due to be reformed in the 1960s. He observed that the teaching of literature and other humanities subjects at Irish secondary schools was a failure of education, because:

---

[164] O'Donoghue 96.
[165] O'Donoghue 97.
[166] Madaus and Macnamara 34.

[education] has been marked by two examinations which test memory rather than thought, judgment, or expressive skill. The examination patterns largely are predictable and the shrewd teacher can prepare the dimmest pupil to get round it with ingenuity and the unscrupulous use of memory. Lines are learned by rote, "appreciations" memorised, model essays prepared, questions predicted.[167]

The problems in the educational *status quo* that Martin pointed out might have foreshadowed the result of Irish canon formation under the strong influences of the Intermediate and Leaving Certificate exams. That is, as pupils could not choose texts for study based upon their interests, nor could they develop their own creative reading of works but had to memorise "potted answers" as part of their mechanical preparation for exams, the development of canons could have become static rather than dynamic. Moreover, as there was only a very limited number of works in the textbooks – the study of which is unlikely to have been a universally pleasant experience – the majority of pupils might have learnt to accept the prescribed perspectives, or biases, presented in the texts without critical opinions. What is also noteworthy is that the exam pressure which pupils constantly experienced in their secondary education would force them to internalise the literary values shown in textbooks and exam papers. In the 1967 Leaving Certificate examination in English, for instance, many of the canonical values were suggested, such as: "Most of Shakespeare's opening scenes are wholly admirable"; "Mangan has been described as the best of the Anglo-Irish poets before Yeats."[168] Except for acknowledging these values or presuppositions, examinees were not encouraged to be honest "non-conformists" but answered questions like "What do you find to admire [. . .]?"; "What [. . .] makes the subject-matter interesting?"; "Mention at least three striking qualities [. . .]."[169] The literary values that pupils learnt by answering these question patterns with repetitive practices would perhaps reinforce the existing canon endorsed by the Examining Board. Nonetheless, the "secondary school" canon might not have survived easily if it had been put into a different educational scenario. Some university teachers, for in-

---

[167] Quoted in Madaus and Macnamara 35. Augustine Martin made this observation in *Irish Times*, 19 Dec. 1967.
[168] Quoted in Madaus and Macnamara 42.
[169] Quoted in Madaus and Macnamara 42.

2. Curricula and Textbooks for Primary and Secondary Schools

stance, have attempted to reformulate the canon in consideration of the various backgrounds of the students and other factors, which will be discussed in the next chapter.

Martin's criticism against the examination-orientated pedagogy in 1967, in my view, might have reflected the general feeling of the public towards the unhealthy state of Irish secondary education. In fact, in 1962, five years before Martin made his observation, members of the Council of Education, an advisory body to the Department of Education and consisting of university teachers, had criticised the state curriculum over the previous twenty years as having been "narrow and uninspiring," so that many students only learnt the "interminable round of compositing, grammatical drill and the minute study of a single prose and poetry text."[170] Nevertheless, not only the pedagogy of literature but also the teaching of foreign languages, history and geography were criticised in the 1970s, when the government of Ireland faced demands from the public to reform Irish education more comprehensively. (These subjects all related to pupils' perception of the nation and the stability of the Irish canon.) The teaching of French, for example, was criticised for placing too much emphasis on grammar and translation and ignoring the spoken language. The textbooks in geography were named as having a very limited number of maps and pictures, but long lists of geographical facts, covering the whole world, for memorisation. According to O'Donoghue, pupils were not encouraged to conduct personal investigations, and the training in analysing statistical information and reading maps was insufficient.[171] David Langridge, in his survey of Irish geography teaching, also observed that the attempt to counter-balance the lack of maps through over-detailed narrations might have served only to "facilitate the creation of phantasms in students' minds."[172] As pupils had learnt geography largely through the traditional approach, these lessons in geography textbooks did not necessarily broaden their horizons.

The pedagogy of history was also a target of criticism in the 1970s, because the mechanical preparation for exams had actually kept pupils from analysing and comprehending historical events by themselves. Their sole task was to memorise standard interpretations in textbooks – from reading lists approved by the Examining Board.

---

[170] Quoted in O'Donoghue 96.

[171] O'Donoghue 95. O'Donoghue's survey shows that the most often used textbooks in geography during the mid-twentieth century were The Christian Brothers' *Outline of Geography* (1928), J. Dennehy's *Ideal Geography* (1930), and Eleanor Butler's *Structural Geography of Ireland* (1948).

[172] Langridge 112.

Although it could be argued that secondary school students might not have been capable of carrying out independent historical research at their age, it is also true that they were not trusted to develop their own views and interpretations. Notably, most questions on history exam papers only demanded that pupils "treat briefly" or "give an account of" the historical events in question. It was therefore not necessary for them to argue for or against their causes and effects, nor to develop an alternative perspective, but to memorise official viewpoints given in textbooks. The pedagogy which corresponded to this type of exam question, presumably, aimed to prepare pupils to have a good memory of "important" dates, names and occurrences. Madaus exemplified one of the answers which received full marks in the 1967 Leaving Certificate examination in history as follows. The answer – given by a candidate – consisted of a list of facts without a consistent or expressive narrative, demonstrating the pupil's good memory of historical incidents at a superficial level. The question with the full-mark answer is: "Excluding Ireland, treat of the expansion of Norman power in Europe during the eleventh and twelfth centuries." Another example is:

The Normans, with Roger Guiscard as leader, invaded Sicily, captured Messina, defeated (sic) the Saracens finally by 1093.

Southern Italy consisting of Apulia, Calabria, Naples, was now by the beginning of the 10th (sic) century under Norman control and later under Roger G. Sicily was joined to the South Italian block of Norman ruled states in Southern Europe.

Norman Rule In Sicily - South Italy
1. The Jews, Latins, Greeks, Moslems were allowed to retain their own laws, customs, religion and so Sicily proposed in
   (a) Economic affairs: new trade routes to Greece, Aegean Islands and the Eastern Mediterrean (sic) were opened.
   (b) Cultural: an increase in prose, poetry.
   (c) New buildings comprising the Arab, Greek, Roman traditions were built.
   (d) New system of provincial organization directly responsible to the King of S. Italy was (sic) set up.
   (e) New Law Courts.[173]

---

[173] Madaus and Macnamara 74.

2. Curricula and Textbooks for Primary and Secondary Schools

Apparently, the answer was not composed in a clear narrative but as a list of brief descriptions of facts, not necessarily unbiased and accurate, and even containing incorrect spellings such as "Mediterrean," and a factual error – tenth century instead of eleventh. However, as this pattern of answers could ensure markers' quick assessment of examinees' familiarity with "textbook knowledge," it could be conjectured that pupils would be encouraged to follow the standard pattern to organise their ideas recalled from books. They did not have to validate the implications or presuppositions shown in exam questions but instead to answer them in "standard" formats and to quote material from textbooks. The standardisation of answering and the grammatical pedagogies – which applied not only to history but also to other subjects – might reinforce the stability of the new nation, its national discourse, and the preferred historiography.[174] It is likely, because the exam pressure was so immense, that many young pupils would internalise the ideologies and perspectives presented in the textbooks without thinking them through for themselves. What is noteworthy is that although this type of pedagogy for exam purposes was also practised in Britain in the national school system – which was introduced to Ireland in 1831 and applied by Irish history teachers with little modification – this might suggest the effects of cultural colonialism on education.[175] Besides, the traditional pedagogies could be considered ideal from the viewpoint of the Catholic Church, which managed most of the secondary schools in Southern Ireland, to ensure that pupils "grasp[ed] fully the established understandings about person, society and God," before they graduated and served in society.[176]

So far this chapter has demonstrated that the making and changes of syllabi and pedagogies were often subject to a wide range of social factors: from the dominance of the nationalistic ideology, religious sentiments, exam pressure, to the difficulty of

---

[174] It is evident that the historiography of which members the Examining Board approved was explicitly nationalistic, as the books by nationalist historians often appeared on its reading lists. For example, Mary Hayden and George Moonan's *A Short History of the Irish People from the Earliest Times to 1920* (1923) and Stephen Gwynn's *The Student's History of Ireland* (1925).

[175] The grammatical approach to the study of Classics was criticised by two English historians in the 1910s, Maurice Keatinge and Norman Frazer, who advocated a new teaching method analogous to the laboratory one for science. However, it was not until the 1970s that the history pedagogy at Irish schools gradually adjusted to allow pupils to express their own views.

[176] Quoted in O'Donoghue 9.

cultural decolonisation. These factors all contributed to the formation of the Irish literary canon directly and indirectly. As the dynamics of these determinants could decide how the facets of the canon should change, how textbook editors responded to them would be worth exploring. The next section will trace those changes in textbooks over the years, in an attempt to see how textbook editors freed themselves from insular ideologies. Some introduced travel writing by European writers; some brought in an international taste of literature; some redefined "Irishness" and "Anglo-Irishness" from a broader sense of Irish culture. Their efforts, as the following discussion will disclose, foreshadowed the potential reformulation of literary canons, producing lasting impacts on the contemporary study of Irish literature.

2.4. Irish Textbooks in Progress and the Remaking of Anglo-Irishness

Jean Anyon in her study of textbooks has suggested that textbooks are "social products that can be examined in the context of their time, place, and function," and pointed to the role of consumer decisions for publishing products.[177] As school textbooks are intended to be read and widely accepted by parents, staff, school boards, and the authorities concerned, editing boards have to compromise over a variety of external forces and expectations. Since compromises are inevitable to ensure the acceptability of textbooks, lessons written by historians, as well as texts selected by literary critics, "often undergo substantial editing by publishing company personnel concerned with meeting requirements of school markets [. . .] and views of individual authors may be altered."[178] That is to say, what is taught through textbooks is not necessarily subject to the personal views and tastes of editors, but to those of people outside the offices of publishers who regard themselves as social élites. The ideologies and sentiments of these social élites are therefore skilfully legitimised, transmitted, and reproduced through the selection of lessons in textbooks, concealing the unequal social structures on which the politically and economically powerful and the powerless are based. With a variety of considerations and compromises, textbook editors hence have to reflect the opinions of the powerful – persuasively but not necessarily objectively. As textbooks have been "censored" by a variety of current social authorities, it is understandable that they cannot usually change their "faces" as swiftly as other cultural products, unless there is a radical political force behind them.

---

[177] Anyon 361-62.
[178] Anyon 362.

2. Curricula and Textbooks for Primary and Secondary Schools

In the case of Ireland, it should be justifiable to say that the radical political force came with the establishment of the Irish Free State in 1922. One of the consequences in literary education – due to the establishment of this Catholic state – was the reformulation of literary tastes, so that pupils were sure to come under the right influences of Irish Catholicism and nationalism. Yearly publications of textbooks therefore became a public educational sphere where pupils acquired "correct" sentiments sanctioned by Catholic nationalists. To be in line with (traditional) Catholic values, some textbook editors managed to demonstrate, or re-demonstrate, what was "proper" literature for Irish pupils, with suitable examples. Take, for instance, a series of English textbooks edited by James J. Carey, who had been in charge of the editing of Intermediate and Leaving Certificate textbooks from the early 1950s up to the late 1960s. His textbooks, which I shall investigate further, suggested a canon of selected good, or accepted texts for Irish pupils. Nevertheless, his nearly three-decades-long career as chief editor for many textbooks also testified to the changes in social ethos, particularly when Ireland became a more active member of international communities in the 1970s.

From my survey, it is clear that there were few significant changes made in Carey's early textbooks. Carey's 1955 edition of the Leaving Certificate textbook was apparently still made in line with traditionalists' notions of "good" literature. In its introduction, he asserted that literature could be dichotomised, and classified, as good or bad literature; the editor's and tutor's responsibility was to "train" pupils to develop a good literary taste. He also expressed his literary views with a tone of authority, defending the duties of literary critics, but possibly underestimating students' own ability to appreciate good literature:

> Literary criticism is the art of judging literature, i.e., of deciding how far and for what reasons a work of literature may be regarded as good or bad. The essential duty of a literary critic is valuation. With criticism in this somewhat professional sense the student is of course not directly concerned. We may take it that the pieces prescribed for our study in this anthology are on the whole well-written; of their period and individual style they are samples of 'good literature.'[179]

---

[179] Carey, *New Senior Prose*, introduction xi.

To have pupils well-acquainted with the standard of good literature, Carey asserted that some training was necessary: "[t]he ability to understand and enjoy a literary work, i.e., to know it, is a matter of experience and learning, just as the solution of a problem in the calculus [. . .] require[s] previous education and training."[180] On the one hand, the school training he prescribed could be seen as an attempt to standardise literary tastes which government officials and the Catholic authorities had endorsed. On the other hand, through standardised literary textbooks, the governmental authority could marginalise, or even censor, that which they regarded as improper literary tastes or social perspectives, labelling them as "bad" literature.

The interests of relevant authorities, such as patriotism, were indeed reflected in Carey's textbooks, even two decades after Ireland became independent. This is the case, for example, in *Intermediate Prose: A new Anthology specially compiled for the Intermediate Certificate Course*, edited by Carey and published in 1941. There were six Irish writers, amongst twenty-nine in the textbook, who were particularly introduced as "Irish patriots" in accompanying notes. They were: Theobald Wolfe Tone, Thomas Davis, John Mitchel, Thomas Francis Meagher, Sir William Francis Butler and the Most Rev. Dr. John MacHale. Works by Irish Catholic clergymen, such as John MacHale, Joseph Farrell and Patrick Augustine Sheehan, were the highlights of the textbook. Notably, these three clerical writers were identified apparently according to their Irish Catholic origin, while writers such as Sir Richard Steele, Oliver Goldsmith and Standish O'Grady were indicated as Anglo-Irish.[181] There were few mentions of their religious orientation, nor whether they had sympathised with Irish nationalists. Only a small percentage of the presented Irish works were non-patriotic or relating to travel.

Another textbook which I would like to examine is D. H. Doak's 1942 edition of *Leaving Certificate Prose*. A major difference between his textbook and Carey's edition was that Doak chose more texts about overseas travel experiences, rather than historical or patriotic lessons. One could assume that Doak's preference for unpoliti-

---

[180] Carey, *New Senior Prose*, introduction xi-xii.

[181] Other writers with an Irish origin included Robert Lynd, Eleanor Hull, William Bulfin, and Conall Cearnach. They were not specified as patriots in accompanying notes, even though Robert Lynd, born in Belfast in 1879, had published *Ireland a Nation* (1919), a work of nationalist historiography. Nevertheless, perhaps due to his birthplace, Lynd was introduced as "one of the most popular English essayists." Eleanor Hull was the only woman writer in the textbook.

cal, neutral, unoffensive travel notes might have had something to do with the ongoing media censorship since 1929 – though not particularly of textbooks, as editors were discouraged from including material of a controversial nature which might be disapproved of by the nationalistic government. Doak's choice of overseas travel notes, therefore, seemed to display his intention of broadening the views and perspectives of the Irish readership. Nevertheless, Doak's own introductions to travel writers, to some extent, still highlighted their patriotic contributions, apart from their travel experiences. Pupils would still have an impression that what made these writers remarkable was their loyalty to their country, rather than their expertise in producing travel writings. These "political" travel writers included Edmund Burke, Stephen Gwynn, John Mitchel, Joseph O'Neill, Robert L. Praeger and Richard Steele. Another interesting fact about this textbook was that one third of the Irish and Anglo-Irish writers selected were from Northern Ireland: Forrest Reid, John Mitchel and Robert L. Praeger. I would argue that Northern Ireland, in the minds of editors, remained an essential part of the Irish nation, while in reality the Treaty could not demand sovereignty over the northern territory.

Having investigated Carey's and Doak's textbooks, I would claim that Irish pupils probably had only two sorts of Irish writing available to them in the 1950s: patriotic and travel material. Both types of material, however, were chiefly written by male authors, while there was only one female writer in each of their books: Eleanor Hull in Carey's, and Emily Lawless in Doak's. Irish female voices were not just marginalised, but almost silenced in the production of patriotic textbooks. In addition, there was a common feature in both textbooks by Carey and Doak. That is, regardless of whether selected materials were travel notes or patriotic writings, the authors' political stances decided whether their works could be studied by Irish pupils. More specifically, since patriotic materials repeatedly appeared in textbooks, it seems reasonable to suggest that what was thought politically correct, such as expressions of a patriotic and nationalistic ethos, could be something producible through textbooks; the function of textbooks was therefore to help the authorities strengthen the foundation of the approved patriotic ethos.

As time went by, the new state began to evolve upon a patriotic foundation, and the social ethos became less "revolutionary"; what concerned the editors of textbooks had therefore changed. Carey's later editions of his textbooks can be used to demonstrate what kinds of change were made, and whether a new literary standard was sweeping the mainstream literary scene, during the period when Irish nationalism began to occupy a less explicit role.

Carey continued to be chief editor of Intermediate and Leaving Certificate textbooks until the late 1960s. However, there were fundamental changes made in the contents of later editions; whether writers were patriots or nationalists was no longer as important as before. In the 1967 edition of the Intermediate textbook, *Exploring English 2: An Anthology of Prose for Intermediate Certificate*, for instance, the number of patriotic works was significantly reduced, and introductions to writers were not now limited to their political contributions alone. A major breakthrough from previous editions can be seen in Carey's general introduction to the book. He made a clear statement as to the reason why he intended to select new writers and works for publication:

> It is clear then that we have in this book a fair cross-section of prose writing in English. The selection, you will have noticed, is of an international character for it includes the work of Irishmen, Welshmen, Scotsmen and Americans, as well as of Englishmen. This gives the reader the opportunity of comparing how writers of different nationality differ from one another in their use of a common language.[182]

Differing from Carey's earlier editions of his textbooks, this new edition had a broader coverage of literary themes, including an extract from James Joyce's *Ulysses*. This edition was published in the same year in which a new bill of censorship was passed, allowing for the release of previously banned books. This year's edition could be considered as more significant than the editions of previous years, in that Carey and his publisher were opening up an old "canon" of selected readings, and intended to introduce an international standard in literature.

The intention of introducing an international taste can be seen in Carey's own article "Correct English," reprinted from *The Times Educational Supplement*.[183] This article stressed the merits of writing good English, and displayed linguistic changes in the English language throughout history. In contrast to the enthusiasm of earlier decades for promoting the Gaelic language, the recognition of English as the common

---

[182] Carey, *Exploring English 2*, introduction xi.
[183] This reprinted article from *The Times Educational Supplement* was from the issue dated 24 Aug. 1962.

2. Curricula and Textbooks for Primary and Secondary Schools

medium through which international literary preferences could be mobilised, suggested a change in Irish society.[184] That is, the political antagonism towards Englishness and the fervour for Gaelicism or Irishness were gradually dying down; Irish people began to see the English language as a means to take part in international matters, rather than as a target for Irish nationalism.

Nevertheless, there were other obstacles that had to be overcome, if Ireland was to be reintegrated into the international literary scene. Since English was, and still is, the dominant language used in Ireland, "international" literary tastes, inevitably, had to be reintroduced through this language. Compared to French-, Spanish-, or Chinese-speaking countries, the concept of "international" tastes might differ from culture to culture. Thus, what French critics deem internationally praiseworthy might not be appreciated, or even recognised, by the critics of other cultures. The emphasis on English as an international language, therefore, reintroduced the English cultural and literary legacy to Irish pupils. Literary textbooks which Carey and his contemporaries edited featured fewer patriotic subjects in later editions, gradually becoming more and more English-orientated. Thus, a canon which contained strong English/British cultural elements was probably being systematically reintroduced into Irish textbooks.

In the *Anthology of English Poetry for Leaving Certificate*, published in 1969, this trend is readily apparent. This textbook was co-edited by J.P. Dunleavy and P.J. Diggin, and included major classic English male poets and some modern (Anglo-)Irish ones.[185] In an attempt to engender a new perspective on the selection of English poets, the editors gave a different, unconventional definition as to who were Anglo-Irish writers, and what kind of works could be classified as Anglo-Irish. The new defini-

---

[184] However, the number of women writers was still small. There were only two female writers amongst the forty writers included in the publication: Jane Austen and Charlotte Mary Yonge. The patriarchy of Irish society had not yet been significantly altered.

[185] Major canonic English poets selected in the textbook, or this type of textbook, included Geoffrey Chaucer, William Shakespeare, Ben Johnson, John Donne, George Herbert, Henry Vaughan, Andrew Marvell, John Milton, John Dryden, Alexander Pope, William Wordsworth, Percy Shelley, John Keats, Alfred Tennyson, G. M. Hopkins, Thomas Hardy, T. S. Eliot. There was only one woman poet to be studied: Emily Dickinson. Amongst these poets, Thomas was born in Wales in 1914, and I assume he would not have liked being called English, although his works were all written in English. Dickinson and Eliot were born in the United States.

tion of Anglo-Irish literature covers those works originally written in Gaelic, but subsequently translated into English:

> In the beginning, Anglo-Irish poetry was crude and inartistic. It comprised ballads and songs, most of them expressing Ireland's stormy history, her sorrows and hopes, her struggle for freedom. The poetry of the Fenian and Young Ireland movements is largely a poetry of patriotic fervour and political propaganda. The relegation of Irish to a minority status in the nineteenth century was a severe blow to Gaelic culture, which was largely an oral tradition. However, a great part of the tradition survived, largely through the work of nineteenth century scholars, translators and poets. Poets like Callanan, Walsh, Moore, Mangan, Larminie and Ferguson succeeded in carrying over into English verse the characteristic features of Gaelic poetry: its rhythms and cadences, its lyrical inspiration, its strong sense of place association.[186]

The new definition seemed to be broader, as it referred to Gaelic works which had been translated into English by Fenians and Young Irelanders who intended to revive Irishness as a concept and style culturally detached from the ideology of colonisation. Nevertheless, Dunleavy and Diggin were not pioneers in giving this broader definition of Anglo-Irishness. Before the establishment of the Irish Free State, Thomas MacDonagh had suggested the term "The Irish Mode" in which Irish writing in English should be incorporated for its shared Irish sentiments, regardless of whether it was penned by Irish or Anglo-Irish writers. A less well-known literary critic and textbook editor in the 1940s, Roger J. McHugh, had also intentionally categorised James Mangan and Thomas MacDonagh as Anglo-Irish poets in his *Matriculation and Leaving Certificate Poetry*, aiming to "denote accurately [. . .] Irish poets in English."[187] In his observation, many Irish and Anglo-Irish writers since the nineteenth

---

[186] *Anthology of English Poetry for Leaving Certificate* 236.

[187] Introduction xxxvii. McHugh specified twenty-five Anglo-Irish writers in this textbook: William Drennan, Thomas Moore, Jeremiah J. Callanan, Gerald Griffin, James C. Mangan, George Fox, Sir Samuel Ferguson, Thomas Davis, Aubrey de Vere, John Kells Ingram, William Allingham, Emily Lawless, William Larminie, Thomas W. Rolleston, Kuno Meyer, W.B. Yeats, Lionel Johnson, George W. Russell (A. E.), William A. Byrne, Thomas MacDonagh, Joseph Campbell, Seamus O'Sullivan, Padraic Colum, James Stephens, Francis Ledwidge.

2. Curricula and Textbooks for Primary and Secondary Schools

century had endeavoured to "express an Irish spirit and [. . .] display certain strongly-marked Irish influences" deriving from "Irish legend and literature, history and tradition, music and speech."[188] It might be appropriate to judge that these critics and editors, unlike those who favoured the racial categorisation of Irish and Anglo-Irish writers, represented a group of the public concerned about the integration of different cultures in Ireland. Dunleavy and Diggin's reinterpretation of their predecessors' ideas of Irishness might hint that Irish society in the 1960s, at the time they published their *Anthology of English Poetry for Leaving Certificate*, had been successfully harmonising various ethnic and cultural divisions. The (not necessarily completely) reinterpreted, concept of "Anglo-Irish poetry" appeared in the introduction of this textbook as follows:

> [Anglo-Irish poetry] is the term applied to poetry written by Irish poets in the English language. It is a distinct body of poetry in that, though written in English, it is Irish in theme, spirit and style. The distinct quality is 'Irishness.' Its themes are drawn from Irish history, life and legend, its spirit and style largely from Gaelic poetry.[189]

Apart from reflecting the cultural *status quo* in Ireland, it was possible that Dunleavy and Diggin's intention of placing Irish and Anglo-Irish writers in one English category, when Ireland was actively seeking out international literary tastes, was to "internationalise" Irish cultural products in order to meet the English standard of the literary market. By broadening the definition of "English" poetry, Irish and Anglo-Irish poetry could give pupils the impression that Irish literature had international merits. Nevertheless, the act of redefining and broadening the meaning of "English" through textbooks for its use in Irish schools, might potentially re-inscribe the English cultural legacy on the psyche of Irish pupils. That is to say, as it was necessary for English to operate as the medium of introducing "international tastes," it was possible that English cultural values and aesthetics would be emphasised over those of other cultures and languages. In any case, the ambiguous redefinition of Irish and Anglo-Irish writings might have shown that insufficient historical considerations had been made to support the new definitions, and critics might not have been aware of the advantages that English writers had secured in regard to maintaining a situation of

---

[188] Introduction xxxviii.
[189] *Anthology of English Poetry* 236.

cultural imperialism. To be more specific, the preference for classic English male poets appeared in many textbooks which were claimed to provide international tastes, such as Augustine Martin's 1969 edition of *Soundings: Leaving Certificate Poetry Interim Anthology*, and Carey's *Leaving Certificate Poetry: Interim Anthology*, published in the same year.

Another reason why the promotion of international literary tastes could potentially reconfirm the English classic canon, instead of the literature of other nations, can be understood in the context of the educational backgrounds in which these editors were raised, and in which they developed their literary perspectives. The Irish editors I have mentioned in this chapter, H.L. Doak, James J. Carey, Augustine Martin, J.P. Dunleavy, and P.J. Diggin, had received their higher education either in England or Ireland. It may well be the case that their university education could have played a significant role in their identification with existing literary standards – initially promoted by the coloniser. Furthermore, as both the English national school system and Catholic schools had historically adopted English literature as their major study materials – as I have shown in Chapter One – English literary standards and tastes therefore formed the "given" model, which influenced the Irish editors' selection of literary readings for local pupils.

In order to more comprehensively understand how higher education had made such a significant impact on the choices of these key textbook editors, there is a need to investigate how literature and history were taught in universities in the 1930s: a time in which the Republic of Ireland had, for the previous twenty years, concerned itself with the restructuring of its nation. I propose to survey the examination papers of major Irish universities, such as Trinity College Dublin (TCD) and University College Dublin (UCD) in the next chapter. Doing so would enable us to picture how literary, political, and religious discourses were competing with each other, and to see how literary discourses circulated within university classrooms, either directly or indirectly influencing the reading appetites of the public. (It is quite possible that university graduates, with their "educated" tastes, become involved in the publishing industry). In the next chapter, I will look into the examination papers used for humanity based disciplines at UCD and TCD in the 1930s, to see how the university faculties used "exams" to promote a preferred literary standard, or to oppose those they considered unconventional.

3. Politics, Literary Canon, and Historiography at Dublin's Universities: The Examination Papers of Trinity College Dublin and University College Dublin in the 1930s as Models

When Queen Elizabeth approved, in 1591, the establishment of Trinity College Dublin (TCD), the first university in Ireland, this institute was set up under a political and religious agenda. It was not only because this college was built upon the foundations of a monastery bestowed in 1538 by King Henry VIII, but because only Protestants – who had kept a firm hand on colonial politics and economics – were allowed to study there. No Catholics were allowed to matriculate at TCD unless they converted to the Reformed Church. For the English government, setting TCD in line with the Oxbridge tradition served not simply to reconfirm its sovereignty over Ireland, but also to ensure that local élites (or future dominant classes) continued to be Anglicised in the way the coloniser expected. There was therefore little provision of "popish" knowledge at TCD. As for the teaching of the Irish language, although TCD set up its School of Irish in 1840, it was primarily to prepare students who intended to enter the ministry for the Church of Ireland. It was not established "for any cultural or nationalistic reasons" in those days but to facilitate the conversion of Irish-speaking Catholics.[190] The teaching of English literature, which was separated from philology at the end of nineteenth century, was to underpin a unified national consciousness. That is, British universities, including TCD, were expected by English intellectuals "to provide lecturers and teachers in English Literature [. . .] not in England only, but in the Colonies," to acquaint local students with "the expression of national idiosyncrasies."[191] One of the petitioners for the teaching of English literature in universities, Matthew Arnold, specified that "no literature except that of our own country [should be added to] to the classical literature." [192] It could be conjectured, then, that the promotion of English literature to other British territories since the turn of twentieth century was to maintain the integrity of the empire. To prompt Irish students to iden-

---

[190] Kiberd, *Synge* 19. Kiberd indicated that the both sides of J.M. Synge's family had produced a few Anglican bishops amongst which, the Reverend Alexander Synge, was a graduate of TCD and had gone to the Aran Islands in 1851 to convert locals there. For Synge's family and many Protestants in those days, "Irish was one of the 'Divinity School Subjects'" with no nationalistic agenda. Quoted in Kiberd 20.
[191] Collins 33, 64.
[192] Quoted in Collins 108.

tify effectively with the superiority of Englishness, TCD, as an institute founded to secure the interests of the coloniser in one way or another, approved English literature as a separate subject for study from 1870.[193] It was also one of the compulsory subjects for examination purposes at both entrance and M.A. degree levels.

What is noteworthy is that the emphasis on English literature persisted from the colonial to the postcolonial era, and students were directed to believe that there were inherent, universal values in literature *by* English canonical writers. They might be required to be acquainted with a second European language, but they were only taught it at the level of everyday communication. As there was no other literary subject which received as much attention as English literature in the curricula of both high schools and universities, the required study of it paved the way for a unified, national consciousness as the coloniser planned. In addition, the hierarchy of educational apparatuses from primary schools to universities helped to construct a correspondent social hierarchy. That is, Irish students had not only to be good at the tongue of the English people but to know their national literature to a relevant extent, in order to enter a state university such as TCD. It is true to say that the entrance examinations to TCD and other British universities had integrated well with the national school system in Ireland for the purpose of circulating English values and sentiments – as I demonstrated in Chapter Two. Notably, those Irish people who studied at national schools and were admitted to British universities had been constantly informed through textbooks that "Great Britain and Ireland formed the most powerful kingdom in the world"; it was also reinforced that "many people who live in Ireland were born in England, and we speak the same language and are called one nation."[194] At national schools, they acquired little of Irish history, language, and tradition, whereas English historiography and culture were the main interests in their textbooks – subsidised by the state. Although the intentional cultural assimilation, or Anglicisation, was systematically operated under the supervision of the English coloniser, it never fully succeeded due to the efforts that Irish (cultural) nationalists made in the Celtic revival since the late nineteenth century.

The consequences of the required studies of English literature and history at both high school and university levels, however, were not completely unrecognised by

---

[193] McDowell and Webb 271.

[194] Quoted in Coolahan, "The Irish" 55. According to Coolahan's survey, these statements were commonly seen in many of the reading books sanctioned by the Board of Commissioners between 1831-1871.

3. Examination Papers of Dublin's Universities

Irish Catholics. Also, because "popish" education used to be under suppression by the British government, and there was no equivalent institute to TCD for Catholics until 1856, Irish Catholic nationalists would therefore assume that the establishment of Catholic colleges could counteract the forces of Anglicisation. Their call for relief of the restraint on Catholic higher education was more or less involved with their plea for an equal political and cultural standing with Protestants. The British government, under increasing pressure from Irish Catholics and in the hope of solving the Irish Question, did show some degree of generosity by setting up a few colleges in Catholic-dominant areas, such as Queen's College in Galway and Cork in 1845, although these schools did not particularly cater for Catholics but admitted students of all religious persuasions.[195] In 1908, the Catholic-based National University of Ireland (NUI) was set up to encompass University Colleges in Cork (UCC), Dublin (UCD), and Galway (UCG), and St. Patrick's College in Maynooth. The establishment of the NUI was particularly welcomed by nationalists, on the grounds that they could offer a wider range of Gaelic-related courses to interested students that the English-orientated TCD could not. (TCD did offer courses in the Irish language since 1840 but not particularly for the purpose of Celtic Revival.) Specifically, from the viewpoint of cultural nationalists – who had endeavoured to revive an Irish culture across the religious divide – the NUI was ideal for those who wanted to acquire knowledge of Irish folklore, music, language, history and archaeology at a more advanced level. For radical nationalists, the establishment of the NUI was seen as a further step towards creating an Irish national identity. However, both cultural and radical nationalists might have overestimated the impact of the establishment of the NUI, in that it was not "Irish-Irish" *per se*; and students still had to sit for exams on the English language and literature for different purposes: admissions, scholarships, graduation, and so on. As English was always a privileged subject in curricula, it could be surmised that the NUI had remained as the establishment where cultural decolonisation had not been well effected – at least in the 1930s.

Nevertheless, the establishment of the Free State in 1922 was not entirely ineffective as far as educational decolonisation was concerned, as it produced moderate but significant effects, directing students' attention to the legacy of their own culture. The reason why the effects were modest, rather than sweeping, in my opinion, was be-

---

[195] In 1879, the Royal University of Ireland (RUI) was established as an examining body, allowing the Irish themselves to publish syllabuses and set papers for non-Protestant colleges in Ireland.

cause the academic faculty were learning to cope with the social and political changes. To explore how the faculty resisted, or compromised with those changes, I propose to investigate TCD's and UCD's curricula in English literature and history; in that the two Dublin universities were primarily set up on different political and religious foundations, the faculty might have perceived the colonial tradition differently. By specifying who chaired the remaking of curricula, I will trace how the teaching of English literature varied amongst the institutes: from regular English and History departments to those at teacher training colleges. I will also compare the teaching of English and Irish history between TCD and Queen's University in Belfast (QUB), to demonstrate the different consequences of political decolonisation in the higher education of Ireland.

3.1. Some Common Features in the Departmental Administrations of TCD and UCD

Before this chapter delves into the way in which the faculty of TCD and UCD coped with or resisted social changes after the establishment of the Irish Free State, it is necessary to bear in mind that how literature and history were taught had a considerable influence on students' perceptions of their social responsibilities. That is, their literary tastes and historical perspectives were usually formed by the selection of texts they studied at school. For university graduates, as a large number of them would enter middle-class professions as civil servants, teachers, editors and engineers, etc, how they realised the tradition they came into would have important effects on those less educated and their values would probably become those of the mainstream. Although university education did not necessarily standardise the perspectives of future élites, it could still be an important channel through which they learnt the favoured values and sentiments of the relevant authorities. More specifically, by studying assigned textbooks and giving "correct" answers to pass examinations, these prospective élites learnt to internalise the viewpoints of the textbooks approved by the authorities.

One of the consequences of studying English canonical literature at Irish universities was that students might learn to justify the inherent values and aesthetics of English literature. Without having many chances of studying the literatures of other nations, Irish students might therefore conceive English literature to be superior and to encapsulate universal values, and would not question its possible colonial/imperialistic agenda. The purpose of university entrance examinations, as a result,

3. Examination Papers of Dublin's Universities

was to identify those students who could, or could not, demonstrate the merits of English literature. Take one of TCD's entrance examinations in the 1930s for instance. Prospective students were required to write an English composition regarding "the Victorian age in Literature."[196] By requiring examinees to write specifically on literature in the Victorian era – the prime age of the British Empire – it could be assumed that the faculty could identify who had, to their best knowledge, acquired an understanding of the political significance of the literature of an imperial power. In addition, as the literary curricula which Irish university students were required to follow in the 1930s were largely in accord with those in use at Oxbridge – examples will be given later – there were further consequences for Irish culture that resulted from students' exposure to these English-centred perspectives. One of these consequences was that Ireland remained a "colony" under the strong influences of British cultural colonisation. Another consequence was that the status of Irish literature and culture, at least at the level of higher education, did not really benefit from political independence but remained on the margin as far as the practice of teaching was concerned. Only a limited number of works by Anglo-Irish writers were introduced to students, and they were not taught as systematically as those of English canonical writers.

However, it might also be true to say that cultural decolonisation was effected, as mentioned earlier, in a moderate manner within Irish academia. This chapter will later explore in what ways cultural decolonisation did, or did not, take effect in university classrooms by looking into a series of examination papers and the choices of textbooks used in the 1930s. This was a crucial period during which the Free State was endeavouring to find its feet and a unified, national voice. I will also suggest who masterminded the limited but relevant changes in curricula.

Compared with the curricula of science studies, making amendments to humanities curricula was a hard task, since the latter were often subject to certain ideologies from politics, aesthetics and ethnicity, and to gender stereotypes. To talk of amending humanities curricula suggests that there were attitudes against those current ideologies, or the tradition(s) behind them. Conflicts, therefore, would be unavoidably incurred between traditionalists and those who questioned the rightfulness of tradition(s). For those who intended to amend the curricula of English literature and history at Irish universities, their struggle with the traditionalist faculty – who had been

---

[196] Trinity College Dublin (TCD), *Entrance Examination*, January, English Composition, −1938, question a-4.

trained to recognise the values of the Oxbridge tradition and only admitted Oxbridge transfers – could be particularly arduous and painful, as they were challenging the very core of the British cultural legacy.[197] To amend, or even slightly modify the curricula, would be regarded as jeopardising the integrity of this existing cultural legacy, which had even been accepted by some of the Irish for its universalism. Any minor amendment, such as to encompass the study of Anglo-Irish literature, the translation of Gaelic literature into English, or Irish-centred historiography, would unsettle the traditionalist faculty who intended to "guard" the passage of the English canon from one generation to another. They might, under the demand of revising curricula suitable for Irish students, have agreed to increase the number of Irish-related subjects in curricula and examinations as a compromise, but many did not genuinely recognise the merits of these non-mainstream literary products at this stage. My survey will later show that many of their compromises, though significant in terms of decolonising Irish higher education, were made with reluctance, since those Irish-related studies were usually accommodated in a subsidiary position in the curricula, and questions relating to them in exams were optional rather than required. The resistance to the revision of English curricula was common at both TCD and UCD in the 1930s, although there were some nuances, as I will demonstrate, between the two universities due to their different religious orientations.

Another common feature of university education at UCD and TCD in the 1930s was that they both continued the academic/general education that students had received at secondary schools. All freshman students of the two colleges, as their university calendars suggest, were required to study a selection of general courses, apart from those of the professional departments to which they were admitted. Take TCD's curriculum for example. Freshman students had to take general courses in Mathematics, Mathematical Physics, Logic, *English*, Latin and Greek as compulsory subjects during their first year. In their sophomore year, although they could be spared from

---

[197] Although the teaching orientation of TCD was akin to that of Scottish universities with four-year programmes and multi-subject first years, that TCD particularly welcomed transfers from the Oxbridge universities was clearly indicated in the section on "Recognition of other Colleges and Universities" in its University Calendars throughout the 1940s. It can therefore be contended that TCD had managed to maintain an equal, or similar, academic status with that of the Oxbridge universities in England. I will further explain this in the next section. I am indebted to Prof. Norman Vance for this information on the curricular differences amongst TCD, UCD, the Oxbridge universities, and Scottish universities.

3. Examination Papers of Dublin's Universities

the studies of Latin and Greek, they had to take Astronomy and one additional course in either Language (any two of Greek, Latin, French, and German), or Experimental Science (Physics and Chemistry) or Natural Science (Zoology, Botany, and Geology). These rules applied to students at both UCD and TCD, while UCD required students to study Irish in their first and second years, which significantly differentiated it from the more Anglophile TCD.[198]

It can be pointed out that the similarities in curricula for first and second year students at UCD and TCD were not a matter of coincidence but stemmed from a shared educational tradition with British universities. The primary aim of TCD was to promote values and knowledge that had been circulated within the centre of the empire. As for UCD, although founded to cater for Catholic students, it was expected to provide education of a similar quality to that offered at TCD and the Oxbridge universities. The major difference was that UCD maintained a strong Catholic ethos on campus. In addition, as university education had been widely expected to prepare "élites-to-be" with advanced knowledge for favourable careers, unlike those who had been channelled to vocational colleges or those not pursuing further studies after leaving – not necessarily graduating from – primary and secondary schools, it was anticipated that these élites, after graduation, would be able to "guide" those from the lower social classes.[199] It is hence fair to contend that the similar curricula for general academic education were also designed to prepare these "élites-to-be," directly or indirectly, to function as the keepers of social order, after Ireland had experienced remarkable revolutionary turbulence.

What is also worth attention is that, amongst the courses in the UCD and TCD curricula for general education, English remained the common subject that students

---

[198] For more details, see Bailey 80. My survey of the examination papers of UCD and TCD in the 1930s shows that the required study of the Irish language was the major difference between the curricula of the two Dublin universities. The choices of other compulsory subjects overlapped to a large extent. Notably, only after 1945 did TCD provide second year students with a "semi-optional" course in Irish.

[199] It should be noted that there were students who, for some reasons, had to leave before the legal school-leaving age, not completing their primary or secondary education. According to a 1971 census, the percentages of full-time primary and secondary school children were only 55.2 per cent and 40.8 per cent, respectively. It could therefore be assumed that during the 1940s, as the period which this chapter dwells upon, the number of students who were able to go to university was very small; those who could enter a university with a scholarship were even fewer. See Horgan 37.

Irish Literary Canon

of both universities had to take in their first and second years. The emphasis on English might be because it was/is the most dominant language in Irish society, and university graduates were expected to have a better command of it than those less well educated. However, the English courses they were offered were not to improve communicative or writing skills but were entirely focused on British/English literature. English writing by Irish writers rarely, or only occasionally, appeared in syllabi. Notably, the highlighting of traditional British/English literature, rather than Anglo-Irish, or Irish literatures, illustrated the fact that cultural decolonisation had not yet taken relevant effect in university classrooms in the 1930s. The coloniser's literature was still thought to have superior, universal values as against the vernacular one(s). As Ireland was not declared a republic until 1949, but remained a dominion of the British Commonwealth, it was understandable that the traditionalist English faculty would insist on teaching English canonical literature for its being "culturally right" for Ireland.[200] It was not until the 1980s, when the first MA taught programme in Anglo-Irish literature was set up at UCD, that "English writings by the Irish" were sufficiently attended to, and cultural decolonisation began to take effect in the university curriculum. This MA programme might have been expected to counteract the misconception by which "Irish literature in English" was subsidiary to the British literary tradition.[201]

---

[200] Nonetheless, UCD's and TCD's curricula were not unique in privileging English/British literature. The traditional English curricula which were adopted outside the British Isles, for instance in the U.S., also highlighted the teaching of canonical English/British writers. It was not until the late twentieth century that "World Literatures in English" were considered by curriculum makers. Specifically, "World literatures in English" refers to the literatures not necessarily written by Britons or Americans. They can be regional literatures written in the English language by writers from Africa, Australia, Canada, the Caribbean, India and some Asian countries, Ireland, New Zealand and the Pacific Islands. The teaching of these regional literatures in English to some extent counteracted the dominance of the traditional English canon.

[201] However, UCD's MA programme on Anglo-Irish literature was/is not confined to the teaching of works by writers from the Anglo-Irish ascendancy but covered "Irish experience in English." Its curricula also touched upon Irish history, folklore and mythology, as well as works written in Hiberno-English, the major dialect of English developed in Ireland over the centuries. The emphasis upon "Irish experience in English" significantly weakened the dominant status of the British/English canon in university curricula. For further details, see the introduction on its programme website: <http://www.ucd.ie/pgstudy/arts_t/arts10.htm>.

3. Examination Papers of Dublin's Universities

In addition to the common curriculum for general subjects with an emphasis on British/English literature, the two universities adopted a similar marking system under which some students were privileged as "Honours" while others were "Pass." It was a system that many British universities also used to encourage students to reach a higher level in their studies. What is dubious about this system, however, is that it potentially reinforced an "intellectual hierarchy" under which knowledge and students were both categorised; some knowledge was only available to Honours students. Take English literature for instance. Honours and Pass students at UCD and TCD were both required to study English literature, but only Honours students had the *option* to study Anglo-Irish literature, while Pass students usually did not.[202] Anglo-Irish literature remained either an élite subject for Honours or a secondary one for Pass in the practice of teaching English literature. (This point will be elaborated upon later.) What is also noteworthy about this marking system is that it was operated in part by pecuniary measures. By getting good marks in English literature and other subjects, Honours students might receive scholarships, or "sizarships," to waive their tuition fees.[203] It was a system that "élites-to-be" strove for out of pragmatic interests to reduce the financial pressure on their families. Although the examinations/competitions for scholarships appeared to be fair by testing students on the same subjects, it is probable that the order of the intellectual hierarchy was reinforced at the same time, as only a limited number of students, namely Honours candidates, could get the awards. My point is that, by competing for scholarships, students were likely to be disciplined by examinations within the academic hierarchy; examinees had to become Honours students first in order to compete for the grants.

However, although UCD and TCD in the 1930s did share some common features in their curricula and marking systems, some faculty members attempted to modify them to meet social expectations, in that the call for de-Anglicisation had been stronger off campus since the establishment of the nationalist government. For in-

---

[202] That is to say, Honours students could choose NOT to study Anglo-Irish literature, but English canonical literature instead, to get a high mark in exams. Pass students, however, were not introduced to Anglo-Irish literature even as an optional subject in the English curriculum.

[203] The word "sizar" originally refers to students at the University of Cambridge who were exempted from paying college fees and other charges by passing certain examinations, according to *Webster's Revised Unabridged Dictionary*. TCD also used this word, as its calendars for the 1930s showed, to describe those students receiving tuition waivers by passing "Sizarship Examinations."

stance, the faculty at TCD's teacher training college adopted curricula dissimilar from those for regular undergraduates, so as to equip prospective (primary and secondary) teachers with proficiency in the Irish language. That the training college faculty could put an emphasis on the study of Irish in their curriculum, on the one hand, should be attributed to the state's support of the revival of the language, which increased the demand for competent teachers. On the other hand, as an affiliated institute of TCD since 1933 – formerly under the management of the Church of Ireland, this training college enjoyed a greater freedom than regular departments of TCD in making curricula to meet social expectations. As TCD had to validate the more Irish-orientated curriculum made by the training college faculty, it could be surmised that there were profound effects on English-orientated TCD itself. (The effects will be elaborated in the next section.) For UCD, the revision of English curricula also underwent an unsettling process, in that not all faculty members shared the same views about the teaching of British/English literature for Irish students. To illustrate how the faculties of TCD and UCD failed and succeeded in modifying curricula, the next two sections will survey the university calendars of the two colleges. The usefulness of university calendars is that they recorded significant changes on an annual basis. The survey of these university calendars is expected to show not only who masterminded those changes, but to what extent cultural decolonisation was effected in higher education. All in all, the way in which the Irish faculty coped with social changes will mirror how they faced, distanced themselves from, or adhered to, the changing faces of Ireland since its political independence.

3.2. De-Anglicisation within Trinity College Dublin

The attempt to transform TCD into an "Irish-orientated" university can be seen from a statement in which Kenneth Bailey, the author of *A History of Trinity College Dublin 1892-1945*, listed the benefits which TCD students could gain, if they studied the Irish language there. According to him, the number of Irish faculty and staff at the School of Irish in 1945 was "larger than that of any of the language schools"; the faculty had not only given "a full course of instruction" in Irish but "succeeded in making important contributions to the scientific study of the Irish language."[204] More importantly, he said that due to "the greatly increased encouragement since the establishment of a native government in 1921," the School of Irish was able to make such

---

[204] Bailey 83.

3. Examination Papers of Dublin's Universities

improvements.[205] What is also noteworthy about this statement, beside its possible propagandism, is its timing. It was at a time when the Catholic clergy explicitly discouraged Catholics from attending TCD, although many Irish Catholics still opted for this university at their own will. Bailey's emphasis upon the improvement of the Irish School, as well as his reference to the native government were likely to counteract the "discouragement" and to convince Irish nationalists that TCD had come up to nationalistic expectations. In contrast to the teaching of Irish for missionary purposes since the mid-nineteenth century, which I have mentioned earlier, TCD had been gradually adapting itself after Irish independence to the nationalistic ethos – perhaps under the influence of the newly affiliated Training College. Nevertheless, the question of whether TCD was genuinely being de-Anglicised should be seen along with the development of TCD's English and History departments during the same period. That is, the "encouragement from the native government" might have de-Anglicised the English department in profound ways.

It could be suggested that the de-Anglicisation of TCD could not have been carried out directly after the establishment of the Free State due to its historical link with English academia. It is a link that maintained TCD in accord with the Oxbridge tradition. The strong association with the Oxbridge universities can be seen from a regulation that appeared as the first item in the section on "Recognition of other Colleges and Universities" – in TCD's university calendars throughout the 1930s. It indicated that no students or graduates of other universities, excluding Oxford and Cambridge, could take the degree of B.A.[206] What is interesting about the "Recognition of other Colleges and Universities" is that a proviso was added to permit students from non-Oxbridge universities to take the degree of B.A, provided they had kept at least two academic years at TCD.[207] In my view, both the regulation and the proviso were unlikely to take relevant effect, for those who had studied for a B.A. at Oxbridge would be unlikely to drop out and come to TCD. It could be considered that the proviso therefore served rather as an alternative to students in Britain who wished to study at Oxbridge but did not gain admission. They might therefore come to TCD after their first year at a university elsewhere, study there for another two years and so become its regular students or graduates. By admitting these students – presumably English Anglicans or Presbyterians – TCD and Oxbridge might have reciprocated

---

[205] Bailey 83.
[206] University of Dublin Trinity College, *The Dublin University Calendar 1930-1931* 81.
[207] *Dublin University Calendar 1930-1931* 81.

each other via their students, on the grounds that TCD could reconfirm its academic superiority and equivalence with the Oxbridge universities. Those from non-Oxbridge universities but willing to study for two more years at TCD might deem that their efforts were worthwhile, in that TCD and the Oxbridge universities had been conceived as establishments with similar academic merits and repute – both in England and Ireland. It might be fair to say that "Oxbridge Englishness" was a cultural ethos well maintained at TCD.

Whether or not TCD reproduced an ethos of "Oxbridge Englishness" in Ireland, the fact is that it distributed the cultural legacy of England/Britain, at least in the 1930s. This judgement is based on the English and history curricula and the specialities of the related faculty. For the English Department, the three successive chairpersons from the turn of the twentieth century to the end of the 1930s – who were responsible for the writing of syllabi and examination papers – were all Shakespearians: Edward Dowden (1843-1913), Dodgson Hamilton Madden (1840-1919), and Wilbraham Fitzjohn Trench (1873-1939).[208] That they succeeded one another with the same research interests suggests the resolute maintenance of the English classic canon in TCD classrooms; not only were Shakespeare's works viewed as the most essential asset in English/British literature, but those who specialised in Shakespeare might expect faster access to a privileged position in the academic hierarchy, such as chairpersonships of English departments.

Nevertheless, the establishment of the Free State had an effect on the appointments of the chairpersons of TCD's English department. Comparing Dowden's publications with Trench's, although they both researched on Shakespeare, Dowden had written works distinctly in favour of Irish unionism, while Trench was sympathetic towards Irish nationalism. A former secretary of the Irish Liberal Union and

---

[208] Bailey 196-97. According to Bailey, Dowden's reputation was established by the publication of *Shakespeare, His Mind and Art* (1875). His other works include *Shakespeare Scenes and Characters* (1876), *The Shakespeare Cyclopaedia and New Glossary* (1902), *Irish Unionists and the Present Administration* (1904), *The Tragedies of Shakespeare* (1922) and so on; Madden was the author of *The Diary of Master William Silence: A Study of Shakespeare & of Elizabethan Sport* (1897), *Shakespeare and his Fellows* (1916), and *The England into which Shakespeare Was Born* (1918); Trench's works on Shakespeare were: *Shakespeare's Hamlet* (1913) and *The Spirit of Shakespeare's Approach to Tragedy* (1925). Nevertheless, he seemed to be sympathetic towards nationalistic causes; one of his lectures on Thomas Moore, delivered in 1934, was published by Three Candles in Dublin.

3. Examination Papers of Dublin's Universities

vice-president of the Irish Unionist Alliance, Dowden in his *Irish Unionists and the Present Administration* (1904) emphasises the benefits which Ireland gained by being under the English crown. Trench, however, by publishing his lectures on Thomas Moore, appeared to clash with his predecessors in political and cultural matters. His lectures on Thomas Moore referred to the poet's argument in relation to English misrule in Ireland, and his contribution to English verse through his Irish folk airs. As the two chairpersons – appointed before and after the establishment of the Free State – had publications that demonstrated different interests, it might be true to say that political independence did matter for the research directions of the academic staff. However, Trench's publication on Moore in 1939 – which was a collection of his transcribed lectures – was his only work on Anglo-Irish writers before he died in the same year. He might have intended to explore in depth the thoughts and life of this particular Catholic poet, but he did not live long enough.

Although Trench's lectures and late publication on Moore might imply that some of TCD's English faculty, by the end of the 1930s, had developed interests in writers who had an Irish origin, this does not mean that English canonical writers were less dominant in syllabi. Moore and Stephen Gwynn, according to my survey of TCD's university calendars, seem to be the only two Irish-born writers who were taught frequently during the entire 1930s, along with English canonical writers.[209] Most of the Anglo-Irish writers, such as Jonathan Swift and Oliver Goldsmith, notably, did not receive much mention, nor did nineteenth-century ones. (However, at UCD, the study of Anglo-Irish writers was more encouraged than that at TCD in the 1930s, which I will discuss later.) The limited teaching of Anglo-Irish literature at TCD might be because its English Department was traditionally modelled after those at Oxbridge. The introduction of Thomas Moore and Stephen Gwynn – the latter was a contemporary nationalistic poet and MP – might have been due to the recommendation of the current chair, whereas Anglo-Irish literature was not the main teaching or research inter-

---

[209] There were no major changes in the English syllabi at TCD in the 1930s, when Trench was the chairperson of the English department. The English canonical writers who were taught included: Geoffrey Chaucer, William Shakespeare, Edmund Spenser, John Milton, Joseph Addison, John Dryden, Alexander Pope, and Francis Bacon. Apart from their texts, students were required to study poetic works from an anthology edited by Francis Turner Palgrave: *The Golden Treasury of the Best Songs and Lyrical Poems in the English Language,* first published in 1888 with revisions in following years.

est of other faculty members.[210] As there was a lack of systematic introduction to Anglo-Irish writers, they were likely taught in the context of English/British literature, on the grounds that the required textbook from which students should study their works in reference was *A History of English Literature*, by Émile Legouis and Louis Cazamian. As there was no other textbook giving the same degree of elaboration on the Irish or Anglo-Irish backgrounds to which Moore and Gwynn belonged, it could be reasonable to judge that their "nationalistic Irishness" might have impressed students only to a limited extent. Having said that, it would be true to observe that the political independence of Southern Ireland had not yet produced relevant effects on TCD's English classrooms, at least in the 1930s. Not only were those writers who were taught all male, but "Irish-Irish" and Anglo-Irish writers – who had written a significant number of English writings about Irish peasantry, folklore, and myths – had not yet been admitted for teaching purposes to university classrooms.

It could be claimed that the emphasis on English canonical writers had largely reinforced English-centred literary tastes; however, the scenario at the History Department was slightly different. To take the reading list for first-year history students as an example, although the number of textbooks on the history of England was still greater than that on Irish history, history students could acquire Irish-centred perspectives more directly than those in the English Department. Three assigned textbooks specifically on Irish history, against five on English and European, were Richard Bagwell's *Ireland under the Tudors* (1885), Edmund Curtis' *A History of Mediaeval Ireland* (1923), and Eleanor Hull's *A History of Ireland and her People* (1926).[211] Nevertheless, English history was technically privileged in the making of history cur-

---

[210] Stephen Gwynn (1864-1950) was born in Rathfarnham, Co. Dublin; son of Rev. John Gwynn and Lucy Gwynn. His father was Regius professor of divinity at TCD. Stephen Gwynn was a Nationalist MP for Galway City, 1906-1918, and the biographer for *Thomas Moore* (1904), *Horace Walpole* (1932), *Dean Swift* (1933), *Oliver Goldsmith* (1935), *R. L. Stevenson* (1939) and *Henry Grattan (1939)*. His *Irish Literature and Drama in the English Language* (1920) was known as an extended survey which charted the tradition of Anglo-Irish literature.

[211] The five textbooks on European and English history were: James Bryce's *The Holy Roman Empire* (1863), Herbert Fisher's *The Medieval Empire* (1898), H.W.C. Davis' *England under the Normans and Angevins* (1905), T.F. Tout's *An Advanced History of Great Britain* (1906), B.A. Lees' *The Central Period of the Middle Ages* (1909), John Masterman's *The Dawn of Mediæval Europe, 476-918* (1909). This reading list was derived from the TCD's university calendars 1931-1939. There were few changes in this reading list during the 1930s.

3. Examination Papers of Dublin's Universities

ricula, on the grounds that it was always listed first in course titles, such as "English and Irish History, 1449-1485," and "English and Irish History, 1485-1801." There was no course specifically on Irish history alone, in the 1930s, according to TCD's university calendars.

What is more interesting is that, on the reading lists for second-year history students, the emphasis on Irish history was largely dismissed and replaced by European history and economic history. The guidelines for students preparing for term examinations did not include any aspect of Irish history, but focused on English constitutional history. For European history, the histories of Germany and France were particularly highlighted. There was no indication in the guidelines that Ireland was taught in a broad European context, even though it did have a long history of cultural and economic interactions with countries on the European mainland before the Middle Ages.[212] What could therefore be surmised was that the dismissal of Irish history (from the European context) and the emphasis on English constitutional history might have subtly strengthened English-centred perspectives in history. It was not only because English history was the main subject on syllabi for both freshmen and sophomores, but because the rules that defined the relationship between the Dáil and the Senate, as well as the roles of many administrative bodies in the Free State "followed British practice very closely [. . .]."[213] As for the teaching of European history to sophomores, some might argue that the makers of the History syllabi might have intended to underpin students' understanding of Irish and English history, before they learnt the history of other European countries. It is noteworthy that Irish history was eventually placed in a subordinate position to English history, as the former was little mentioned on syllabi for second-year students, nor was it mentioned on those for freshmen.

Another notable fact about TCD's history syllabi can be illuminated by comparing them with those used at QUB during the same period of time. Although QUB and TCD are both located in Ireland and both have an English foundation, they experienced different decolonising effects stemming from the political partition in 1922. As the former had been separated from the Catholic NUI since 1908 and was commonly

---

[212] The two specific periods in German and French history which were dealt with were the Ages of the Hohenstaufen, 1137-1250 and France in the Seventeenth Century. The two periods were listed in the guidelines for students preparing for term examinations. Irish history was mentioned little in the teaching of European history throughout the 1930s.

[213] Lyons, *Ireland* 474.

identified as a university catering more for the Presbyterian population in Northern Ireland under the British system, this university was more or less expected by unionists to promote the political alliance between Northern Ireland and Great Britain.[214] This "expectation" persisted through to the 1930s and was reflected in the history syllabi. Unlike TCD's history syllabi, which itemised courses as "English and Irish" history or "English" constitutional history, the syllabi of QUB named these courses "History of Ireland and the Empire" and "Constitutional History of Great Britain and Ireland."[215] The nuance lies in the different connotations of the choices of words: Great Britain, the Empire, or English. It could be stated that the former two emphasised the political unity with which Ireland was associated – under a shared constitutional model. However, the juxtaposition of English and Irish – which appeared on TCD's syllabi – suggested a rather equal comparison between two political entities. It might therefore be reasonable to judge that the naming of course titles could be varied from one political standpoint to another. Notably, only Honours students at QUB were tested on Irish history, while Pass students were not. This suggests that at QUB, perhaps due to political reasons, the teaching of Irish history was not deemed essential, while at TCD, freshman students, regardless of Honours or Pass, were required to study Irish history to some extent in the 1930s.

The early part of this chapter has argued that the History Department at TCD was more pioneering in accommodating Irish subjects than the English Department. Nonetheless, the most significant decolonising effects on teaching practises, in my observation, might have come from TCD's own teachers' training college, which was established in 1933 and admitted students who were formerly registered with the Church of Ireland Training College.[216] As students of the two-year training college were expected to teach at primary and secondary schools and be able to conduct Irish language classes, it is understandable that the curricula for them would be different from those of regular TCD students. The courses that training college students were

---

[214] However, it cannot be denied that some faculty members at QUB were supporters of Irish nationalism; notably R.M. Henry, Professor of Latin, was a prominent Irish nationalist. I am thankful to Prof. Norman Vance for the information.

[215] Queen's University, *The Queen's University of Belfast Calendar for 1932-34* 189. The curriculum for History did not vary much during the 1930s, according to my survey.

[216] It is hard to know why the Church of Ireland Training College was affiliated with TCD in 1933. But those "teachers-to-be" could thereby have access to the same learning resources as those of TCD.

3. Examination Papers of Dublin's Universities

required to take were as follows: Irish, Mathematics, English, Geography, Religious Knowledge, the Art of Teaching, Latin, and Logic. Amongst them, English, Latin, and Geography were optional in the second year, but Irish remained a required course in both years. Although the particular emphasis on Irish was doubtless to make these prospective teachers competent in this language for future use in schools, it was groundbreaking for TCD to approve Irish as a required course – to any internal or affiliated department of TCD. (Contemporaneously, Irish was an *optional* course for regular students.) What is more interesting is that this training college, affiliated with TCD, became an institute which gave future teachers a proper command of this native language; English, on the contrary, was not an emphasised subject in its curricula. It might therefore be appropriate to judge that TCD was under the pressure of becoming de-Anglicised, although this decolonialising force emanated from the marginal, affiliated teacher training college, rather than the regular English department. I will later elaborate on how this decolonialising force was substantiated in examination papers.

3.3. Moves towards Decolonisation within University College Dublin

Some people might argue that there was no need for UCD to be decolonised, as it had laid a strong foundation in encouraging Celtic studies since the mid-nineteenth century.[217] Not only was its predecessor, the Catholic University, set up to counteract the Protestant-orientated TCD, but its co-founder, John Henry Newman, was particularly supportive of Celtic studies.[218] At the turn of the twentieth century, UCD even cooperated with the Gaelic League in providing courses on the Irish language and history for its staff and interested students. These courses, according to UCD's official records, were conducted by Patrick Pearse, Douglas Hyde, and others.[219] These facts illustrate that UCD did contribute, with nationalist encouragement, to the making of a

---

[217] The Catholic University was the predecessor of UCD, established in the mid-nineteenth century by Paul Cullen and John Henry Newman. In 1881, under the Royal Universities Act, the university was renamed University College Dublin. In 1908, UCD was incorporated as a constituent college of the National University of Ireland (NUI).

[218] Newman gave Eugene O'Curry and W.K. Sullivan relevant support in leading Celtic Studies at the Catholic University. O'Curry was appointed Professor of Celtic history and archaeology in 1845.

[219] *Story of University College Dublin 1883-1909* 183, 186.

different cultural identity from that of the English, along with the movement of de-Anglicisation.

This generalisation might be right in some respects, but it appears open to question when we observe how the call for de-Anglicisation was effected within UCD's English and History departments. It is because the two departments, unlike the "new" schools for Irish music and archaeology, were to a large extent modelled, since the mid-nineteenth century, on those of British universities. They contributed to the circulation of English values and perspectives by adopting curricula that had been used at British universities. However, as with TCD, the establishment of the Irish Free State did have some effect on the remaking of UCD's curricula. Some modifications in curricula were minor but important; some were expedient. In this section, I will explore these modifications in curricula and their significance, in attempting to argue that UCD was not always consistent in responding to the movement towards de-Anglicisation, due to the various political standpoints of faculty members.

I would first like to examine the English curricula used at UCD in the 1930s, as the two successive chairpersons of the English Department seem to have had dissimilar opinions regarding the teaching of the English canon in university classrooms. Robert Donovan, who chaired the department from 1928 to 1936, for instance, was known not only as a friend of Roger Casement but also as a researcher in Irish literature in English.[220] He developed an interest in Anglo-Irish literature many years before he was appointed chair of the English Department.[221] His special interest in Irish writings in English was, as could have been expected, reflected in the curricula approved during his term of office. He not only encouraged students, both Pass and Honours, to study Anglo-Irish literature, but also specified the names of nineteenth-century Anglo-Irish writers in the guidelines for students preparing for B.A. degree examinations. The nineteenth-century Anglo-Irish writers he listed were: Thomas Moore, George Darley, Aubrey de Vere, James Clarence Mangan, Samuel Ferguson, Thomas Davis, Denis MacCarthy, Percy Fitzgerald, William Allingham,

---

[220] His correspondence with Roger Casement is now archived in the library of UCD. Casement had written to him, elaborating his ideas on Home Rule, education, the use of the Irish language, and so on.

[221] In 1884, he gave a speech at the inaugural meeting of UCD's Literary and Historical Society. The title of the speech was "The Irish Genius in Literature: A Forecast of its Work in the Future." It should be safe to say that he had developed an interest in Irish literature earlier than 1884.

3. Examination Papers of Dublin's Universities

Gerald Griffin, William Carleton, and John Mitchel.[222] It could be argued that he was attempting to differentiate Anglo-Irish writers from English ones, and to pave the way for an Anglo-Irish canon to emerge.

However, the important thing about his list of Anglo-Irish writers was not who was on the list and who was not, but whether it did in fact counteract the English traditional canon. On the one hand, the list seemed unprecedented, in that most of the English curricula, whether those used at TCD or at universities on the British mainland, had not acknowledged the necessity of teaching Anglo-Irish writers as a separate category from the English. They were largely ignored or taught along with English writers. On the other hand, the number of them fortunate enough to be included in curricula was usually very small. Without a separate categorisation, students might not be able to come to the proper understanding that an Anglo-Irish origin might matter in terms of how a writer approached literature. (At TCD, as I have demonstrated earlier, Thomas Moore and Stephen Gwynn were the writers who apparently received more mentions than others). It could be observed that Donovan's specification of a remarkable number of Anglo-Irish writers demonstrated his attempt to draw students' attention to writers in English whose origin was not English, but Irish. Notably, the writers he selected had a more or less strong inclination towards Irish (cultural) nationalism. Some translated Gaelic poems into English; some presented the misery of Irish peasantry; some rewrote Irish myths, and so on. Donovan might therefore have expected to underpin students' recognition of a distinct Irish identity, at least at a cultural level.

Although Donovan and his colleagues in the 1930s might have attempted to reinforce a cultural identity that was different from the English one, their efforts were actually circumscribed or counteracted by the traditional forces that persisted in the English department. It was expected that English graduates would improve both their writing technique and their knowledge of canonical literature. For Honours and Pass freshmen at UCD, English grammar and English prose composition were two major required English subject areas. Seniors were tested on how they appreciated and analysed different English prose styles since Dryden as a composition topic for B.A. de-

---

[222] University College Dublin, *Calendar for the Session 1931-32* 197. It was very likely that he endorsed the guidelines, because not only was he the chairperson at the time but his name was printed on the guideline sheets. It is interesting to know that William Carleton was included in Donovan's list for Anglo-Irish writers. He was usually deemed an Irish-Irish writer, rather than Anglo-Irish.

gree examinations.[223] Apart from the language requirement, Honours seniors were expected to study specific texts by English canonical writers, so as to demonstrate "a more detailed knowledge of the History of English literature" at degree examinations.[224]

It is fair to say that the study of English language and literature, as a matter of fact, remained predominant in English curricula, despite the attempts of Donovan (and some of his colleagues) to act against the overpowering English canon. Notably, as the Anglo-Irish canon was pretty much in its infancy in the 1930s, it was likely that Donovan at this stage had not been able to specifically point out which texts should be studied but suggested who might be worth looking at. In other words, his list of Anglo-Irish writers with unspecified texts might have implied a "canon in progress." Nevertheless, due to his nationalistic background and early association with Roger Casement, the "canon in progress" was never open-ended but was unavoidably tinted with a nationalistic ethos. That is to say, the writers he chose were more or less concerned with the making of a cultural identity through literature, and some in particular endeavoured to translate Gaelic works into English, as a method of counteracting Englishness. It might therefore be fair to contend that mainstream, nationalistic social interests were involved in his attempts at creating an Anglo-Irish canon in the 1930s – one decade after the establishment of the Free State. Notably, the eighteenth-century Anglo-Irish writers on the syllabi he approved, such as Jonathan Swift, Oliver Goldsmith, Edmund Burke, were usually mixed with canonical English ones. That these writers were not differentiated from English-born writers might be because their works, though some of them sympathetic to Irish Catholics under the suppression of British rule, were mostly written for English audiences, and not always explicitly in reference to Irish patriotism or the Celtic revival. The nineteenth-century Anglo-Irish writers that Donovan specified, however, had shared a more distinct nationalistic attitude.

What should not be ignored with regard to Donovan's attempt to formulate an Anglo-Irish canon is that his successor, Jeremiah Hogan, who was appointed chair-

---

[223] *Calendar for the Session 1931-32* 197.

[224] Specific texts included: Chaucer's *The Knight's Tale*, Spenser's *The Faerie Queen Book I*, Marlowe's *Dr. Faustus* and *Edward II*, Shakespeare's *Richard III*, *Macbeth*, and *The Tempest*, Milton's *Samson Agonistes* and *Lycidas*, Ruskin's *The Harbours of England*, Arnold's *On Translating Homer*, and Butcher's *The Poetics of Aristotle*. See *Calendar for the Session 1931-32* 198.

3. Examination Papers of Dublin's Universities

person of the English Department in 1936, did not seem to share the same interests as Donovan. During Hogan's term of office, the curricula he approved referred to few Anglo-Irish writers or their texts, and were essentially English-orientated. Only on the curricula for Honours students were Matthew Arnold's "essays on Celtic literature" required for study.[225] The sudden dismissal of Anglo-Irish literature from curricula during 1936-1940 might imply some backlash from the traditionalist faculty against Donovan and his "comrades." Hogan, as Professor of Philology with an interest in Romanticism, might presumably have been appointed to "rescue" the traditional English canon from being opened up too quickly to accommodate "new" Anglo-Irish writers.[226] On the other hand, although the subject matters of Arnold's essays were Celtic-related, his views of Celtic culture as "feminine" could not be more stereotypical and traditional. The introduction of Arnold's essays therefore potentially strengthened the standpoints of the traditionalist English faculty who expected the English canon to remain essentially English, rather than to be hybridised with Irish characteristics.

It may be observed that English Departments, whether at UCD or TCD, were likely to be the most difficult arenas in which the movement towards decolonisation could have made progress. History Departments, however, could have different scenarios according to which the teaching and interpretation of history would more often be subject to mainstream political values. It is true to say that at UCD, as an educational institute with an aim to counteract the consequences of Anglicisation, the faculty of the History Department had, understandably, endeavoured to produce curricula that cultivated an Irish-centred historiography. The emphasis on Irish-centred historiography was reflected in the choices of textbooks and the subject matter taught to students. Notably, during Mary Hayden's term of office as the chairperson of the

---

[225] Matthew Arnold's views on Gaelic literature are/were regarded as being very biased, in that he saw the Celtic psyche as "essentially feminine," and ambiguously praised the Celts for their incapability of dealing with the "despotism of fact."

[226] Jeremiah J. Hogan was the author of *Romantic Poets and the English Language* (1923), *The English Language in Ireland* (1927), and *An Outline of English Philology* (1934). Hogan was particularly interested in the philological study of Hiberno-English and had proposed the formation of a "Dictionary of the English of Ireland." In his view, "Hiberno English [. . .] ha[d] received no systematic study." It could be assumed that he, as a philologist, was more interested in the language *per se*, rather than literature. His lack of interest in Anglo-Irish literature, therefore, seems understandable. Quoted in Montgomery 27.

Modern History Department until 1944, the curricula she approved did not seem particularly English-orientated, nor was English history particularly prioritised. Instead, the history of Europe and Ireland were often emphasised more in curricula, while English history was always given a lower priority. The textbooks assigned for history students encompassed a greater number relating to Irish and European history than to English. To name a few: *The Patriot Parliament of 1689* (1893) by T.O. Davis, *Modern Europe, 1815-1899* (1901) by W.A. Phillips, *Europe in the Nineteenth Century* (1916) by Ephraim Lipson, *Last Independent Parliament of Ireland* by George Sigerson (1918), and *Illustrated History of Ireland* (1919) by P.W. Joyce. As students were apparently not expected to study English history intensively, there was only one textbook assigned for it: S.R. Gardiner's *A Student's History of England* (1923).

The reason why UCD's History department could have a more pioneering achievement with de-Anglicisation, by having students acquire knowledge of Irish history within a European framework rather than an English one, was not, in my view, simply because of the nationalistic ethos but was also due to Mary Hayden's own standpoints on educational, cultural and political issues. She was the first woman to serve on the senate of the National University of Ireland (from 1909-1924), and had greatly encouraged women to go to university. She had taken part in the Gaelic League in which she "rejoiced in the freedom" due to its non-sectarian, non-political, and mixed-sex activities.[227] It is therefore reasonable to judge that her participation in the Gaelic League foreshadowed her attempts to make history curricula more pertinent to Irish experiences. It could also be pointed out that it was her unconventional standpoints that facilitated the decolonisation of UCD's History Department in the 1930s, while the English department, contemporaneously, remained greatly dominated by the traditionalist faculty.

The next two sections, on TCD's and UCD's examination papers, will demonstrate how the movement of de-Anglicisation took effect in a more sophisticated manner. My survey will show that examination papers were sometimes not in accord with changes in curricula, and were probably designed to counteract decolonial forces within the History and English Departments. The lack of accord might be because the setting of examination papers was subject to a wider range of social and academic determinants, and some teachers attempted to demonstrate their diversified opinions by including questions that reflected their particular interests. Examination papers

---

[227] Quoted in Paseta 140.

3. Examination Papers of Dublin's Universities

therefore served as a more expressive forum in which different political concerns were testified. In this connection, they will serve as channels through which we can trace how decolonialism did, or did not, have a greater effect in the 1930s at the two pre-eminent universities in Dublin.

3.4. (De)Colonising Examination Papers: Trinity College Dublin

The early part of this chapter has demonstrated that TCD was a university firmly based on an Oxbridge tradition by admitting transferees only from the Oxbridge universities. It was also an establishment that aimed to circulate and preserve knowledge, values and perspectives favoured by the upper-class English, and primarily catered for Protestants.

With its historical background and links with the English Crown, it is understandable that some TCD faculty members would attempt to keep the institute from being decolonised too quickly, so as to subtly continue its superiority in both Irish and British higher education. The way in which TCD was subtly maintained as a colonial institution was, in my view, typified in examination papers which mirrored power interrelations amongst the faculty. An analysis of the contents of examination papers composed by the English and History Departments during the 1930s, therefore, will demonstrate how different powers/ideologies grew, interacted, or diminished amongst tutors and students, and whether some faculty members were still subject to colonial biases and values.

It is true to say that the establishment of the Irish Free State did result in radical changes in Irish politics, and facilitated that nationalists took over political positions that the former coloniser, or supporters of continued British rule, had occupied. In the early period of post-Treaty Ireland, however, as I demonstrated in Chapter One, political changes took effect on a more external, rather than internal level: "neo-colonialism" had taken its form with similar hegemony inherited from the former coloniser. Education, which played an important role in the formation of students' internal and external perceptions of their being and society, was not properly restructured so as to be able to free itself from colonial consequences.

As TCD had been the top university to which both Catholic and Protestant Irish pupils could be admitted (since 1793), there was always an entrance examination which students were obliged to take. In particular, Irish pupils who would like to study at TCD had to pass its entrance exams which tested their appreciation of English literature, history, and so on. The exams, therefore, enabled TCD to screen out those students who failed to meet the faculty's expectations for absorbing English knowledge. It could be suggested that exams, no matter whether for admissions, scholarships, or graduation purposes, would be means through which TCD maintained its favoured perspectives in history, literature, and so on.

It could be assumed that there were preferred answers which examinees were expected to produce. Questions which appeared on a series of 1930 entrance exams on the subject of "History and Geography," for example, to a large extent were written in line with the sentiments shown in history curricula. Notably, there were always many more questions on examination papers that related to English history than there were on Irish history. Those questions that did concern Irish history were composed more or less in accord with the viewpoints of the English. It could be argued that, to pass the entrance examination, students had to recognise the presuppositions behind questions, and avoid giving answers that were creative but obviously politically incorrect. Questions relating to the reciprocal relationship between Great Britain and Ireland were frequently included, such as:

> Account for the superior development of non-agricultural industry in Great Britain as compared with Ireland.[228]
>
> In what circumstances was the Union of Ireland with Great Britain effected?[229]
>
> Illustrate from British History the importance of sea power.[230]

For the first question, it may well be the case that students would need to admit that Ireland was good at agriculture, and that having non-agricultural industry was the advantage of a developed country like Britain. The cooperation between Ireland and Britain would have to be described as one serving as a food supplier and the other as "superior" protector, with mutual benefits to each.[231] That the second question re-

---

[228] TCD, *Entrance Examination in Arts*, January 1930, History and Geography, question 9.

[229] TCD, *Entrance Examination in Arts for Medical School*, Hilary Term, 1930, History and Geography, question, A-6.

[230] TCD, *Autumn Entrance Examination Arts and Science*, October, 1930, *History and Geography*, question B-8.

[231] It is also true that the lack of indigenous raw materials, such as iron and coal, was one of the reasons why Ireland could hardly be highly industrialised before the twentieth century. Nevertheless, the fact that the British government relied heavily on food supplies

3. Examination Papers of Dublin's Universities

quired examinees to find evidence from the social and political context in which unionism was fostered might have suggested that, possibly in the view of the British the Union of Ireland with Great Britain was reciprocal and expectable. There is apparently no room for students, as the question stands, to argue the undesirability of the Union.[232] To answer the third question, it is possible that students would be expected to acknowledge the military advantages of the British Empire so that Ireland, as an agricultural state, should rely on its military protection. Nevertheless, although it is undeniable that the question reflected the imperious demands for sea power before and after the First World War, the British-centred sentiments were obvious here in the focus on British history. This question might seem awkward to some radical Irish nationalists who might be uncertain about the necessity of having Irish students demonstrate their knowledge of, or comment on, the sea power of their neighbouring state and former coloniser.

The favoured, English-centred perspectives were also reflected in the titles of history examinations at TCD – the same as the course titles given in the curricula discussed earlier. Notably, most of the examination subject titles were given as either "History" or "English History." If neither, it would usually be "English and Irish History" – with a large number of questions about England, and a very limited number about Ireland. From these given titles and the lack of balance in the number of questions on English and Irish history, respectively, it is fair to assume that examinees were expected to acquaint themselves more with Anglo-centric historiography than with an Irish-Irish one. After all, university entrance examinations were not a forum for students to dispute with the markers about the legitimacy of a particular historiography, but to give answers according to "textbook knowledge."

---

from Ireland should be acknowledged. The large amount of Irish agricultural produce exported to Britain, for instance, was one of the causes of the Great Famine (1845-1848). Liam O'Flaherty in his historical novel, *Famine* (1937), illustrates the mixture of causes of the Great Famine; Britain's traditional reliance on Irish farm products was one cause to be underlined.

[232] The passing of an Act of Union in 1800, which abolished the Irish Parliament by providing for Irish representation at Westminster in London, seemed a desirable solution to the Irish Question in the aftermath of the Rebellion of 1798. The voices of Irish MPs could therefore be more attended to at Westminster, whereas Irish political agitation was staged there, too. By identifying the historical background of this Act, in my opinion, students might have to acquaint themselves with the sentiments of unionism, as a solution broadly beneficial to both Ireland and Britain.

Irish Literary Canon

My survey of TCD's curricula earlier in this chapter has shown that the establishment of the Irish Free State did not seem to have a decisive impact on the Anglo-centric TCD, even though TCD did offer language courses on Gaelic amongst other foreign languages. English perspectives still dominated the creation of both curricula and examination papers. In addition to the subject of history, which more or less favoured English historiography, the teaching of literature was also English-orientated and intended to pass on to students the knowledge of the English classic canon, rather than that of an Irish or Anglo-Irish one. Notably, the English literary canon was constantly reinforced by exams with questions about writers originating from England. In my survey, the literature examination papers used from 1930 to 1935 addressed very few writers of Irish origin. Also, only a very limited number of Anglo-Irish writers were taught to undergraduates, although many of them had produced a significant amount of writing from the early eighteenth century onwards. The stress laid upon the English canon could be seen from the examination papers designed for degree examinations, as well as those compiled for the purpose of scholarship competitions. That is, students in different school years, from entrance scholarships to senior student exhibitions, all had to be familiar with the English canon if they wanted to stand a chance of winning TCD funding, or be considered to have academic merit. These exams included: *Junior and School Exhibitions*, Michaelmas Term, 1930; *Entrance Examination*, Midsummer, 1930; *special B.A. Degree Examination*, Trinity Term, 1934; *Supplemental B.A. Degree Examination*, Trinity Term, 1934.

At TCD, the absence of Anglo-Irish literature, or Irish literature in English – including works translated into English – was slightly redressed in the middle of the 1930s. Questions about Anglo-Irish writers started to appear in examination papers for senior undergraduates, such as, describe "the life and works of Jonathan Swift" in *Senior Sophisters Examination: English Literature*, Hilary Term, 1936,[233] and an essay topic: "Famous Irish men of letters of the eighteenth century" in *Senior Sophister Term Examination*, Hilary Term, 1937.[234] Nevertheless, these were not a required question that examinees had to answer, but optional ones. Students could complete the examination and achieve a high mark without having to deal with any Irish-related questions. One question which more explicitly referred to a number of

---

[233] TCD, *Senior Sophisters Examination: English Literature*, Hilary Term, 1936, question 3.
[234] TCD, *Senior Sophisters Term Examination*, Hilary Term, 1937, question 1-C.

3. Examination Papers of Dublin's Universities

Anglo-Irish writers appeared as follows on the bottom of the exam paper for *Entrance Scholarships and Junior and School Exhibitions*, Trinity Term, 1938 – a location which might signify a new but marginal position given to these writers in the teaching of English literature:

> Here follow the names of a few writers of Irish birth. Restricting your attention to two of these, explain the importance of their contribution to English literature. Suggest also approximate dates. Any sign (very briefly given) of first-hand acquaintance with any of the work of these two will be particularly valued: Swift; Goldsmith; Sheridan; Burke; Thomas Moore; W. B. Yeats.[235]

These few references to Anglo-Irish writers in English literature exams did not necessarily mean that the faculty of TCD in the 1930s was redressing its traditional literary perspectives in an attempt to hold out an olive branch to Anglo-Irish literature; that is to say, to place it on an equal basis with the existing English canon. On the contrary, probably in response to the public call for attention to native literature, TCD had to make some adjustments to its teaching and examination materials. The small adjustments, however, did not affect the dominant position of the English canon in TCD's curricula. As a matter of fact, TCD took the opportunity to further subjugate non-canonical Anglo-Irish literature. The integration of Anglo-Irish or Irish literature (in English) into English literature can be seen from the *B.A. Degree Examination*, Hilary Term, 1936:

> assume that you are asked to write a long essay on 'the contribution of Irish writers to English literature.' Sketch a plan to show how you would proceed, and add any rough notes that may occur to you.[236]

The question seemed to imply that English literature had benefited from Irish writers, and an Irish-interested perspective was taking its form. However, it could be argued that Irish writers were more likely to be seen as contributors to English literature, rather than to Irish/Gaelic literature as a separate cultural legacy. More specifically, as "English literature" might connote the literature of a foreign political entity – in the

---

[235] TCD, *Entrance Scholarships and Junior and School Exhibitions*, Trinity Term, 1938, question 10.
[236] TCD, *B.A. Degree Examination: English Literature*, Hilary Term, 1936, Question 7.

view of fundamental Irish nationalists – rather than merely literary works in the English language, it could be observed that Irish literature (in English) was being subjugated to the English canon as a side product contributed by writers from the neighbouring state. The English classic canon still remained the core of English curricula at TCD, and Irish "contributors" had not yet counterbalanced the dominance of the English classic canon.

It could therefore be assumed that, although Irish literature (in English) had found a space in TCD's English curricula, it was no more than subsidiary to canonical English literature. The inclusion of non-canonical Irish writers in the examination papers, therefore, did not mean that TCD had opened up its academic canon to new texts and writers, but in fact sought "to stabilise itself [. . .] in the face of its present crisis by accommodating the non-canonical."[237] The reluctance to make the merits of Irish writers better known probably stemmed from the sense of English and Protestant superiority, which had historically resided at TCD. In other words, the inclination to put the teaching of English literature in the foreground of the curriculum was still strong in the 1930s, as English interests had traditionally been the prime concerns of TCD. Concerns about English or Protestant contributions to Ireland were constantly shown in examination questions. Questions on Protestantism, rather than on Catholicism, suggested a Protestant-centred perspective with which students were required to be familiar, regardless of their denomination. For instance, history students in their B.A degree examination were asked to show their understanding of "how the 'Protestant interest' [was] affected by the commercial legislation applied to Ireland in the eighteenth century."[238] In an examination for the scholarships competition, examinees were required to give an answer as to why partition was needed to suit Protestant needs: "what is the historical background of the solidarity of Ulster Protestantism in favour of 'Partition?'."[239] Regarding the answer to the first question, although students could demonstrate the advantages Catholics derived from the 1792 Relief Act, this question was mainly concerned with "Protestant" interests.[240] As to the second

---

[237] Guillory 485.
[238] TCD, *Special B.A. Degree Examination: History*, Trinity Term, 1936, Question 12.
[239] TCD, *Entrance Scholarships and Junior Exhibitions (A)*, Trinity Term, 1938, Question 8.
[240] The 1792 Catholic Relief Act allowed Catholics the right to buy land, vote, and hold most civil and military offices, except in parliamentary boroughs. It also removed most restrictions in the Penal Laws affecting Catholic education. However, Catholics were

3. Examination Papers of Dublin's Universities

question, examinees were expected to illustrate the necessity of partition from the viewpoint of Ulster Protestants. It was unlikely that examinees – if sympathetic towards Irish nationalism – could write an answer disapproving of the link between partition and the solidarity of Ulster Protestants. What is noteworthy is that this question – which appeared on the 1938 entrance examination – seemed to contradict the new 1937 Irish Constitution in which Northern Ireland was confirmed as the territory of Éire. Hence it is possible that the Protestant faculty at TCD did not agree with De Valera's call for decolonisation but intended to counteract it. More specifically, it was a question not simply concerning the solidarity of Ulster Protestants, but the Protestant tradition of TCD. For Protestant students, including Anglicans and Presbyterians, this question could not be easier, in that the partition was primarily made to secure their direct or indirect interests in Ulster, but not those of Catholics.

However, the faculty's resistance to, or conformity with, the movement of decolonisation always remained dynamic in the 1930s. The regular English Department, which was essentially in step with the Oxbridge tradition, had to cope with the newly affiliated teachers' training college – previously under the management of the Church of Ireland before 1933, offering English courses to prospective teachers. Although the faculty of the regular English department might not necessarily overlap with that at the training college, the latter seemed to be more willing to teach Irish-related subjects. The regular English and History Departments, however, were more confined to the English literary canon and historiography as this chapter demonstrated earlier. A lot of the titles of a series of exams for training college students in 1930, for instance, prioritised the word "Irish," as in "Irish and English Literature," "Irish and European History," and "History of Irish and English Literature." The questions put were more Irish-related than those endorsed by the regular Departments of English and History. There were more Irish events and writers mentioned in the exams, as opposed to English and Anglo-Irish ones. For example:

> Give some account of the authorship and contents of any two of these books of ancient Ireland: - Lebar-na-Haera; Book of Leinster; Lebar Brec; Yellow Book of Lecan.[241]

---

still barred from sitting in parliament, from the offices of Lord Lieutenant, Chief Secretary, and Chancellor of the Exchequer, and from other senior positions. It was not until the last Catholic Relief Act of 1829 that these remaining restrictions were removed.

[241] TCD, *Examination for Training College Students: Irish and English Literature*, Trinity

Irish Literary Canon

Give some account of the Colleges and Monasteries of ancient Ireland to show how widespread learning was from the sixth to the tenth century. Or, discuss the claims of Columkille to be considered a poet.[242]

Discuss the statement that even during the period of the Danish invasion Ireland was not without learned men and poets.[243]

The first two questions were more literary-orientated, while the third statement involved some arguments which Irish revivalists formerly employed to shape their historical perspective on the Gaelic civilisation. This statement suggests that Irish culture had developed independently, before the Danes invaded. English historians from the regular Department of History, however, might assert that the Danes had a more significant impact on what Irish people thought of their culture. This view was reflected in a B.A. degree examination in the regular History Department: "Did the Danes make any permanent contributions to the growth of civilisation in Ireland?"[244] Although students could certainly negate the Danes' contribution to Irish civilisation, the two assignments contained statements which were true to some point and suggested two different interpretations of the Danish invasion.

On the other hand, as students at the training college were mainly trained to be primary school teachers and were expected to be proficient in the Irish language, they encouraged the faculty there to differentiate themselves from those of TCD's regular departments, which held on to a traditional English canon. The explicit intention of confronting the "regular" English perspective/faculty could be seen in an unusually lengthy nationalistic statement which appeared at the beginning of an examination paper in English literature for training college students which I quote as follows. Students were required to write a note on the style of the following passage, before they proceeded to other questions on the examination paper:

On this gloom one luminary rose, and Ireland worshipped it with Persian idolatry; her true patriot – her first – almost her last. Sagacious and intrepid,

---

Term, 1930, question 1.

[242] TCD, *Supplementary Examination for Training College Students: History of Irish and English Literature*, Michaelmas Term, 1930, question 1.

[243] TCD, *Examination for Training College Students: History of Irish and English Literature*, Trinity Term, 1930, question 2.

[244] TCD, *Special B.A. Degree Examination: History*, Trinity Term, 1936, Question 11.

3. Examination Papers of Dublin's Universities

he saw – he dared; above suspicion, he was trusted; above envy, he was beloved; above rivalry, he was obeyed. His wisdom was practical and prophetic – remedial for the present, warning for the future. He first taught Ireland that she might become a nation, and England that she must cease to be a despot. But he was a churchman; his gown impeded his course, and entangled his efforts. [. . .] As it was, he saved her by his courage, improved her by his authority, adorned her by his talents, and exalted her by his fame. His mission was but of ten years, and for ten years only did his personal power mitigate the government; but though no longer feared by the great, he was not forgotten by the wise; his influence, like his writings, has survived a century; and the foundations of whatever prosperity we have since erected are laid in the disinterested and magnanimous patriotism of Swift.[245]

The most relevant point of the statement was not necessarily about Jonathan Swift, nor its tenability, but the clear-cut nationalistic declaration of the making of the Irish nation. Although this statement was made to test examinees' recognition of a specific writing style, the unusual lengthiness suggests that some faculty members might have intended to produce a forum through examination papers in which a favoured historical interpretation could be uttered. The above quote was therefore more like a nationalistic testimonial, which examinees should not have doubted in itself, but simply have recognised in what style it was written.

Nevertheless, it might be suggested that the incorporation of the teacher's training college with TCD, as years went by, gradually destabilised the distinct English tradition which had been securely maintained in the regular departments. In the same year in which the above statement appeared, not only was there an increase in the number of questions about Irish history and literature, but some of them were placed on the title page. Although some of the Irish questions were still asked from a colonial perspective, the increasing number and the re-location of those questions suggested that the decolonial forces within TCD were becoming more effective as the decade drew to its end. This "opening-up" of the traditional perspectives of TCD can be seen in an unconventional question on one of the 1937 examination papers (for regular students) about the current censorship placed on literary publications. Examinees had to write

---

[245] TCD, *Examination for Training College Students: English Literature*, Trinity Term 1937, question 1.

an essay to demonstrate "[a] case against (or, for and against) a censorship of literature."[246] With this sort of question, students were allowed to show their concerns with current issues outside the classroom, and with those that were not traditionally confined to the studies of the classic English canon. Nevertheless, it is more likely that TCD was reluctant to endorse the current censorship which reflected Catholics' interests, rather than Protestants.'

The "opening-up," however, proceeded within a difficult environment, still dominated by the traditionalists in the English faculty. The forum, which allowed the faculty to try out a variety of viewpoints, through the means of examination papers, became increasingly crowded with diversified discourses. For example, the faculty members from the regular college of TCD who held on to Anglo-centric views of Ireland might have sensed the "unorthodox" perspectives that the faculty of the training institute might be promoting to students. Some of them continuously tested students with questions which particularly favoured English perspectives. The ideology of Ireland in servitude to England appeared in a question on a 1938 B.A. degree examination paper in history:

> What has contributed to the success of the Act of Union between England and Scotland? Would the Act of Union with Ireland have been more likely to succeed if it had been enacted a century earlier?[247]

It could be argued that, in this question, the Act of Union between England and Scotland had been presupposed a success, and the reason why the Irish Question was present was because the Union with Ireland did not succeed a century earlier. However, it is unlikely that this presupposition was tenable since rebellions had occurred before 1700 in Ireland, and the Union of England and Scotland did not entirely solve "the Scottish Question."[248] It is difficult to say whether the passing of the Act of Union between England and Ireland would not have prompted Irish rebellions earlier, thus altering the course of Irish history. As a result, the fictitious proposition in the above question would, most probably, suggest how those History faculty members reasoned

---

[246] TCD, *Junior Sophister Term Examination: English*, Hilary Term, 1937, question c.

[247] TCD, *Senior Sophisters and Supplemental B.A. Degree Examination: History*, Trinity Term, 1938, question 16.

[248] For instance, the 1715 and 1745 Jacobite rebellions in Scotland, following the 1689 Jacobite Rising, recurred in attempt to restore the Stuart descendants of King James II of England to the British throne.

3. Examination Papers of Dublin's Universities

the Irish Question from the unionists' points of view. Examinees should therefore have assumed not only that the union between England and Scotland was a success but that the Scottish experience was readily applicable to Ireland, despite the fact that this assumption is arguable.

In the next section, I would like to tackle examination papers from University College Dublin, which was run by Jesuits, to observe how the colonial and decolonial conflict proceeded in a Catholic institute. I aim to see whether the colonial atmosphere, which James Joyce experienced – before Ireland became a Free State – had lingered on into the mid-twentieth century.

3.5. (De)Colonising Examination Papers: University College Dublin

UCD was formally established in December 1908, in accordance with the Irish Universities Act of the same year. It was founded on St Stephen's Green, Dublin, in buildings that had housed the Catholic University of Ireland since 1854.[249] However, The Catholic University lasted for only four years, under the rectorship of Cardinal John Henry Newman. Twenty-five years later – in 1879, under increasing pressure from the Catholic clergy and Irish middle class – the British government agreed to set up the Royal University of Ireland on the same site that the Catholic University had occupied. Catholic concerns for the foundation of the Royal University were not only to ensure equal educational opportunities for Irish Catholics, but also to have them educated in a non-Protestant Episcopalian atmosphere, which prevailed at TCD. With its strong link to Irish Catholicism and nationalism, how the faculty of UCD faced and dealt with social changes, particularly in the 1930s when the new nation had just found its feet, is a matter worth reviewing. The examination papers used at the time, therefore, should be relevant to this discussion.

Compared to TCD, which held on to the traditional English perspective and canon, UCD in the late 1930s offered more opportunities for learning Celtic history and other related subjects. Students could choose to study for a B.A. degree in Celtic Archaeology, Early and Medieval Irish History, or Modern Irish History. These degrees suggest that the promotion of such subjects was indeed a major feature, which dis-

---

[249] Since 1882, the Catholic University of Ireland consisted of the following six colleges located for the most part in or near Dublin: St. Patrick's College, Maynooth; University College, St. Stephen's Green (Jesuits); University College, Blackrock (Holy Ghost Fathers); St. Patrick's College, Carlow; Holy Cross College, Clonliffe; and the School of Medicine, Dublin.

tinguished the Catholic-based UCD from TCD. However, one might detect a chronological weakness shown in the examination papers used at the institution, which suggested the conservatism of some of UCD's faculty members in tackling nationalistic issues. Take the 1930 B.A. Degree Examination in Modern Irish History, for example. The examination was divided into two chronological sections: 1485-1652 and 1652-1870. The focus on the early part of Irish history was not a problem, as the faculty might have intended to give students a coherent understanding of the course of early Irish history. Nevertheless, the six-decade gap from 1870 to 1930 left the most decisive period of the emerging nation completely absent. Causes for the chronological gap might have been, on the one hand, because this period was politically turbulent with competing discourses, and few historians at the time were able to find an objective view, or views, to summarise what the new nation had just experienced; on the other hand, it might have been because the educational authorities in Ireland were trying to keep controversial discourses and political issues – which were still present in most people's memories – from young students. The reticence in tackling recent historical events, such as the Civil War (1922-1923), could have been a way for the government to stabilise the new-born nation as quickly as possible.

The passing of the Censorship of Publications Act in 1929 allowed the Irish government to lawfully censor materials which might potentially damage the security of the new nation. Although the Act was initially meant to ban indecent publications, some incidents had shown that it also provided legal support for the government to suppress unorthodox ideas. Besides, as the teaching and reviewing of recent national events in universities might re-awaken antagonism in politics, the Catholic faculty at UCD would, possibly intentionally, self-censor teaching materials to avoid jeopardising their Catholic government. The self-censorship within universities, not only at UCD but also at other Catholic colleges throughout the country, had therefore forced the discussion over politics out of its traditional university forum.[250] This could ex-

---

[250] UCD's Literary and Historical Society, for instance, was set up in 1855 by John Henry Newman as a literary academy. However, it gradually became a debating society for political issues at the turn of the twentieth century, bringing together men of diverse beliefs and principles: John Dillon, Thomas MacDonagh, Arthur Clergy, James Joyce, Rory O'Connor, Kevin O'Higgins, Patrick Pearse, John O'Leary, W.B. Yeats, Tim Healy, Jim Larkin, Eamon de Valera, and so on. The president of the society gave inaugural addresses every year, while between 1914-1927 there were no addresses given. The absence of inaugural addresses might be because "the Chancellor of the University, who was also the Archbishop of Dublin, regarded debating societies as nests of disaffection."

3. Examination Papers of Dublin's Universities

plain why the debate on public affairs became less and less enthusiastic inside the traditional university forum.

As to the teaching of Celtic and English literatures and cultures, there were departments specialising in Celtic Archaeology and Early and Medieval Irish History, as well as a group within UCD's faculty which promoted the traditional curricula adopted at TCD and Oxbridge. Similar to TCD's 1930 examination papers, those used for undergraduate students in the English Department of UCD included few Anglo-Irish or Irish writers – even though these had been producing works in English since the eighteenth century.[251] Writers who appeared on the examination papers for undergraduates were mainly English: Geoffrey Chaucer, William Shakespeare, John Milton, John Dryden, Alexander Pope, etc. The choices of writers to be taught were little different from those in TCD's classrooms. Some references to writers of Irish birth only appeared in M.A. degree examinations, while Thomas Moore was referred to as an English satirist, and Aubrey De Vere was listed among other English writers.[252] The two questions referring to Moore and De Vere appeared in the last two lines of the examination paper, and were optional ones which examinees did not have to answer. Examinees could simply answer questions about classic English writers to get a good mark. Also, it is noteworthy that there was no clear distinction among Irish, Anglo-Irish, and English writers on examination papers produced by the English department; writers tended to be classified as either Irish or English. Moreover, if a writer had an Anglo-Irish origin, it was usually either not mentioned or he was included with the English writers. (The lack of a clear national distinction was only redressed after the establishment of the Department of Anglo-Irish Literature during the 1980s.)

The scant references to "Irish literature in English" – by which I mean Irish experiences, expressed or translated through the English language in the teaching of literature at UCD, suggests several things. Firstly, that the English department in early post-Treaty Ireland made few distinct changes to its teaching materials, which had

---

For details, see Meenan xvii.

[251] It is interesting to note that the 1980s were a watershed for the study of Anglo-Irish literature in the English Department of UCD, as an M.A. programme in "Anglo-Irish literature and drama" was established and differentiated from the study of English literature.

[252] University College Dublin (UCD), *Autumn Examinations: M.A. Degree Examination*, 1930, pp. 2-c, d.

most likely been duplicated from Oxbridge. In particular, before undergraduates could continue pursuing an M.A. degree for which a limited number of Irish-born writers were introduced, they were required to study English classic literature intensively as the basis for understanding Irish literature. In addition, since English literature dominated the content of exams in those days, and questions relating to Irish literature were not required to be answered, UCD could have successfully built up an English-to-Irish literary relationship in which the latter was subsidiary. Irish Catholic students at UCD before the end of 1930s were not able to get away from this colonial relationship in literature.

Secondly, in contrast to the generous introduction to Celtic studies in the departments of Celtic Archaeology, Early Irish History, and so on, limited references to Anglo-Irish writers in English Department exams suggest that these writers were in fact doubly marginalised in the practice of teaching. That is to say, due to their political identity involving "sitting between two stools," Anglo-Irish writers were not given a proper position in the two major cultural courses of study at UCD: English studies and Irish studies. Although some Anglo-Irish writers had indeed made profound contributions to Irish independence, they were not given a special status within the whole apparatus of Irish literature. It may have been because the social ethos was more Irish-Catholic orientated, so that a Catholic institute like UCD would structure its curriculum around the assumption that a writer was either English or Irish. The efforts to initiate intensive Irish studies can be seen in the establishment of three departments for Celtic studies in the 1930s, namely Early and Medieval Irish Language and Literature, Irish Folklore, and Modern Irish and Welsh. Before they were set up, there had been departments of Celtic Archaeology, as well as of Early Irish History.

The neglect of Anglo-Irish literature in the Department of English was gradually remedied as time went by. In 1932, in one examination paper for Honours undergraduate students, an optional essay question relating to "Irish Tradition in Anglo-Irish Literature" appeared in the last line of the last page.[253] The whole examination paper consisted mainly of questions about classic English literature. However, English literature exams taken by students from other diploma courses, as well as Pass, but not Honours or undergraduates from the English department, largely consisted of the works of English writers, with few Irish authors included. The slight improvement of allowing Honours students to answer an optional question about An-

---

[253] UCD, *Summer Examinations: English Literature – Honours*, 1932, p. 2-d.

3. Examination Papers of Dublin's Universities

glo-Irish literature, on the one hand, seemed to suggest the broadening of the English canon. On the other hand, the location of this question on the examination paper seems to imply that the study of English literature was the basis on which students should build their literary knowledge before they acquired other national or regional literatures.

An interesting amendment to the 1932 advanced level Irish literature exams was that, as well as putting an optional question relating to it on examination papers, M.A. students were now required to compose a short essay on Anglo-Irish writers. What made the amendment significant, compared with the 1930 paper, was that, not only could examinees no longer skirt questions on Irish literature (in English), but also that the Irish questions were moved from the last line of the third page of the examination paper to the bottom of the first page – although still placed under questions relating to English literature (Usually examination papers were two to three pages, and in my opinion they displayed a relationship between dominant and subsidiary literatures). The re-location of Irish questions indicates that some faculty members at UCD had started to re-think the academic status of Anglo-Irish literature. However, faculty members who had come from an English literary convention somehow intervened in the act of re-positioning Anglo-Irish literature within the English department – by continually including questions about Matthew Arnold's Victorian-orientated literary criticism in examination papers. For instance, students sitting the 1932 M.A. degree examination in English literature were required to write an essay on "Matthew Arnold's Theory of Criticism."[254] The particular reference to Arnold's poetry, prose, and literary criticism often appeared in exams at both UCD and TCD, applied to various components of English and Irish cultures, throughout the decade of the 1930s. In brief, the shared interest in Arnold's literary perspective in both colleges' examinations suggests that there was a group in both faculties keen on preserving the English convention, and worried about opening up the English canon to (Anglo-)Irish literature. The English canon, to this group of faculty members, might symbolise a literary and cultural authority whose merits were supposed to be transcendental and universal, with the recognition of the authority being associated with the political and economic colonisation of Ireland. It is unlikely that the Anglo-Irish canon would have been recognised, at a time when some members of the English faculty were so reluctant to fully open their arms to Irish literature in English.

---

[254] UCD, *Autumn Examination: MA degree in English*, 1932, p. 3-a.

It is interesting to compare this attitude to that of other humanities departments. The English Department in the 1930s, where the English canon still had the upper hand, was slow to introduce its students to a new wave of literary and social criticism from the European mainland, but instead persisted in maintaining the status of "literature of the past." The Departments of Sociology and Economics, on the other hand, attempted to bring in new cultural perspectives from Europe, and drew Irish students' attention to events more relevant to Irish history. Making students engage in new criticisms, such as socialism, though not directly relevant to reading literature, was revolutionary to some extent for a Catholic university. This was because the materialistic theory of socialism potentially put religious belief in jeopardy, and in later years socialism became "a taboo concept within Irish political culture"; and publications on socialism were largely censored.[255] The intention of introducing new waves of thinking, as well as history relevant to Irish people, could be seen from the following questions from examination papers for non-English major students. It could be argued that at the same time teaching and examination materials in the English Department suggested or dealt with these issues only to a limited extent:

> In what respects does the price of labour differ from the price of other things?[256]
>
> What do you understand by the term 'socialism'?[257]
>
> What were the principal causes and consequences of emigration from Ireland?[258]
>
> Briefly summarize the development of land purchase in Ireland.[259]

The encouragement of students to review specific facts about Ireland did not begin in the English department. Nevertheless, as I demonstrated above, within this department was a group of faculty members insistently seeking to re-position Irish literature. In one 1934 examination paper for Pass students, the choice of answering questions relating to Irish literature was given, and this privilege was no longer re-

---

[255] Ó Drisceoil 244. That socialism was a target for censorship is elaborated in 243-57.
[256] UCD, *B.A. degree examination in Political Economy, 1932*, question 2.
[257] UCD, *B.A. degree examination in Political Economy, 1932*, question 4.
[258] UCD, *B.A. Degree Examination in National Economics of Ireland*, 1932, question 1.
[259] UCD, *B.A. Degree Examination in National Economics of Ireland*, 1932, question 2.

3. Examination Papers of Dublin's Universities

tained at Honours level, as examination papers of previous years have shown.[260] Moreover, students who sat for scholarship competitions were required to answer questions about specific Anglo-Irish writers and their contributions to drama, and sometimes these questions were placed before those relating to English literature. The re-location of Anglo-Irish questions in this examination tends to suggest that the historical relationship between the dominant English and subsidiary Irish literatures was being reversed. Questions specifically relating to Anglo-Irish contributions to the revival of Irish literature include:

> Compare Moore, Mangan, and Yeats as Irish poets.[261]

> How far do you consider the use of Irish mythology by modern writers characteristic of the Irish spirit?[262]

The reversed Irish-to-English literary relationship can be exemplified by this essay question:

> Write an essay on one of the following subjects: -
> (a) The modern Irish Drama
> (b) Pilgrimages
> (c) The English nineteenth-century Novel[263]

The significance of these changes is made clearer by a comparison with examination papers used at TCD in the same period. As the early part of this chapter has demonstrated, not only were there limited questions about Anglo-Irish literature on TCD's examination papers, but those present were also put in a way that suggested some English or Protestant superiority over Irish literature (in English). On the contrary, at UCD, the ways in which the faculty put Anglo-Irish examination questions were more neutral, as the above quoted questions reveal.

---

[260] This particular exam was UCD, *Summer Examinations: B.A. Degree Examination in English Literature – PASS*, 1934.

[261] UCD, *Summer Examinations: The Dr. Henry Hutchinson Stewart Literary Scholarship Examination*, 1934, question 8.

[262] UCD, *Summer Examinations: The Dr. Henry Hutchinson Stewart Literary Scholarship Examination*, 1934, question 9.

[263] UCD, *Summer Examinations: The Dr. Henry Hutchinson Stewart Literary Scholarship Examination*, 1934, p. 2.

On the other hand, in contrast to the majority of UCD faculty members who adhered to the English literary canon, a small number of teachers were in fact more open-minded, like their colleagues in other Humanities departments, in linking students with Irish colonial history by prescribing specific texts. Jonathan Swift's satire "A Modest Proposal," as well as *Gulliver's Travels*, were frequently tested subjects in examination papers in 1934. Examples include:

> Describe the circumstances under which Swift wrote 'A Modest Proposal.' What was his motive? Show how effective was his irony revealing the serious thought underlying his argument. Give some examples.[264]

> The same characteristics of mind and style are discernible in both *Gulliver's Travels* and 'A Modest Proposal.' Do you agree with this criticism? Give your reasons.[265]

Jonathan Swift's satirical works were presumably favoured by the nationalistic faculty at UCD, due largely to the fact that this author had written prolifically about Ireland's misery under English colonisation.[266] The specific references to "A Modest Proposal" and *Gulliver's Travels* suggest, in my view, that some faculty members intended to focus Irish students' attention on relevant facts about Ireland, rather than on canonical (literary) pictures sanctioned by English authority. It could be argued that this particular group of faculty was supported by its then chairperson, Robert Donovan, who, as I discussed earlier, had carried out research in Irish literature in English. Unlike their colleagues in the Departments of History and of Economics, and possibly because they had to rely on literary works as teaching media, the English faculty who were interested in Anglo-Irish literature had to be very specific about texts for students to work on. The faculties of the History and Economics Departments, as the questions quoted earlier from their examination papers revealed, could require examinees to look into the cause and effect of the land issue, the Famine, and emigration (moreover, in 1934 the period covered by the course in *Modern* Irish History

---

[264] UCD, *Summer Examinations – Pass: B.A. Degree Examination in English Literature, 1934*, p. 2.

[265] UCD, *Summer Examinations – Honours: B.A. Degree in English Literature*, 1934, p. 1

[266] I do not suggest that Jonathan Swift was a nationalist, but his discontent about the British misrule of Ireland might have been seen as a nationalistic gesture – through the eyes of Irish nationalism.

3. Examination Papers of Dublin's Universities

moved significantly forward to 1900, whereas in earlier years this course ended in 1870.[267]) However, both faculty groups – one within the English department and the other from other Humanities departments, shared a similar aim of pedagogy – which was to enable Irish students at UCD to regain their national consciousness.

The year 1934 was significant for the pro-nationalistic faculty of UCD, in that it was probably the first year in which they managed to successfully reverse the relationship between English and Irish literature, and were able to pose specific examination questions relating to the Irish experience. However, the traditionalists in the English Department did not passively accept the rise of non-canonical Irish literature, but skilfully expressed their disapproval by making students examine the presupposed weaknesses of Anglo-Irish literature. For example, in a 1934 B.A. examination paper for English literature Honours, a disparaging question appeared:

> What, in your opinion, are the chief limitations of Anglo-Irish literature? Mention the principal writers of the nineteenth century.[268]

This question not only reflected negatively on Anglo-Irish literature but also hinted at the competition between the traditionalist and less-traditionalist faculties at UCD.[269] This rivalry involved other Anglo-Irish writers, such as Sir Samuel Ferguson and James Clarence Mangan, who, like Swift, frequently appeared on examination papers – although the actual space for Irish writers was still limited, but growing. The reason why Ferguson and Mangan were included was possibly their remarkable contributions to English translation of Gaelic poetry.

Having suggested some possible reasons underpinning the less-traditionalist faculty's bias towards Swift, Ferguson, and Mangan, I would maintain that their rivalry with traditionalist faculty members was essentially based on conflicting political ideologies, rather than on aesthetic considerations. In other words, the movement of decolonisation, to some extent, might have been permeating through the traditionalist faculty. A large number of Irish writers, therefore, who did not write for (cultural) na-

---

[267] The expansion can be seen from UCD, *Summer Examinations – PASS: B.A. Degree Examination in Modern Irish History*, 1934.

[268] UCD, *Summer Examinations – Honours: B.A. Degree in English Literature*, 1934, p.1.

[269] The reason why I termed this group of faculty "less traditionalist" was because, like Robert Donovan, they were interested in Anglo-Irish literature but were not anti-English, nor were they necessarily nationalists. It is not appropriate to dichotomise the faculty simplistically, based upon their research interests.

tionalistic causes would not be favoured by this group, and later were left out of the nationalistic canon of Irish literature.[270] The less traditionalist faculty, in my view, gave their academic endorsement in order to enable (cultural) nationalistic literature to be at the core of a new literary canon for the purpose of teaching. In addition, the academic acceptance implicitly displayed through UCD's examination papers resulted in the way in which editors of Leaving Certificate textbooks judged the value of a work for Irish pupils to study. Works by Swift, Mangan, and Ferguson all frequently appeared in textbooks which featured a (cultural) nationalistic canon that was emerging as the national one.

My survey of UCD's examination papers suggests that the rivalry between the less traditionalist and traditionalist faculty members was very likely an ideological one. However, the latter group seemed to gradually compromise with the former in the late 1930s. The compromise could be seen from the repetitive references to Matthew Arnold on examination papers. As demonstrated earlier, students used to be tested on his Victorian perspective in English literature, but the following questions reveal that Arnold's study of Celtic literature became a new topic of examination interest:

> Discuss what seems to you the most interesting and valuable of the theories put forward by Arnold in *The Study of Celtic Literature*.[271]

> Discuss some of Arnold's opinions in the light of your own reading in early Irish or Welsh literature.[272]

The shift of emphasis in Arnold's works from Victorian criticism to Celtic literature suggests that the two groups of faculty might have come to a compromise. That is, Arnold still remained as an English critic to be studied, while the interest had moved from English literature to Irish. However, this *modus vivendi* could still be problem-

---

[270] In Chapter Two, by examining textbooks I have exemplified some of those writers eligible for the nationalistic canon, in that they often wrote with patriotic sentiments. Supposedly, nationalistic writing was not the only type of writing that Irish writers would have contributed to, but political events have seemingly directed how publishers, editors, teachers, and students appreciated their "national" literature.

[271] UCD, *Summer Examinations – Honours: First University Examination in Arts and Commerce*, 1936, pp. 2-6.

[272] UCD, *Summer Examinations – Honours: First University Examination in Arts and Commerce*, English, 1938, pp. 2-5.

3. Examination Papers of Dublin's Universities

atic in fundamental Nationalists' eyes, as Arnold's views on Celtic or Irish literature were often tinged with colonial biases. That is, he viewed Celtic people and literature as feminine and emotional, while Anglo-Saxons were masculine and phlegmatic. The fundamental questioning of Arnold's problematic assumption is revealed in the second question above. What is noteworthy is that, as this chapter demonstrated earlier, Arnold's criticism had a prominent place in the curricula approved by Jeremiah Hogan, Donovan's successor, but this could only be said for very few Anglo-Irish writers. Hogan, as professor in philology and not particularly interested in Irish literature, might have been expected by the traditionalist faculty to counteract the growing emphasis on Anglo-Irish literature. It might therefore be reasonably assumed that the introduction of Arnold's criticism of Celtic literature was a compromise between the two groups of faculty, in that examinees had to familiarise themselves with Arnold's views but were allowed to develop their own reading, as the above questions demonstrate.

One success that the less traditionalist faculty and their colleagues in other humanities departments should be credited for, as evidenced in examination papers and curricula during the 1930s, was the broadening of the definition of the word "English" and the scope of English literature. Specifically, English examination papers and curricula in the early 1930s were very much confined to literature written by English-born writers, but as time went on Anglo-Irish writers who wrote or translated Irish texts appeared in increasing numbers. What was successfully decolonised within the English departments of UCD and TCD, in my opinion, was not so much an ideological literary canon, or canons, but the concept of "English." Hence, the special interest in other post-colonial societies shown by English readers across cultures and nations should be attributed to the less traditionalist faculty of UCD who, from the early 1930s, strove to tactfully, rather than radically, decolonise the word "English."

4. Practices of the Theory of Canon: Irish Anthologies Revisited

In 1912, James Joyce, outraged by a printer who smashed up the type of his *Dubliners*, lampooned Ireland in "Gas from a Burner" as a place "where Christ and Caesar are hand and glove!"[273] What concerned Joyce, as someone who expected to write "a chapter of the moral history of [his] country," was that the conscience of Irish people was, in his view, paralysed by the conspiracy of religion and politics.[274] In particular, in Joyce's view, the hand and glove of "Christ and Caesar" worked together to keep the Irish from being aware of their deep-rooted habit of betraying leaders, stooping to foreign powers, and sending artists into exile. Although Joyce's observation may contain some degree of truth, the majority of the Irish reading public was not unshackled by Joyce's "scrupulous meanness" in criticism.[275] This chapter will explore a special literary production, the anthology, to look at how it mirrored, resisted or conformed to prevailing political ideologies, particularly during the early half of the twentieth century. My focus will be on how Irish literary canon formations were asserted, adjusted, reformulated, or disclaimed by anthologists during those turbulent decades during which the Free State fought for its political independence.

4.1. Some Consequences of Canon Formation in Ireland

In order to discuss literary canon(s) properly, it is necessary to trace the origin of the *concept* of canon, as well as relevant debates on its changing definitions. According to *The Concise Oxford Dictionary of Current English,* the word "canon" is derived from Greek.[276] It was a word originally used for secular Greek works of recognised quality before it was applied to biblical books.[277] Contextually, it suggests something

---

[273] "Gas from a Burner" 466.
[274] *Letters of James Joyce* 2:134.
[275] *Letters of James Joyce* 2:134.
[276] "Canon," *Concise Oxford Dictionary.*
[277] The canonical status of the Latin translation of the Old Testament was confirmed in 1546 by the Council of Trent, which, in response to the Protestant Reformation, initiated a general reform of the Catholic Church and precisely defined its essential dogmas and edition of the Old Testament to be used. This Latin edition of the Old Testament, the Vulgate – which means "popular edition" in Latin – was pronounced "authentic" by the Council of Trent. The Vulgate was translated from the Greek *Septuagint* used by the early Fathers of the Church. The Greek *Septuagint* was translated from the ancient Greek translation of the Hebrew Old Testament. However, the issue of which edition of

straight or something to be kept straight; and therefore indicates a rule, or something ruled. It was initially applied to the Scriptures rather than to other sorts of written works, meaning "the authoritative rule of faith and practice, and the standard of doctrine and duty," according to *Easton's 1897 Bible Dictionary*.[278] Interestingly, although this definition of canon was originally religiously orientated, the editor(s) of this 1897 version of *Easton's Bible Dictionary*, were reserved about *who* owns the authoritative right to the Scriptures.[279] The editor(s) remarked that "such a right does not arise from any ecclesiastical authority, but from the evidence of the inspired authorship of the book."[280] A key point in this definition is that interpretations of the Scriptures are needed, but no legitimate institution is necessary in order to provide decisive and authoritative interpretations. Although entries in *Easton's 1897 Bible Dictionary* only cover signifiers in the biblical context, when it comes to defining what a canon is, it seems to allow some degree of flexibility in recognising alternative meanings.

The literary critic and historian Frank Kermode has explored the social background in which the Scriptures received canonical status. He claims that the "gradual replacement of the oral tradition by writing was the necessary prelude to establishment of a canon, with all the consequences of that development"; the Scriptures therefore exemplify the development of human civilisation from the oral to the written tradition.[281] As the biblical canon was transformed to writing from speech, later generations gradually demanded authoritative interpretations to fix the biblical canon. Hence, the demand for interpretations hinders the interpretation from being "neces-

---

the Scriptures was to be used by the Church had been disputed for some twelve centuries before the Council of Trent confirmed the rightness of the edition in Latin. The recent issue relating to which literary work(s) were to be canonical was, to some extent, similar to the debate on the choice as to which biblical edition was to be canonical and authentic. The latter is still ongoing amongst different Christian denominations. The above information was derived from *Encyclopaedia Britannica* and *Encrata Encyclopedia*. See the entries of "Council of Trent," "Vulgate," and "Septuagint."

[278] "Canon." *Easton's 1897 Bible Dictionary*.
[279] The chief editor of the *Easton's Bible Dictionary* is M.G. Easton, but I suspect that the 4,000 entries in this dictionary might not all have been written by this single person.
[280] "Canon." *Easton's 1897 Bible Dictionary*.
[281] Kermode 602.

4. Irish Anthologies Revisited

sarily open rather than closed," and the canon at this point begins formulating wstern culture in a written form.[282]

The development of the word "canon" to include negative connotations occurred during the last few decades of the twentieth century, when deconstructionists began to call for a re-examination of explicit or implicit social hierarchies. The publishing industry, as an agent manoeuvering cultural representation, unavoidably becomes one of the examined targets, in that it operates within, or reacts to, external social frameworks. The word canon began to be referred to as a set of literary texts with distinguishable merits, other than the Scriptures. Nevertheless, as the oral tradition had already faded out from the modern perception of canon, alternative but arbitrary interpretations for the support, re-evaluation, or even attack of existing canonical works gradually took their form.

Various arguments concerned with upholding, redressing, or dismantling the canon have given rise to a series of debates. An assessment of these debates on the canon will be reviewed before this chapter considers canon formation(s) in early twentieth-century Ireland. However, the primary intention in dealing with these polemics is not to display their weakness or to privilege any party, but rather to suggest that there could be a variety of ways to reshuffle canonical or non-canonical texts in Irish literature.

A conventional stance on the canon is that canon(s) exist, and literary works with remarkable, intrinsic merits deserve inclusion in it. Intrinsic values are usually aesthetic, and defenders of aesthetics invariably stress their ability to transcend a particular time and place. Paisley Livingston describes such a conventional position as follows:

> To be a work of art, some item must have been made with the right sort of intentions and under the right conditions, or it must serve artistic functions in the right sort of way. [. . .] there are instances of works that are clearly not canonical, just as there are clear-cut cases of works that definitely are and should be canonical.[283]

However, this absolute distinction between canonical and non-canonical works surely has to be tested, if aesthetic idealists want to defend the superiority of their belief.

---

[282] Readings 156-57.
[283] Livingston 145.

Irish Literary Canon

In the case of mid twentieth-century Ireland, school textbooks used for Leaving Certificate examinations, as discussed in Chapter Two, suggest that the official canon – circulated at educational institutes of the Free State – underwent a process of opening up to texts with strong Irish patriotic elements. It was fairly recognisable that works by Romantic and Victorian authors were juxtaposed with patriotic texts by Irish and Anglo-Irish writers, though the number of the latter was apparently small. The juxtaposition suggests that Romantic and Victorian literatures were perceived to contain transcendent values, so that their colonial agenda could be easily ignored. Nevertheless, it is also important to note that the introduction of the English cultural heritage to Irish pupils had been a tradition since 1831, when the National School System started its operations in Ireland. In particular, the Commissioners of National Education in Ireland at the time, though mostly Irishmen, "saw their task as anglicisation [. . .] and provided a curriculum that almost ignored the Irish child's own culture and environment."[284] Therefore, it may be reasonably assumed that the artistic values conveyed through the teaching of the English language and English literature were systematically instilled in Irish pupils through national but colonial education. One of the consequences, a century later, was that few disputes occurred regarding the inclusion of canonical texts by British authors in textbooks. The textbooks introduced by Eamon de Valera in the 1930s and used for the next three decades in Ireland testify to these consequences. It could be contended that Irish people's notion of literary excellence, in general, was founded on the alleged merits of English literature.

The editing of Irish literary textbooks and anthologies is an example that demonstrates the interactions between the canonical and the non-canonical. The accommodation of nationalistic works suggests not only the increasing pressure on the traditional English canon, but also the gradually more emphatic call to formulate an exclusive canon for the Irish people. As Ireland's recent conflict with England was still fresh in people's memory, it is understandable that editors would opt for works that reflected mainstream experiences and values. It is no surprise that works by writers with acknowledged patriotic contributions were included in textbooks and anthologies. Their achievements were usually referred to in the introductory notes to their texts, and these authors included Theobald Wolfe Tone, John MacHale, Thomas Davis, Thomas Francis Meagher, and William Francis Butler.[285] It could be claimed

---

[284] Coleman, "'Eyes'" 177.

[285] These authors often appeared in James Carey's editions of textbooks. Carey was the chief editor of literary textbooks from 1941-1956. The authors I named were from his

4. Irish Anthologies Revisited

that the mention of their identities as patriots was so recurrent that pupils might (mis-)perceive that the relevant literary works must be nationalistic ones. It might be true to say that, as pupils were required to study and be tested on nationalistic works during their school years, they would have been equipped with a sense of Irish patriotism as the authorities expected. On the other hand, they might have acquired a sense of victimisation with which they continued, in a conceptual manner, the bitter experience of the older generation against the coloniser. They might therefore still be shackled with political ideologies, and unable to acquire Irishness without patriotic sentiments.

However, although a number of nationalistic works had been significantly juxtaposed with English canonical works in textbooks, this did not necessarily suggest that Irish literature in English gained the same artistic value as the English works, but it did indicate that the values of the traditional English canon might be being reinforced. The fact that English authors and their works were the main subjects to be tested in university entrance examinations was a striking example. After all, the canon did accommodate new texts, while newly included works might solidify the artistic standards ordained by the former coloniser; nationalistic materials were read but had not yet undermined the dominant position of English literature (which was also apparent in the syllabi). It might be because, as Readings suggested, "cultural imperialism [was] incarnated in the English literary canon."[286] In particular, since the national educational system in Ireland had long adopted the model used on the UK mainland, the decolonisation of mind was in view but could not take effect immediately following political uprisings. In other words, the emerging nationalistic canon had not been capable of counterbalancing the traditional English one, as the aesthetics of the latter had been in Irish people's perceptions of classic literature since the colonial era.

It could be observed that, in the canon, there could always be some force of subjugation deciding what deserved more attention, despite the fact that the canon had opened up to accommodate new texts, such as Irish nationalistic materials. Nonetheless, the subjugation was not necessarily enacted under the shadow of a dominant, traditional canon, but could be enforced by the non-canonical itself. That is to say, to gather non-canonical texts as a group might be to label "the category of the

---

Intermediate Prose: A New Anthology, specially compiled for the Intermediate Certificate Course in 1941.
[286] Readings 150.

non-canonical as a set of actively excluded works."[287] As a result, the collection of the non-canonical would not redress the pitfalls of the traditional canon, but might doubly marginalise them. Textbooks and anthologies which highlighted patriotic materials, except for those suggesting a sense of victimisation to pupils, were to form an exclusive Irish canon that was parochial in essence. Pupils might still not be able to perceive "Irishness" from multi-cultural perspectives, but could gain a simplified version of it in line with either "Irish-Irish" sentiments or the one-sided, nationalistic stances exemplified in the textbooks.

It is essential to consider the ways in which canons were forced to open. As I suggested, the traditional English canon and the emerging Irish one were inevitably being (re-)positioned for political causes after the establishment of the Free State. Having no need to meet expectations established by educational boards, critics and editors off campus had greater freedom in presenting Irish canons without being burdened by the conventions of English literature. Some editors, for example, were dedicated to anthologising works with patriotic elements; some selected works which pictured an idyllic, nostalgic Western Ireland; some favoured stories that particularly caricatured the English in contrast to stage Irishmen. Detailed discussion of these anthologies will be provided later in this chapter. Nevertheless, I would argue that the re-anthologisation of Irish works as a means to decolonise Ireland did not necessarily reflect a "genuine" Ireland, but arose from a political reaction against the coloniser. My survey will show how anthologists created *their* images of Ireland by abridging long works or eliminating what they thought to be superfluous paragraphs. Notably, the editing of anthologies could involve personal tastes, and that factor might inevitably render their canon(s) subjective.

The active anthologisation of Irish works for different faces of Ireland suggests a demanding pressure from outside the educational institutes in regard to the amendment of traditional canons. The addition of patriots' works to textbooks and anthologies, on the one hand, can be seen as a response to the mainstream expectation laid on the English curricula through which pupils would learn recent Irish history from literary examples. On the other hand, such additions might imply that the traditional English canon was forced to open up under social pressure, so that it only allowed a limited number of Irish texts with narrow subject choices to be included in textbooks. It could be assumed that traditionalists who chaired the editing of textbooks had be-

---

[287] Guillory 485.

4. Irish Anthologies Revisited

haved conservatively, when the calls from outside the classroom became more and more unrelenting as to the revision of English textbooks.

To return to the early discussion on the repositioning of "canons" and their consequences, the Irish experience in canon (re-)formations provided a concrete example testifying how canonisation works under political or other external pressures. Nevertheless, some critics were sceptical about the necessity of formulating another canon against the traditional one. To them, both traditional and emerging canons could be "ideological constructs," due to "a transcendental negativity inherent to the canon."[288] The negativity stems from the artificiality of a canon in its making; as Charles Altieri argued, the canon is "a repository of humane ideals which function negatively rather than positively and work to make us struggle rather than to confirm our smugness." In his view, although the canon may confirm the literary elements which are aesthetically good and humanly salutary, it can also, when becoming most ideological, justify the smugness that prompted critics to disfavour certain literary works for religious, political, and moral considerations.[289] That is, some works or some voices may be expelled from the endorsed canon due to their unwelcome, politically incorrect, and non-mainstream features. In addition, canon formation may incur "injustice" in selecting works; Altieri observed that "the negative functioning of the canon must generate the injustice that its acknowledgement of extrinsic claims condemns as unacceptable."[290]

Some might contend that the "repository" is not necessarily unhealthy in that it may contain intrinsic values of conventional canons. However, some critics' insistent opposition to any canon (or reformulated canon) might be due to their assumption that no canon can survive without political or religious interference. Moreover, it might seem to them that, if canons can co-exist, then this co-existence in fact serves to create a stalemate in which new and old canons potentially decanonise each other in order to attain a recognisable, authoritative position. If canons do not decanonise but acknowledge each other by annexing the canonical and the non-canonical, then, in Guillory's opinion, the annexation is an act of creating a hegemonic tradition and an impasse, in that the concept of canonicity does not change. Guillory has a negative view about the collection of the non-canonical, claiming the following: "It may be

---

[288] Quoted in Readings 151. Readings refers to Charles Altieri's article: "An Idea and Ideal of a Literary Canon" when making this point.
[289] Quoted in Readings 151.
[290] Readings 151-52.

possible to defer the impasse by the establishment of alternative canons – canons of the non-canonical – but these pedagogic constructions also do not escape the formal features of canonicity. Rather they suffer the deuterocanonical fate of "ghettoized" programs."[291] He does not accept that the competition between the canonical and the non-canonical can produce any satisfactory result. Non-canonical texts would still be omitted from the conventional canon, rather than being placed within the same category without acknowledging their diversities. On the one hand, this competition amply demonstrates "the exercise of power" of canons.[292] On the other hand, if canons do not compete but annex each other, then the ideology of canonicity underpinning annexation still involves hegemonism – to be a privileged and centralised canon. Hence, Guillory contends:

> The delegitimation of the canon is premised upon a structural homology between, on the one hand, the distinction of the canonical from the non-canonical, and on the other, the process of inclusion or exclusion by which social groups are represented or not represented in the exercise of power. [. . .] Yet the pragmatic struggle moves quickly to an impasse that takes the form of an unreflective annexation of non-canonical works to a hegemonic tradition – a phenomenon of co-optation.[293]

In post-Treaty Ireland, faced with criticism for having neglected the contributions of Irish writers in the teaching of literature, institutions of the higher education sector such as Trinity College Dublin and University College Dublin did more or less adjust their syllabi to accommodate some Irish or Anglo-Irish writers. However, my investigation into the exam papers used at both universities in the 1930s shows that the number selected was still limited, and the general choice of works did not always present Ireland from an Irish, but rather the English traditionalists' perspective. Besides, Irish writers who were newly included were mostly male and Anglo-Irish. Female voices were rarely heard properly. I would contend that the swift annexation of canonical and non-canonical writers was perhaps merely to pacify temporarily, like an expedient, the attack on the coloniser's canon for the sake of anti-colonialism.

---

[291] Guillory 484.
[292] Guillory 483.
[293] Guillory 483.

4. Irish Anthologies Revisited

Thorough consideration of the reasons for which a particular work should be included now, and why many others were still left out, was bypassed without adequate debate.

This chapter will examine three aspects of the re-anthologisation of Irish literature. Firstly, I will survey those anthologies made at the turn of the twentieth century, to explore how diverse the literary images of Ireland could be, and how they were largely invented by anthologists. Secondly, I will consider two genres, poetry and the short story, as these were highlighted forms of writing during Irish nation formation, while both were used by political and religious propagandists to construct their ideal but ultimately unreal Ireland. Thirdly, the general methodology of producing anthologies will be examined, since it is relevant to how a mythic, sentimental, entertaining, or political Ireland was created through literature.

4.2. Inventing Irish Anthologies

The editorial board of an anthology, before the collection is published, would have made specific choices of themes. This selection may differ for diverse reasons, such as who chairs the editorial committee, which institution financially backs the publisher, what sort of theme is particularly welcome and politically correct at the time, and so forth. Some anthologists may claim that their collections represent the most authentic depiction of prescribed themes, so that this particular anthology outshines other anthologies. In some cases, a specific anthology would be much valued, or canonised, as a classic work offered for appreciation. Notwithstanding this, editors are not always completely autonomous in their role of selecting appropriate works. They act under the constraint of publishers, the reading public, or the relevant authorities, to comply with moral and social expectations, and not to contravene political taboos.

According to Robert Graves and Laura Riding, "the Anthology of the days before cheap books were printed was justified as a secure portfolio for short poems that might otherwise be lost."[294] Indeed *Carmina Burana*, (a thirteenth-century collection of goliardic verse in Latin), for example, accomplished this purpose so well that contemporary scholars are still able to delve into medieval literature and culture. With the passage of time, the printing industry prospered and the production of books was no longer as costly, yet the tradition of producing anthologies continued. Anthologies became "strategic weapons in literary politics," and were edited to fit in with particu-

---

[294] Quoted in Lampe 3.

lar social and political expectations.[295] Editors may therefore prescribe certain ways of reading by listing the peculiarities of the anthology in the preface, so that the reader can identify with the agenda which the editors wish to convey.

As to the formation of anthologies, at the dawn of the twentieth century, Ireland was troubled by issues of nationality, and the literary revival intoxicated many critics, with the result that the editing of anthologies inevitably involved patriotism and Celticism to a large degree. Publishers were keen to bring out anthologies relevant to these questions, following the trend of anti-imperialism. Infused with the passion for emancipating Ireland, nationalistic concerns, rather than intrinsic artistic elements, were often the principal concern for works to be anthologised. Some patriotic editors concentrated on bringing out new anthologies with the purpose of confronting colonial conventions, such as Victorian aesthetics, as an act of decolonisation.

To demonstrate how the publishing business was intertwined with Irish politics, and vice versa, it suffices to name a few anthologies before and just after the turn of the twentieth century which contain political appeals. It is obvious that the tradition of producing anthologies in Ireland was not simply concerned with keeping texts from being lost, but was also used as part of the struggle for a national identity, political independence, and Catholic emancipation. Taking patriotic themes, for example, an early collection for Irish patriots dates back to as early as 1795, when a Belfast-based newspaper and publisher, *The Northern Star*, compiled *Paddy's Resource: Being a Select Collection of Original and Modern Patriotic Songs, Toasts and Sentiments,* "for the Use of the People of Ireland." The significance of this anthology is that it is probably the first anthology produced with the expressed aim of counteracting the Orange Order, which was also founded in 1795 to secure the English coloniser's interests in Ireland. I suggest that this encouraged the convention of compiling anthologies as political propaganda.

The sentiment of patriotism was lasting. In 1844, two years after the weekly journal *The Nation* was founded by Thomas Davis and his comrades, John O'Daly compiled *Reliques of Irish Jacobite Poetry*. In this collection, O'Daly edited and translated eighteenth-century political poetry, *aisling*, written in Gaelic, into English. The motive underpinning the process of reissuing Jacobite poetry was to consolidate the cause of the newly established Young Ireland movement, in that Jacobite poets foretold the restoration of the Irish Kingdom when a rightful king returns. At one level,

---

[295] Mulhern 23.

4. Irish Anthologies Revisited

the compilation of this anthology mirrored national consciousness, which *The Nation* tended to call forth. At the same time, the anthology secured a source from which Young Irelanders could bolster the nationalist ideology by drawing on the political myth in Jacobite poetry.

As the Young Ireland movement developed, the call for re-ensuring the national consciousness became more and more intense during the late nineteenth century and the early part of the twentieth century. Numerous anthologies were dedicated to Young Ireland or to the emerging Irish Nation. Among these were: *Poems and Ballads of Young Ireland*, edited by W.B. Yeats and T.W. Rolleston in 1888; *The New Spirit of the Nation* and *Songs and Ballads of Young Ireland*, collected by Martin MacDermott in 1894 and 1896 respectively; *The Spirit of the Nation*, compiled by Grattan Flood in 1911; *Emerald Gems: Selected from the Poetry of "The Nation," "The Weekly News," and "Young Ireland"* and *Irish National Poems by Irish Priests*, compiled by T.D. Sullivan in 1885 and 1911.

The above-mentioned anthologies were politically linked with Young Ireland. Notwithstanding this, they can also be viewed as products of the literary revival movement whose aim was to stimulate and encourage a trend of reviving Irish culture as a means of affirming cultural and racial identity. Many anthologies, as a result, were produced in the context of these political and cultural concerns, as well as to strengthen the collective sense of being Irish. These anthologies covered a variety of Irish interests from fairy tales, folklore and stories about Irish peasantry, to bardic poetry, love songs and Celtic music, producing a number of canons for these Irish themes. I would argue that, owing to a radical appeal for political reform, these canons, which emerged at such a rapid speed, may have lacked scrupulous consideration or enough deliberation surrounding their formation, and were confined to political ideologies to replace the English canon. The English/colonial canon, with the exception of English-based academia, was consequently targeted for decolonial purposes. Political propaganda was involved, whether implicitly or explicitly, with the production and promotion of these anthologies.

The collective imagination of being Irish has been constructed throughout the history of Ireland by a variety of means, while the increasing number of anthologies demonstrated that being Irish was no longer a factor of the imagination but rather was something to be enacted. One abiding effect of these anthologies was that they accelerated the development of Irish nation-formation, providing nationalists with a literary weapon alternative to the military one with which to recapture the Irish kingdom.

While this alternative weapon had a durable effect on the psyche of the Irish people, it also left issues of aesthetics little explored.

According to Gerry Smyth, many revivalists, such as W.B. Yeats and Standish O'Grady, drew upon an existing canon contained in *The Cabinet of Irish Literature*, edited by Charles Read and published in 1880 in four large volumes.[296] However, although this late nineteenth-century anthology was endorsed by the Royal Irish Academy, the canonical grounds it provided were more problematic than authentic. Some literary critics and anthologists accused it of lacking a precise definition of Irishness – from the nationalists' points of view. Works such as Stopford Brooke's ten-volume *A Treasury of Irish Poetry in the English Tongue* (1900), Stephen Gwynn's *The Scholar's Treasury: A Book of Irish Poetry* (1927), Justin McCarthy's *Irish Literature* (1904), and Thomas MacDonagh's *Literature in Ireland* (1916), all participated in the discourse on what should constitute the Irish tradition.[297] Their editors declared their literary and political views in the introductions to the anthologies, putting their ideas into practice by selecting favoured texts to appropriate the decolonial canon. Key issues that concerned these anthologists included the following: Who was or was not qualified to be an Irish writer? What elements should be contained in an Irish text? What is inherited in the Irish tradition? A contest for drawing the public's attention to their anthologies was implicitly involved.

An example that illustrates how the editor refined his argument by contrasting other shades of nationalistic opinion on canons is Thomas MacDonagh's *Literature in Ireland*, published in 1916. In this book, MacDonagh introduced "the Irish mode," as a way to break down Young Irelanders' parochial views on Irish literature. However, his intentional dismissal of their views suggests that there was a fierce struggle amongst anthologists for gaining an elevated status for their literary products.

To delineate the attributes of the Irish mode, MacDonagh first of all sets out those writers who are disqualified from it. He excludes "Hibernian-English writers of the eighteenth century," as "they do indeed form a band apart in English Literature, with

---

[296] Smyth 164.

[297] The first part of Thomas MacDonagh's *Literature in Ireland* (1916) was a critical study of Irish literature in English. The author defined Irishness in a sense of Irish cultural nationalism. The second part of the book was a collection of thirty-three works – some were English translations of Irish verse – which exemplify MacDonagh's idea of Irishness. The book serves as a critical study and anthology.

4. Irish Anthologies Revisited

the common characteristic of adventurous and haughty individualism."[298] These excluded writers are principally those who are accused of producing stage-Irish characters for the amusement of English audiences. Their portraits of Irishmen tended to stigmatise the native Irish, who were caricatured as savages or traitors. The reason why MacDonagh called them "Hibernian-English," instead of "Anglo-Irish writers" of the eighteenth century, was that he supposed that many of them "going to England, adopted English manners, expressed English or European life, referred to themselves as Englishmen"; what they occasionally wrote about English-speaking Irishmen were "either caricatures or were obviously only half articulate in their new speech."[299] Due to their perceived lack of seriousness in dealing with Irish themes, MacDonagh left them out of the Irish mode. However, he insisted on including Jonathan Swift, Richard Steele, Richard Brinsley Sheridan, Edmund Burke and Oliver Goldsmith, since these writers displayed "an attitude rather of dissent from an English orthodoxy than of consent in an orthodoxy of their own or of Ireland" owing to "their Irish birth or upbringing."[300] These eighteenth-century writers, in his opinion, deserved the title of "Anglo-Irish."

Nevertheless, MacDonagh did not endorse a particular "segment" of Anglo-Irish literature to be included in the Irish mode, nor did he hold that the place of birth should be the only factor in deciding who is or is not an (Anglo-) Irish writer. According to MacDonagh, the idea of Anglo-Irish literature should include writers of Gaelic stock, so that the literature is "from, by, of, to and for the Irish people."[301] Certainly, his re-definition of Anglo-Irish literature was not welcomed by radical nationalists who wanted to purify Irish literature from any alien trait, including at an linguistic level.

One of MacDonagh's prime targets was the "Celtic Note," a term used by Matthew Arnold, who suggested that femininity was a common feature in Irish literature. In MacDonagh's view, the "Celtic Note" was a generalisation about Irish literature, being derived from the racial theory promulgated by English colonialism. Through Arnold's stress on the "Celtic Note" or Celticism as the racial trait of Irish people, the Irish were culturally segregated from the masculine and colonial ruler. MacDonagh

---

[298] MacDonagh vii. MacDonagh was executed in 1916 for being a leader of Easter Rising. This book was published posthumously.
[299] MacDonagh 16.
[300] MacDonagh vii.
[301] MacDonagh viii.

therefore viewed the "Celtic Note" as "an attempt to construe a Celtic culture as a manifestation of an underlying racial or national 'character'."[302] It is true to say that MacDonagh's criticism of the "Celtic Note" was with nationalistic concerns, while many of his comrades were more radical and tended to view the Irish Question in an over-simplified and dichotomous way. He therefore perceived that narrow, exclusivist Irishness, over-emphasised by radical nationalists, would result in another racial-orientated hegemony in Ireland. To break through this nationalistic myth of Irishness, he proposed the notion that Irish literature written in English was "not less authentic than the native Gaelic mode," since "'Irishness' was not a genetic or racial inheritance [but] something to be achieved as part of a concerted, cultural effort."[303] In other words, his introduction of the Irish mode was an attempt to distance Irish literature from racial distinctions.

MacDonagh, as a liberal latitudinarian who intended to "rescue" the Irish canon from a nationalistic impasse that he foresaw, was not the only anthologist who was opposed to the British colonial discourses on literature. His contemporary, W.B. Yeats, experienced a similar struggle when compiling *A Book of Irish Verse* (1895). In its preface, Yeats painted a vivid picture of how political forces made him almost yield to pressure to produce an exclusive collection of Irish patriotic verse:

> I compiled it towards the end of a long indignant argument, carried on in the committee rooms of our literary societies, and in certain newspapers between a few writers of our new movement, who judged Irish literature by literary standards, and a number of people, a few of whom were writers, who judged it by its patriotism and its political effect. [. . .] I have endeavoured [. . .] to separate what has literary value from what has only a patriotic and political value, no matter how sacred it has become to us.[304]

Yeats' record of external forces surrounding the formation of literary anthologies demonstrates some aspects of canon formation at a period when the Irish nation was taking its shape. During this time, the dividing line between political propaganda and

---

[302] Quoted in Gibbons 563. Gibbons paraphrases MacDonagh.
[303] Gibbons 563.
[304] Preface xiii. Yeats wrote this preface to the 2nd edition of the collection, which was published in 1900. The reason why Yeats had to add this preface to this edition might be that his choices of Irish verse in the first edition were not well received by some critics, so he had to defend himself.

4. Irish Anthologies Revisited

the arts became indeterminate, since external social values gained the upper hand in evaluating literary works. These social values may be disguised as values of "patriotic aesthetics." For example, the editor of *Emerald Gems* (1885), an anthology exclusively of patriotic poetry, blurred the dividing line – probably intentionally – by claiming that patriotic poetry could liberate the minds of colonised people. According to the editor, "patriotic aesthetics" could internally fulfil Irish people's expectation of right art, and externally serve to the political benefit of Ireland. "Patriotic aesthetics" was seen as an exclusive standard for Irish national literature, becoming a tradition which Yeats intended to fight against:

> [The poems in this volume] are of a patriotic character, love of country being one of the strongest and noblest feelings of the Irish heart. The beauty of particular scenes and places specially dear to those who sing of them, the pangs of parting from Ireland, the sorrows of exile, the job of battling for Irish freedom, the hopes, the resolves, the triumphs of the nation – these supply the inspirations of the following spirited and tuneful compositions, which cannot fail to cheer and nourish the sentiment of nationality in Irish hearts. We intend to issue a volume of this kind annually from the NATION office – the headquarters of national literature in Ireland – and we commend this pioneer of the series to the good will of true-hearted Irishmen "all the world around."[305]

By its very nature, a nationalistic anthology manifested the *zeitgeist* in which further collections of patriotic writings were produced in great numbers in the period leading up to and following Ireland gaining its independence.

4.3. Short Story Anthologies in Irish Literary Politics

It is fair to say that in the process of decolonising Ireland at the turn of the twentieth century, political discourses had to be exemplified through more than political slogans or poems. Discourse makers had to find more demonstrative and powerful media to persuade and call up followers effectively. Poetry, drama, and the short story were frequently the forms of writing chosen to testify to political ideals. Nationalists with either an Anglo-Irish or native Irish origin, taking a radical or moderate stance, more or less relied on literary productions to express their anti-colonial attitudes. The

---

[305] *Emerald Gems* 1.

anthology was inevitably seen as a form of publication which could collectively endorse a particular political agenda. In this section, I will focus on the development of the short story and the application of it, on the grounds that the particular genre helped produce a canon, or canons, favoured by Irish nationalists and literary revivalists in early twentieth-century Ireland. I will also survey short story anthologies made in the US to see how an Irish canon was conceived of overseas, and what caused canons inside and outside Ireland to be vulnerable and problematic.

In the case of Irish literature, the literary revival did attract attention to the ignored but still surviving folk tradition in the west of Ireland. Anglo-Irish revivalists, such as Yeats and Lady Gregory, compiled volumes of fairytales, stories about the peasantry, and wrote plays based upon legendary figures, like Cathleen Ni Houlihan, Cuchulainn, and Deirdre. J.M. Synge applied the distinctive rhythms of the Irish language and speech patterns of Hibernian-English to produce bilingual effects in his drama.

The call for attention to the native tradition indeed stimulated more critics, mostly Irish Irelanders, to verify the political and racial significance of native culture. Many collections of Irish tales started coming out, as there was a trend for Irish writers finding inspiration from the Gaelic and rural culture in the far west side of the country. Although some of these collections included first-hand stories transcribed from native speech, they went through a process of re-editing and rewriting. Many editors, some of whom were distinguished writers too, were involved with the re-editing and re-writing, possibly sub-consciously, when they had an urge to discover authentic Irishness. Such re-editing and re-writing produced a number of canons which mirrored the mainstream literary values promoted by some members of the social élite.

I would like to explore this point by taking Yeats' short story "The Twisting of the Rope" as an example. This story is about a bardic poet, Hanrahan the Red, who joins a party without invitation, as the hostess knows that this poet has a reputation for infatuating young girls by telling them lots of alluring stories. In order to separate her daughter from the unwelcome poet, the hostess and other female neighbours manage to trick him into twisting a rope. When the rope is twisted long enough, the poet has to stand outside the door to hold it. When this happens, the hostess shuts the door and keeps him out of the house. This story was from an old folk anecdote, and Yeats rewrote and published it at least twice.

The first version came out in 1892, and it was re-collected with other folk tales in *The Secret Rose* (1897). Yeats probably was not satisfied with the story. In 1903, he

4. Irish Anthologies Revisited

re-published it in a revised version, and later collected it with other Hanrahan stories as a series, giving this collection the title *Stories of Red Hanrahan*. These two versions of "The Twisting of the Rope" differ in the ways Yeats tells the story. The early version is more realistic, while the later one was lengthened with more conversation and is distinctly poetic. To be more specific, the song which Hanrahan sings to allure the daughter at the party is completely different in the two versions. In the early version, the lyric of the song is

> O Death's old bony finger
> Will never find us there
> In the high hollow downland
> Where love's to give and to spare;
> Where boughs have fruit and blossom
> At all times of the year;
> Where rivers are running over
> With red beer and brown beer.
> An old man plays the bagpipes
> In a gold and silver wood;
> Queens, their eyes blue like the ice,
> Are dancing in a crowd.[306]

In the 1903 version, the lyric is replaced with another more allegorical one:

> I never have seen Maid Quiet,
> Nodding her russet hood,
> For the winds that awakened the stars
> Are blowing through my blood.
> I never have seen Maid Quiet,
> Nodding alone and apart,
> For the words that called up the lightning
> Are calling through my heart.[307]

---

[306] *The Masterpiece Library of Short Stories: Irish and Overseas*, ed. by J. A. Hammerton, 240.
[307] *W.B. Yeats: Short Fiction*, ed. by G. J. Watson 146.

Yeats may have wanted to embellish the song with a mythic atmosphere. The intentional embellishment can also be seen from the way in which Hanrahan's sorrow is described differently in the two versions. The early version shows that Yeats tends to describe Hanrahan's sentiments in a less poetic way. Take the ending for example:

> And then he got free of [the rope], and went on, shaking and unsteady, along the edge of the strand, and the grey shapes were flying here and there around him. And this is what they were saying, "It is a pity for him that refuses the call of the daughters of the Sidhe, for he will find no comfort in the love of the women of the earth to the end of life and time, and the cold of the grave is in his heart for ever. It is death he has chosen; let him die, let him die, let him die."[308]

In the second version, Yeats refined the ending with more artistic and mythic elements, narrating the death of Hanrahan with a rather sympathetic tone:

> Grey forms, half seen, half felt, seemed to gather about him and to walk upon the sea. And among them Cleena of the Wave passed by, no longer marred by a human body, but laughing and mocking under a crown of rubies. Then it seemed as if the Rope of Human Sorrows changed in his dreams into a great serpent, coiling about him and taking him always more closely in its folds till it filled the whole earth and the heavens, and the stars were the glistening of its scales. [. . .] He imagined the grey forms to be flying round and round the coils. And behold! they were singing, "Sorrow be upon him who rejects the love of the daughters of Dana, for he shall find no comfort in the love of the daughters of Eve. The fire has taken hold upon his heart. Cast him out, cast him out, cast him out."[309]

Although in the early version Yeats did intend to create a mythic aura by mentioning the Sidhe, fairies who presage a death by wailing, I would argue that the mythic imagery and allegory in the second version – with references to "Cleena of the Wave" and "Dana," are more metaphorically associated with the death of Hanrahan. That is, Yeats associated the hostess' daughter with Cleena, who was lulled by fairy music and swept by a great wave of the sea to fairyland; her lover was devastated by her

---

[308] *Masterpiece*, ed. by Hammerton, 242.
[309] Yeats, *Short Fiction* 150.

4. Irish Anthologies Revisited

disappearance. In other words, with its features of Irish folk tales and Celtic myths, this more mythic version was seemingly revised to fit in with revivalists' expectations of revitalising Irish literature, so that readers could politically differentiate the literature of the Irish (in English) from that of the coloniser. Notwithstanding this, rewriting and embellishing a tale, with certain expectations, can potentially distort the nature of the original story. The second version of "The Twisting of the Rope" is potentially a new short story which Yeats produced with ideas from the Gaelic folk inheritance.

However, some critics believe that the use of folk tales provides the grounding for modern Irish literature. The claim is only partially credible since there are other political and religious concerns involved in the retelling of a story. Máirtín Ó Cadhain, an Irish novelist and critic, once observed that "he would prefer to read a single folk-tale in its original form than twenty listless adaptations of that tale in the shape of the short story."[310] Such appeals were recognised by some critics in an attempt to present authentic Irishness through the form of anthology. Yeats' second version of "The Twisting of the Rope" was thus regarded with disfavour by the editors of the *The Masterpiece Library of Short Stories: Irish and Overseas* (1923). Although this anthology is problematic in a way that I will discuss later, I would suggest that the editors' choice of this early version, rather than the embellished one, reflects their expectation of largely unembroidered Irishness. As the chief editor, J.A. Hammerton, commented in the introductory note that this story is "very charming and characteristic," I would suggest that the revised, more mythicised version was not deemed characteristic enough of Irishness.[311] It lacked the plainness and simplicity of the earlier version.

The Irish literary revival drew people's attention, to some degree, to the Gaelic cultural legacy in both oral and written forms. Translations and transcriptions of Gaelic tales and verses offered an alternative perspective from which people could hear a great diversity of native and Anglo-Irish voices. The coloniser's English literary tradition, as a result, was gradually losing its mainstream position. On the one hand, the "submerged population groups" (Frank O'Connor's term is meant to connote the politically and geographically marginalised Irish), started being viewed and examined in the medium of the short story.[312] On the other hand, the core issue of

---

[310] Quoted in Kiberd, "Story-Telling" 22.
[311] Hammerton, "Irish Story-tellers" 14.
[312] Frank O'Connor, *Lonely* 26.

what was authentic Irishness, along with the increasing number of anthologies published in Ireland and overseas, was gradually paid more attention to.

Yeats' two-volume collection of nineteenth-century Irish fiction, *Representative Irish Tales*, is one of the major anthologies he produced in his early career.[313] As he said in its introduction, he "made the selection in such a way as to illustrate as far as possible the kind of witness they bear to Irish character."[314] He tended to record, for not only political but historiographic ends, what had not been "discovered" in anthologies. In a letter to Father Matthew Russell regarding his anthology, he declared that "I am trying to make all the stories illustrations of some phase of Irish life, meaning the collection to be a kind of social history."[315] In the preface to *Stories from Carleton*, which he anthologised, and which came out two years before *Representative Irish tales*, he praised the short story writer, William Carleton, thus: "William Carleton was a great Irish historian. The history of a nation is not in parliaments and battlefields, but in what the people say to each other on fair-days and high days, and in how they farm, and quarrel, and go on pilgrimage. These things has Carleton recorded."[316] This obviously suggests that Yeats' aim in making anthologies about the Irish peasantry was not purely art for art's sake, but an act of historiography, which aimed to re-write history so as to include ignored social communities. Moreover, Yeats used anthologies to testify to his political and literary points of view. As we know, he disagreed with Young Irelanders about the use of literature merely as political and religious propaganda. He objected to English critics' view of the Irish as a sentimental race – a view upheld by Matthew Arnold. He also disliked the stage-Irish humour with which the English audience was entertained. Bearing these concerns in mind, Yeats selectively anthologised the works he deemed reflective of true Irishness. In *Representative Irish Tales*, he gave each writer a short introduction to explain why his/her work was chosen, regardless of the reputation the writer had gained for having caricatured the Irish or for being a propagandist of Young Ireland. William Carleton, for instance, was a Protestant convert writer who had more works selected than any other writer in *Representative Irish Tales* (four as opposed to one or two in the case of other writers). His numerous stories were supposed to have been

---

[313] Yeats produced three anthologies of Irish folk tales: *Fairy and Folk Tales of the Irish Peasantry* (1888), *Stories from Carleton* (1889), and *Representative Irish Tales* (1891).
[314] Yeats, *Representative Irish Tales*, 25.
[315] Yeats, *Letters* 143.
[316] Yeats, introduction xvi.

4. Irish Anthologies Revisited

written in a condescending tone towards Catholic Irish peasants, which gave him a mixed reputation for his dubious anti-Catholic position and lack of artistry.[317] Hammerton showed his objection by including none of Carleton's work in his *The Masterpiece Library of Short Stories*, on the grounds that "careful examination of his work has failed to discover an example suitable for inclusion, as they lack both invention and narrative art, and are told with unnecessary circumlocution."[318]

Nevertheless, Yeats admired Carleton because he identified with Carleton's appeal for (re-)popularising Irish peasantry stories – though not all critics agree with Yeats; he might have wanted to alter the inaccurate impression of Carleton that people had. Carleton's own appeal, with which Yeats identified, is revealed as follows: "[I] disclaim subserviency to any political purpose whatsoever. [My] desire is neither to distort [my] countrymen into demons, nor to enshrine them as suffering innocents and saints, but to exhibit them as they really are – warm-hearted, hot-headed, affectionate creatures."[319] This statement partially illustrates the intention with which Yeats compiled this anthology, as he tended to present Irish characters who were capable of deep passion, joy, and tragedy, instead of uncivilised, sentimental, and superficial stage Irishmen. However, not only could there exist a subtle line – in the choice of stories – dividing deep passion and sentimentality, as well as tragedy/drama and melodrama, but also the process of selection may involve personal bias. To be more specific, *Representative Irish Tales* does anthologise most of the major Irish writers in the nineteenth century, including Maria Edgeworth, John and Michael Banim, William Carleton, Samuel Lover, Gerald Griffin, Charles Lever. Nevertheless, these writers often assume an English reader and many of their works involve crude representations of Irishness. Interestingly, Yeats only chose those works which did not appear to stigmatise the Irish. Some of the works he selected obviously portray the English as laughing-stocks, such as "Trinity College," by Charles Lever, and "The Pig-Driving Peelers" by Charles Kickham.

"Trinity College" is a story consisting of four episodes which ridicules scholars' corruption and students' misconduct. This story gives the impression that Trinity College is a school where money talks; students can be admitted as long as parents make large enough donations; professors visit the Bank of Ireland more often than tutoring students or conducting research. Some good-for-nothing students trick pe-

---

[317] Welch 50.
[318] Hammerton 11.
[319] Carleton xxv.

Irish Literary Canon

destrians outside Trinity College, and end up causing a massive riot in the city. "The Pig-Driving Peelers" caricatures two Irish policemen who run breathlessly after wild pigs, presenting Irish peasants who have more sense of humour and wits than those who work under the English order. I would argue that the stories Yeats selected present either favourable images of Irish peasants or ideas of anti-English authority. These stories can hardly even be categorised as "comedies of manners," which are meant to satirise the manners of certain social groups. On the contrary, they echo the anti-English ethos by gathering or making up ridiculous "stage Englishmen" anecdotes.

This sort of replacement of comic "stage Irishmen" with "stage Englishmen" appears in other anthologies as well. A 1932 anthology entitled *Irish Short Stories*, edited by a cultural nationalist, George A. Birmingham, was compiled particularly to combat the image of stage Irishmen.[320] In its introduction, he pointed out that the stereotype of Irishmen, which was consolidated by English critics, dichotomised the Irish into two simplistic types, "either amusing or deeply depressing":[321]

> There are a good many Englishmen [. . .] who hold strongly that an Irish story must be amusing, preferably broadly comic, if possible rollicking. Otherwise they think it is not Irish at all [. . .]. [. . .] Then there are other Englishmen [. . .] who hold that Irish stories ought to represent melancholy saints with enormous haloes round their heads, made of Celtic glamour, persecuted creatures who move the sensitive to tears. [. . .] These gentlemen get exceedingly angry with anyone who dares to put into a book an Irishman who is either gay, or even cheerfully vicious.[322]

As a cultural nationalist, and someone who had been working with Douglas Hyde and Arthur Griffith in the Gaelic League, Birmingham was active in re-making the image of Irishmen in literature. In *Irish Short Stories*, most of the works he chose are about childhood experiences, glances of country life, or incidents in cities, and none of them are particularly amusing. As Birmingham intended, these stories were to form a

---

[320] George A. Birmingham was born in Belfast, and was also a novelist, playwright, and religious writer. He worked with Arthur Griffith and Douglas Hyde in the Gaelic League. Many of his works are concerned with the notion of Irish nationhood such as *The Search Party* (1909) and *Irishmen All* (1913).
[321] Birmingham 11.
[322] Birmingham 11.

4. Irish Anthologies Revisited

unity of impression "that the amusing Irish story is dying out and the grim story occupying the whole field."[323] Stories in this collection may not all be so unpleasant or grim as he put it, but they more or less touch the shadowy sides of Irish life. James Joyce's "A Painful Case" and Michael McLaverty's "Wild Duck's Nest" are cases in point. The former is about an affair between two Dubliners, and the woman protagonist dies miserably in a train accident due to the loss of love. The latter nostalgic story takes place on an isolated island in County Antrim, Rathlin Island and is about a child taking care of a wild duck in the beautiful countryside.

Birmingham's battle against the stage Irishmen, and his insistence upon the realistic representation of Irishmen, is exemplified in two stories in *Irish Short Stories* which explicitly mock at the English. They are William Carleton's "Bob Pentland," and Somerville and Ross' "Lisheen Races, Second-hand." In "Bob Pentland," English officials attempt to seek out illegal whiskey distillation stations run by native Irish, never outdoing the witty Irish. Instead, they are insulted constantly by the Irish throughout the story. "Lisheen Races, Second-hand" even more pronouncedly replaces stage Irishmen with "stage Englishmen." In the story, an English lord pays his first visit to Ireland, but makes a fool of himself in public due to either bad luck or his ignorance of Irish culture.

Stories like these which are critical of the English suggest that the Irish, in the period of post-independence, were amused to see Englishmen ridiculed. This might involve some sort of literary revenge for the falsely-produced image of stage Irishmen. By selecting anti-English stories – one by Anglo-Irish writers, Somerville and Ross, the other by Carleton – the editor seems to suggest that the key power of ridiculing their political foes has been handed over to the Irish. Furthermore, given that both Somerville/Ross and Carleton had written a great number of stories which were not particularly anti-English, Birmingham's choice of the two stories suggests his political concerns. That, as a result, supports my earlier argument that anthologies can act as "strategic weapons in literary politics."

Apart from anthologising anti-colonial works for the sake of re-making the Irishman image, re-editing stories was one of the strategies that served this purpose. That is, editors may choose stories that they suppose relevant to the re-made image; they may also modify a story to fit in with that new image. Mary Helen Thuente claims for Yeats' *Representative Irish Tales* that the re-editing of stories makes this anthology

---

[323] Birmingham 15.

"more 'representative' of [Yeats' own] conception of the peasant than of Irish fiction in general."[324] As Thuente traced the first-hand sources from which Yeats made his selection for *Representative Irish Tales*, she found that the editor omitted nearly twenty-three pages from Michael Banim's novel *The Mayor of Wind-Gap* to piece together an excerpt short enough for his anthology. The omitted part, in Thuente's view, is significant in that it gives accounts of the cause and effect of the appearances of characters. Yeats' omission of the twenty-three pages, as a result, "introduces an aura of mystery which was not in [Banim's] source," and "the sense of mystery thus achieved is similar to [what] Yeats had sought to convey in *Fairy and Folk Tales*."[325] Yeats also re-edited Thomas Crofton Croker's "The Confessions of Tom Bourke" for the anthology. He added two paragraphs selected from Lady Wilde's *Ancient Legends* to the end of Croker's story, because he wanted to draw the reader's attention to "the aesthetic, religious, and mysterious character of Irish fairy doctors."[326]

On the whole, to privilege stories with certain themes and to re-edit them results in a deliberate act of re-interpretation. Specifically, this re-interpretation may alter the authors' intended messages, and invent a new image through which anthologists suggest political concerns. However, the "copy and paste" procedure seems to be recognised by some anthologists as a legitimate means for anthologisation, and they inevitably "mangle the text[s]" to achieve "public canonisation of private taste."[327] Arthur Quiller-Couch, the editor of *The Oxford Book of English Verse*, first published in 1900 and including many poets with Irish origin, admitted that the way in which he produced this collection was based upon his individual tastes: "I have often excised weak superfluous stanzas when sure that excision would improve [the poem]."[328] Nevertheless, the parts he reckoned weak and superfluous may still carry important messages to the reader. The reason for omission may be just that there is something unfitting for current aesthetic standards, or something politically sensitive, such as anti-English sentiment.

Therefore, it is justifiable to say that the trend of producing anthologies in early twentieth-century Ireland involved political ambition – which was not just to rescue works from being lost but to ground the Irish nationalistic ideology. However, if Irish

---

[324] Thuente 17.
[325] Thuente 16-17.
[326] Thuente 16.
[327] Lampe 3.
[328] Quiller-Couch viii.

4. Irish Anthologies Revisited

anthologies collected at the time have to be seen collectively as a political reaction against colonialism, anthologies produced outside Ireland, in my observation, were not more objective in dealing with "the Irish Question." I would like to take the series of *The Best British Short Stories*, which was compiled annually by Edward O'Brien, an Irish American, and published in Boston and New York from 1915 to 1939, as an example.[329]

The significance of this series is that its publication spanned those crucial decades in which Ireland struggled for political independence. An interesting fact about this series is that it tended to provide a specifically British cultural imperialistic perspective on modern literature written in English, in that not only British, but also Irish, Canadian, and American-born writers were selected for inclusion. Also, this series of anthologies suggests how a "British" literary canon was conceived overseas: writers from the regions mentioned above were regarded as constituting the British/English canon due to their historical associations with the British Empire. (However, English works by Indian writers were excluded, although India belonged to the British Empire. Here it could be suggested that only white-skinned writers qualified for the title of British writers in the first place, although many of them were obviously born outside Britain). Nevertheless, changes made in the appearances of each year's *The Best British Short Stories* document conflicts between colonial and anti-colonial discourses at the time.

As I have mentioned above, the editor of this series of anthologies seemed to hold to a cultural imperialistic view to present what he thought were the best British/English short stories since 1915. Nevertheless, the anti-colonial call for political reforms was so intense that the organisation of the anthology had to be amended. Starting from 1922, the year in which the Irish Free State was established, there were two appendices added to the end of each yearly anthology: "The Yearbook of the British and Irish Short Story" and "Volumes of Short Stories Published in Great Brit-

---

[329] Edward O'Brien (1890-1941) was an Irish American author, poet, editor and anthologist. His works include "The Dance of the Machines" (1929); "The Guest Book" (1935); "White Fountains" (1917); "Modern American Short Stories" (1932. O'Brien and John Cournos co-edited this series of anthologies from 1915-1925, which were published by Small, Maynard Publishing, Boston. After 1926, O'Brien edited it alone, and published it with Dodd, Mead & Company, New York; from 1930 onwards, with Houghton Mifflin Company, Boston.

Irish Literary Canon

ain and Ireland."[330] The titles of the two appendices seemed to recognise that Ireland and Britain were now two different states. Nevertheless, looking into the two newly-added appendices, we find that the editor simplistically classified writers into two kinds: "English writers" and "American and Canadian writers." Writers with an Irish origin were put under the category of "English writers," and there seems to be no way to single out who is *not* English in O'Brien's categorisation. Edward O'Brien indeed showed his awareness of current political changes between Ireland and Britain, but the mixed list of English and Irish authors exposes his cultural imperialistic viewpoint about what constitutes English literature. That is, literary works written in English but by Irish writers were subsumed under the broad British/English cultural and literary tradition. The editor of this 1922 anthology from the USA, which is also an Anglophone country, would erase, possibly unconsciously, the distinctions between Irish and English writers. Cultural imperialism also inevitably resulted in the marginalisation of non-English, for instance Gaelic, literature. Not surprisingly, the appendix entitled "The Yearbook of the British and Irish Short Stories" does not include works written in Gaelic or those translated into modern English, while that is what the Gaelic League in Ireland was keen to revive and promote nation/island-wide.

The recognition of Irish writers in this series of anthologies was slightly enhanced after three years. The title of the 1925 edition was amended as "The Best British Short Stories of 1925: with an Irish Supplement." The contribution of Irish writers was therefore superficially acknowledged, while it served as a supplement to British literature. The amended title seems to suggest that Irish literature should always be linked with British literature as its sub-product. As to the appendix "Volumes of Short Stories Published in Great Britain and Ireland," it excludes Canadian writers from this year on; nevertheless, the editor still categorised selected writers into two kinds: "English and Irish Authors," and "American Authors." No reason is offered for the exclusion of Canadians. Regarding the category of "English and Irish Authors," Irish writers were still mixed with the English without reference to their origins. Furthermore, Scottish and Welsh writers were taken for granted as English. I would argue that if the word "English" here has more linguistic than geographic connotations, the

---

[330] In the two appendices, the editor listed titles of short stories he had read from newspapers, magazines, and other sources, in order to compile the anthology. He marked some titles with an asterisk to indicate distinction, but did not provide information on writers' origins or nationalities as the titles of the appendices suggested.

4. Irish Anthologies Revisited

latter do not apply to Irish authors, as apparently none of the works selected were written in Gaelic but many were in (Hibernian-)English.

This "British" anthology was not re-named for three years until 1927; the subtitle "with an Irish Supplement" in smaller print was kept. After 1926, a new appendix, "Biographical Notes," was added. Only then could the reader distinguish writers' nationalities. In 1928, the anthology was renamed again and the title lengthened into "The Best British Short Stories of 1928: with an Irish and colonial supplement." From this year onwards, the problematic appendix of "English and Irish Writers" was renamed as "British and Irish Authors," while the category of "American Authors" remained. The replacement of "English and Irish" with "British and Irish," as the editor explained in the 1930 collection, was intended to cover more "colonial work" for the Great British canon. He said: "What interested me [. . .] is the fresh, living current which flows through the best British, Irish, and Colonial work. [. . .] I have sought to select from the stories published in British, Irish, American, and Colonial periodicals those stories by British, Irish, and Colonial authors."[331] The amended title acknowledges an enlarged British canon, in which writers from New Zealand, Australia, and South Africa were formally recognised by being given a supplementary place. (In fact, works by writers from these regions had been included in previous years' collections, but were not mentioned in a separate supplement, as the Irish had been.) Interestingly, the "Biographical Notes" appendix was removed after the title of the anthology was lengthened in 1928 to cover colonial writers. Again, writer's nationalities were omitted. The last time the anthology was re-named was in 1933. The word 'Supplement' was dismissed, and the title was lengthened again into "The Best British Short Stories of 1933: And the Yearbook of the British, Irish, and Colonial Short Story." From this year onwards to 1939, the title remained unaltered.

The re-naming of the annual British anthology published overseas shows that the Irish canon, which was being formed by Irish Irelanders and Anglo-Irish critics within Ireland, was in fact vulnerable outside Ireland. This was because some critics identified with the ideology that the British culture was superior and should supplant other regional literatures, even though this idea was spread more by military means in the beginning. The nearly three decades long series of British anthologies spanned those turbulent years during which the British Empire had to cope with anti-colonial pressures mounted in many of its colonies, and with World War I. The dwindling size

---

[331] Edward O'Brien, introduction ix.

of the "Irish" in the title of the anthologies apparently ensured that British cultural imperialism still survived. However, no re-named title could escape from political assessment. That is, in Irish nationalists' eyes, Irish literature was not supplementary to British literature, and from a post-colonial point of view, no national literature should be grouped and simplified under the category of colonial literature. The traditional perception of British literature can therefore be re-scrutinised from these two perspectives.

Having explored anthologies produced in Ireland and overseas for different political aims in the early twentieth century, I would contend that most of the anthologies present Ireland, or Irishness, in problematic ways, since they involve personal biases, political confrontations, censorship, economic factors, education, and other external forces. As to the trend of producing anthologies for nationalistic or colonial ends, Peter Lennon points out that it is largely owing to "desperate narcissism," and its result is likely to be "a unique patchwork" or even a "Domesday Book."[332] Seamus Deane is concerned about the way in which anthologies are produced and about their influences, though he has chaired the editing of a few Irish anthologies himself, including the voluminous *Field Day Anthology of Irish Writing*. He says: "The work of putting together the anthology was itself an exercise in dismantling [those texts], in escaping from their coercive and disheartening power. [. . .] Selection is not made from a preordained "tradition"; it is selection which ordains the tradition(s)."[333] Deane seems to suggest that although the making of anthologies is one way to free certain works from a "coercive and disheartening power," they are in fact forming a potentially hegemonic tradition.

However, an anthology can at least serve as a strategic weapon in literary politics for the editors and the reader to contribute to social reforms, while social concerns are at times more highlighted than aesthetic ones. Anthologists from different generations have been acting as historians reflecting the social discourses of their times through literary examples which presented unsolvable ideological confrontations. The anthologies they produced might no longer be popular, but they still offer some significant historical lessons for later generations.

---

[332] Lennon 23.
[333] Deane, introduction xx.

5. Historiography and the Motif of the Rising
in Some Irish Short Stories and Novels

There is an anecdote about the 1921 peace negotiations during which Eamon de Valera, who was the president of Sinn Féin and the Irish Volunteers at the time, strongly opposed an Anglo-Irish Treaty which excluded Northern Ireland and included an oath of loyalty to the British crown. In order to make his opposition clear, he "lectured" British Prime Minister David Lloyd George on the history of Ireland. This lesson did not please Lloyd George much, so that he complained while walking out of the meeting venue: "Mr. De Valera has been talking non-stop since eight o'clock this morning, filling me in on the background to the Irish fight for freedom. And after eight hours and sixteen minutes he hasn't even reached the Norman invasion of Ireland yet." Hearing this, de Valera responded, "Aye, he needed a lesson in Irish history."[334]

This anecdote is not intended to indicate that de Valera lacked a sense of humour, but rather to show that he and his anti-colonial comrades were obsessed with Irish history and intended to interpret it for the sake of decolonising Ireland. One year later James Joyce published *Ulysses*, and portrayed Stephen Dedalus asserting that "[h]istory is a nightmare from which I am trying to awake"; in the same year the Republican wing of the IRA failed to realise their dream of a united Ireland in the Anglo-Irish War. Joyce's observation on his countrymen's "obsession with Irish history," however, seemingly only received further attention overseas when he was in exile in Trieste.[335] Notwithstanding this, the obsession with Irish revolutionary history, and the bitter memories it evoked, continued even after the Free State took its form; official or unofficial commemorations of political events, such as the Rebellion of 1798, the Lockout Strike of 1913, and the Easter Rising of 1916, were held annually in order to perpetuate and renew their significance in Irish history.

Furthermore, the fact that Ireland was a Catholic state meant that some political figures, such as Patrick Pearse, were sanctified by the Church. A mosaic in Galway Catholic Cathedral displays the praying figures of Patrick Pearse and John F. Ken-

---

[334] "Eamon De Valera Quotations."
[335] In Trieste, Joyce was invited by Attilio Tamaro to give lectures to local university students in 1907. He supported nationalism but denounced the hypocrisy of some nationalists and Irish parliamentarians, as well as the over-dominant Catholic Church. For more details, see Ellmann 255-59.

nedy on either side of the risen Christ.[336] The association of these two figures with Jesus Christ seems to idealise their deaths. These events and figures illustrate that the emerging Catholic state of Southern Ireland needed a celebratory interpretation of history in order to produce a sense of community, while Ulster Protestants might emphasise and commemorate different things.

For publishers, writers, and historians, the (re)writing of Irish history and (re)collection of works containing patriotic themes are always popular subjects for publication. As discussed in Chapter Four, a Belfast-based newspaper and publisher, *The Northern Star*, had been intentionally compiling anthologies to promote an anti-colonial viewpoint in the late eighteenth century. The anthologisation of patriotic works was not undertaken to prevent them from being lost, but rather for the purposes of anti-colonial politics. In other words, although anthologists did not eventually take up their pen, as historians, to write history, they and their publishers were involved with a project of history (re)making. As part of this project, short stories and poems whose themes were relevant to politics were often grouped together by anthologists; novels featuring historical events were placed into the category of "Irish historical novels," and some were even valued as "epics," regardless of their faithfulness to actual incidents. This chapter will further explore the formation of an Irish canon by looking into a specific and popular motif in modern Irish prose writing: the Easter Rising.

Irish revisionists have always targeted the obsession of the public with nationalistic politicians and revolutionaries. Many influential figures of the Easter Rising and other social movements, such as Patrick Pearse, James Connolly, and Eoin MacNeill, were reappraised by revisionist historians in the 1960s and 1970s. By unearthing many ignored and private documents, revisionists found that these "rebels" in fact had disparate ideas about an armed rising at Easter 1916, and not all behaved honestly to each other or kept to a single political line as their supporters liked to believe. According to F.X. Martin's survey, Pearse deceived MacNeill into thinking that the latter had succeeded in dissuading James Connolly from leading his Citizen Army into rebellion on its own, whereas MacNeill was actually an anti-Rising figure who believed that "to kill any person in carrying out such a course of action is murder."[337] Ruth Dudley Edwards contends that Patrick Pearse's extraordinary devotion to a

---

[336] This particular piece of mosaic was also noted in Laffan 108.
[337] Quoted in Boyce 165.

5. The Motif of the Rising

foreseeable, tragic uprising resulted from his failures "on personal, family and financial grounds," and to die heroically was a method to "compensate for [his] failure in life."[338] As for James Connolly, who had been seen as a hard-line socialist, Austen Morgan declared that after a thorough reading of the last twenty months' worth of Connolly's own writings, "it is very difficult to associate Easter 1916 with an international proletarian revolution," as he had tried hard to "marr[y] socialism and nationalism."[339] These new findings potentially alter the perception of many major revolutionary events, including the Easter Rising, and certainly unsettled traditionalist historians who had previously credited these leaders with the emancipation of the Irish nation.

However, Irish revisionists' scepticism of the "nationalist" historical narrative is not completely tenable; one of the revisionist historians, R.F. Foster, expressed reservations about the way in which Irish history was reviewed. In the 1980s, he put this question to his colleagues in *The Irish Review*: "We are all revisionists now. But who will revise the revisionists?"[340] His self-interrogation most likely resulted from *re*-revisionist historians' suspicions of those narratives highlighted by both traditionalist and revisionist historians. That is to say that, although revisionist historiographers had carefully surveyed neglected material to rebuild the facts of key events and figures, their approach to history was still called into question with regard to the limits of objective presentations of history.

Postmodern historians such as Saul Friedlander troubled Irish revisionists because the former argued that facts could obtain significance through being narrativised; "the narrativisation in its emplotment and troping confers on the facts a significance which a different emplotment and troping could take away."[341] In other words, what makes historical reality perceivable is that most historians and their readers believe, as Hayden White observes, "events themselves possess a 'story' kind of form and a 'plot' kind of meaning."[342] As a result, historians who harbour different concerns for a national history might try to convince their readers with different uses of emplotments. Thus, with the leaders of the Easter Rising, nationalistic and religious historians would stress their heroic acts, portraying their execution by the colonisers as being as

---

[338] Boyce 168.
[339] Boyce 169.
[340] Foster 4.
[341] Friedlander 385.
[342] White, "Historical" 394.

sacred as Jesus' death. These historians would also express an antagonistic attitude towards non-nationalists or anti-home rulers. However, the Rising's leaders would be depicted as rebels who jeopardised the integrity of the United Kingdom, if the historians did not accept a romantic reading of the Easter Rising but looked at it from an imperialist or Orangeman's view of "the Irish Troubles."

One postcolonial critic, Paul Carter, asserts that the writing of history is similar to that of a theatrical performance, in that historians "reduce space to stage" and unfold events with chosen emplotments.[343] He argues that historians "may think of the performance, [but] do not question the stage conventions."[344] The illusion of the theatre, therefore, sustains, and "reveal[s] heroic man at his epic labour on the stage of history."[345] The stage conventions that Carter mentions quite likely refer to the way in which facts are narrated subject to linguistic limits. As Luke Gibbons analyses in "Identity without a Centre," "[what] speech possesses [. . .] is historically bounded."[346] This means that few historians can freely and objectively present historical reality without falling into a linguistic format, a format which has been passed down for hundreds of years. Reconstructing history through language has its limits, in that linguistic formats which contain figurative, poetic, comic, or tragic expressions are "historically-bounded." Historiographers and readers must, whether unconsciously or consciously, follow these linguistic conventions. Disputable historical issues, "within a limited range of canonical and emergent allegories available to the competent reader [and writers]," would be argued, documented, or narrowed down to a linguistically presentable extent.[347] Therefore, since language and history, in terms of the theory of postmodern historiography, are bound together, it is not possible to present a history fairly without "legitimat[ing] 'us' and not others," on either a nationalistic, colonial, imperialistic, or Orangemen's level.[348] The "nightmare" of history from which Stephen Dedalus tries hard to awake is actually made up of these components. In the Irish context, as I have already mentioned, an alternative approach to history as such puts both revisionist and traditionalist historiography at stake. However, some may argue that those historians who tend to "redress" revision-

---

[343] Carter 376.
[344] Carter 375.
[345] Carter 375.
[346] Gibbons 371.
[347] Clifford 110.
[348] Ashcroft, introduction to "Part XI: History" 355.

5. The Motif of the Rising

ist historiography should dissect more subtly the ways in which history is written and read by exemplifying actual texts, in order to make their theory less sweeping and more convincing.

5.1. Varying Sentiments in Historical Representations

Before moving on to discuss specific texts, it is necessary to clarify the use of literary texts to analyse "historiography," by which in this context I mean historical novels and stories, rather than historical monographs or documentation. Some might argue that historical novels and stories are fictional works, and as such, should not be relied on for an understanding of history; historians should be more well-trained and professional than writers in producing authentic depictions and objective observations of events which have taken place. These arguments may be partially correct, but it is also possible that Ulster Protestant historians would make less favourable comments about nationalistic issues, though historians from both the South and the North could claim to have interpreted history in a professional manner. As there is always room for free interpretations, it can be assumed that historical monographs and documentation by themselves cannot provide an unbiased viewpoint of past events. Historical stories and novels, therefore, with their more sophisticated depictions of characters and background, as well as their narrative variations, will endow the reader with more individualised responses to relevant events.[349] Readers' responses and observations are be the result of complex interactions among characters in the course of events, which is not always within the control of authors.

Another reason to favour historical novels and stories lies with the Structuralists' breakdown of the binary "reality against fiction." For them, "human experience is grounded in language as an institution,"[350] and human existence is "made out of words."[351] As language is widely used to comprehend existence, Structuralists believe that both historians and novelists can produce comprehensible reality through a narrative. However, it is a narrative that has an artificial "consistency of character, and combin[es] episodic immediacy with over-all coherence" in a formal linguistic

---

[349] Historical monographers, even though they may set out their works in a thoughtful manner, have a rather limited number of narrative variations to apply, when compared to the choices regarding narrative point of view that is possible in fictional writings.
[350] Brown 40.
[351] Culler 140.

organisation.[352] For decided Structuralists, real history is not only unknowable, but the binary concept of "fiction against reality" is also not tenable; "reality" is just another text, a verbal construct; thus, the (re-)writing of "reality" merely serves to "add fictions to fictions."[353] Nevertheless, although Structuralists deny the possibility of reproducing reality in writing, renouncing the differences between novelists and historians, they do not however reject the idea that society has a history. It is not a history that exists in a text, but rather a history that composes the texture of everyone's life, though it is not dependent on individual realisation. As a result, history may be redefined along the lines proposed by David Lodge: "History may be, in a philosophical sense, a fiction, but it does not feel like that when we miss a train or somebody starts a war."[354] Having said this, I believe it is arguable that historical novels and stories deserve equal treatment with historical monographs, as means to understand the complexities of the human past.

In early twentieth-century Ireland, there was a diversity of political discourses over the settlement of the Irish Question, and it was common for novelists, poets, and dramatists to put pen to paper to express their views of the contemporary political situation. Their works were often concerned with public events, such as W.B. Yeats' poem "September 1913." I would like to compare this particular poem with Joyce Kilmer's riposte "Easter Week," to suggest that historical interpretations are subject to political and personal sentiments. Readers of these two poems, which have competing historical interpretations, may, in the words of Hayden White, perceive history as "a chaos of forms."[355]

In "September 1913," Yeats expressed his sympathy with the exploited working class who suffered the 1913 "Great Lockout." The poet's resentment at hirers who locked out "Larkinites" from the Irish Transport and General Workers' Union also stemmed from his frustration over missing financial support from employers to build an art gallery to house the Lane collection. Disappointed with mercenary employers with no interest in the arts and outraged by the workers' deteriorated, uncultured living conditions, he wrote this poem to denounce employers' materialism and lament

---

[352] Bergonzi 43.
[353] Bergonzi 44.
[354] Lodge 33.
[355] White, "Politics" 122. Hayden White suggests in this article that postmodernist readers should be aware of "the variety of ways of configuring a past which itself only exists as a chaos of forms" (120).

5. The Motif of the Rising

the less than spirited Irish nationalism of the time. In this poem, 1913 Ireland appears thus: "Romantic Ireland's dead and gone / It's with O'Leary in the grave." In addition to the Fenian John O'Leary (1830–1907), he refers to such nationalist Irishmen as Edward Fitzgerald, Robert Emmet, and Wolfe Tone, deploring the fact that Ireland, at the time he wrote this poem, has failed to deserve the blood they sacrificed under the prevailing materialist ethos.[356] The poet's regret over the commercialisation of Ireland displays only one aspect of the country; however, his portrait was not much appreciated by one contemporary poet, Joyce Kilmer (1886-1918).

Kilmer was born in New Brunswick, New Jersey, in 1886, and often claimed that he had Irish blood on both sides of his family.[357] He converted to Catholicism in 1913, and became an ardent supporter of Home Rule, often contributing to articles on Irish nationalistic issues from America.[358] His poem "Easter Week," written in 1918, was to exalt the heroic conduct of Irishmen sacrificed during the Easter Rising. He begins his poem by interrogating Yeats: "Romantic Ireland's dead and gone, / It's with O'Leary in the grave. / Then, Yeats, what gave that Easter dawn / A hue so radiantly brave?"[359] Kilmer begins "Easter Week" by quoting Yeats' lines in "September 1916": "Romantic Ireland's dead and gone, / It's with O'Leary in the grave." Kilmer's poem suggests that he, as an ardent Irish nationalist, did not agree with Yeats' pessimistic attitude towards the future of Ireland. His use of Yeats' lines questions the latter's views on the strength of Irish nationalism and seems highly patriotic with a romantic vision of war and death. In contrast to Yeats' anguish over a materialist Ireland with a negative interpretation of history, Kilmer's poem affirms past and present nationalist endeavours with a somewhat surrealistic image of the resurrection of the

---

[356] Lord Edward Fitzgerald was an Anglo-Irish United Irishman who jointly led the 1798 rising with Wolfe Tone.

[357] However, in 1993 Joyce Kilmer's son, Kenton Kilmer, published a biography, *Memories of My Father, Joyce Kilmer*, in which he found there was no evidence to prove Irish blood in his father's veins. He was mostly German; his mother predominantly English, while most people now recognise Joyce Kilmer as an Irish American, as he identified himself. See "Joyce Kilmer: FAQs and Fancies."

[358] Most of his manuscripts and correspondence are now archived in the library of Georgetown University, Washington D.C. One cluster of his manuscripts is categorised as "Irish-American Opinion on the Home Rule Deadlock."

[359] Yeats, "September 1913" 55.

dead: "Lord Edward leaves his resting place / And Sarsfield's face is glad and fierce. / See Emmet leap from troubled sleep / To grasp the hand of Padraic Pearse!"[360]

Kilmer's patriotic "Easter Week" lives up to the passionate nationalist interpretation of the Easter Rising: the rebels whose names appear in his poem should now be justified as heroes whose blood gave life to a new nationalistic country. Needless to say, this poem could serve as patriotic propaganda to demonstrate the necessity of war and rising against the English.

In keeping with the sentiment of patriotism running through this poem, writings which presented a reserved view of the Rising, such as Yeats' "Easter, 1916," were omitted from Leaving Certificate textbooks before the 1950s.[361] This poem, along with "September 1913," was not received well by zealous patriots, since the poet admired the bravery of revolutionaries but was not explicitly supportive of the necessity of a bloody rising. He named a few revolutionaries who died or were executed for the Rising, but at the same time suggested that these people had failed to avoid the tragic consequences they brought on themselves and society. The question he asks about them – Thomas MacDonagh, John MacBride, Patrick Pearse, and James Connolly – is: "And what if excess of love / Bewildered them till they died?"[362] The "excess of love" cited here represents Yeats' reluctance to acknowledge the desirability of the Rising in the face of less bloody solutions. The phrase "A terrible beauty," rather than a "glorious" one, suggests Yeats' reservation about a form of militant patriotism which might have produced a "terribly fragile" beauty.[363]

Since the 1960s, commemorations of the Easter Rising have increasingly met with severe criticism from revisionists, as some believed that an over-emphasis on 1916

---

[360] Joyce Kilmer, "Easter Week." Patrick Sarsfield was the leader of the 1691 rising of Limerick; he had fought the army of William of Orange to a standstill, but was unwillingly exiled to France after signing the Treaty of Limerick.

[361] According to my survey of Leaving Certificate textbooks published before the 1950s, "Easter, 1916" was rarely included. Yeats was one of the few Anglo-Irish poets whose work was consistently well represented. In James Carey's edition, the most frequently selected poems by Yeats are: "No Second Troy," "September 1913," "The Fisherman," "Sailing to Byzantium," "The Circus Animals' Desertion," and "Among School Children." One of the common features of these poems is that, with the exception of "September 1913," they do not deal with a distinctively political event, but are more metaphysical and romantic in tone. "September 1913," however, can be read as recalling the heroism of United Irishmen.

[362] "Easter, 1916" 93.

[363] "Easter, 1916" 93.

5. The Motif of the Rising

had produced a culturally unhealthy society in which Irish people lived in the glory of the past. Some argued that the Easter Rising of 1916 could never pass into history, as it had been inscribed on the Irish psyche under the supervision of the nationalistic government, so that "[i]t can be present here and now as an element in the imagination and the subjective experience of the individual."[364] Richard Kearney therefore proposed that the Easter Rising, amongst other Irish cultural and political myths, might have become "something that can imprison the mind [. . .] of the myth's devotee in a kind of idolatry."[365] In Kearney's view, this was because the state had not only allowed traditionalist historians to over-simplify the historical context of the Easter Rising, but it had also discouraged creative uses of these national icons "in an open-ended process of cultural emancipation."[366]

Revisionist historians attempted to provide an alternative reading of the Easter Rising. The most distinctive feature of the new reading was that it explored how ordinary people felt about and reacted against social upheavals. However, long before revisionism emerged, some short story writers had already begun to reassess nationalistic issues from ordinary people's viewpoints and experiences. These stories included: Liam O'Flaherty's "The Mountain Tavern" (1929), Frank O'Connor's "Guests of the Nation" (1931), Denis Johnston's "The Call to Arms" (1936), and Mary Lavin's "The Patriot Son" (1956). Daniel Corkery's short story "The Ember" (1920), written at the time of the Anglo-Irish War, will also be examined here.

Through rereading these texts, I would like to explore the way in which Irish writers approached historical subjects personally and independently. To what extent did they succeed, or fail, in keeping a reasonable distance when portraying political conflicts? Along with short stories, I will also look at novels, such as Iris Murdoch's *The Red and the Green* (1965), James Plunkett's *Strumpet City* (1969), and J.G. Farrell's *Troubles* (1970), in order to gain a closer picture of how early twentieth-century Irish history was constructed, deconstructed, or documented in these texts. Last but not least, I wish to ask, is it possible to "revise the revisionists"?

---

[364] Ó Grualaoich 58.

[365] Ó Grualaoich 51.

[366] Revisionists named some of the traditionalist Irish historians who were opposed to alternative readings of the Easter Rising: notably Brendan Bradshaw and Desmond Fennell. See Ó Grualaoich 51.

5.2. Fictional History: The Decentralisation of Historical Narratives in Some Irish Short Stories

"The Patriot Son" is a story by Mary Lavin which has an armed rising as its backdrop. The text concerns a young man, Matty, who is strictly forbidden by his mother, a grocery-shop owner, from attending any nationalistic meetings, including a weekly Gaelic language course held at a local school in the evening. Although Matty does not really grasp what the rising is about, he much admires Sean, who appears to be an active campaigner against English rule in Ireland. Matty always wants to give Sean a helping hand behind his mother's back, both as a response to her dominance as well as to fulfil his heroic aspirations. One day a group of policemen from the Royal Irish Constabulary trace Sean to the shop of Matty's mother's and shoot him dead. As Matty is afraid that the policemen have been aware of his secret help to Sean, he escapes to the roof of a pig-shed in the backyard. In order to save her only son from being shot by the policemen who have seen Matty's attempt to flee, the mother creates a scene by crying out: "He must have been frightened out of his wits."[367]

The key character in this story is neither Sean nor Matty, but rather the dominant mother whose presence is constantly on her son's mind, even when he discreetly meets Sean far away from home. The climax of the tale is not the fatal shooting of Sean, but the fact that the mother bravely interferes by crying out to the policemen in good time. While this account features maternal love and a mother's dispassionate response to the campaign for Home Rule, it also deals with a woman's opposition to the violence brought about by colonial and nationalistic ideologies imposed upon ordinary people. Similarly, concern for individuals was probably the reason why Lavin selected this as the title story of the volume *The Patriot Son and Other Stories*, published in 1956.

However, it is true to say that "The Patriot Son" was one of the very few stories that Lavin wrote against a nationalistic background. As she rarely presented political themes in her short stories and novels, nor portrayed them favourably, as "The Patriot Son" exemplifies, some traditionalist critics found that her stories did not "fit into comfortable categories, [. . .] lack[ing] direct political or historical material [. . .]."[368] In other words, critics, as well as anthology makers whose intention was to present a patriotic Ireland, may have judged that a story like "The Patriot Son" was somewhat

---

[367] Lavin, *Patriot* 14.
[368] Donnelly.

5. The Motif of the Rising

out of focus and that readers might therefore not get an accurate historical picture of Home Rule, but be "more at a loss than a foreigner would be."[369] These critics might prefer a typical pro-Rising story, such as Daniel Corkery's "The Ember," to demonstrate the Fenian tradition to which the revolutionaries of the Easter Rising came to belong.[370] This story portrays an unnamed revolutionary who is being harassed by the English due to his participation in the Easter Rising. He is on the run in the countryside, while soliciting donations to assist his revolutionary comrades in Dublin. Someone introduces him to a reclusive old man, Muirish, who is highly respected by local villagers because of his Fenian background. After learning that the Rising in Dublin needs financial support to carry on, Muirish produces a bag full of "Fenian gold," which he has successfully hidden for fifty years. The elderly veteran is glad that this money can finally be used for the revolutionary cause, before he either throws it into the river or dies without peace: "I [. . .] may throw [it] into the river [. . .], 'tis them very same young lads made the fight in Dublin. [. . .] But 'tis in ease I'll lay my head down in my empty house this night [after handing it over to you]."[371]

This story is open to potential disapproval by revisionist critics, since it not only presents an Irish-Ireland ideology, but the author also creates a narrative with a nationalistic emplotment to convince its readers of the strength of the Fenian tradition. (Corkery himself was always a target for revisionists due to his Irish-Ireland stance.) Notwithstanding this, the story does not objectively present the fact that Ireland was formerly a multi-cultural state with English, Irish, and Anglo-Irish inhabitants, with a resultant diversity of opinions on Home Rule. "The Ember," however, intentionally keeps readers in line with a revolutionary tradition in Ireland passed down from the Fenians to the Easter Rising "rebels." The highlighting of this tradition is thus involved in creating "the 1916 myth," whose possible negative effects on culture have been discussed earlier.

---

[369] Frank O'Connor, "Girl" 25.
[370] "The Ember" is the first story in the anthology *Tears of the Shamrock*, edited by David Marcus and devoted to "Ireland's struggle for nationhood." This anthology was published in 1972, the year of the Bloody Sunday events in Derry. The Fenian movement was a secret revolutionary organisation established by James Stephens in 1858. Stephens had participated in the Young Ireland rising of 1848 and planned a rising for 20 September 1865. This group is also known as the Irish Republican Brotherhood (IRB), which was revived by Thomas Clarke in 1907 and continued as a secret organisation within Sinn Féin and the IRA.
[371] Corkery 23.

Some readers may find that Lavin and Corkery do not offer in-depth observations on the military situation surrounding the Easter Rising, although the latter does create a sense of urgency throughout the story as the unnamed revolutionary is on the run. There are some other short stories which deal with Irish militarism more from a non-traditionalist angle, such as Frank O'Connor's "Guests of the Nation," Denis Johnston's "The Call to Arms," and Liam O'Flaherty's "The Mountain Tavern."

"Guests of the Nation" features two Englishmen, Belcher and Hawkins, held as hostages by Irish military men. Two of the Irish abductors are reluctant to kill them, as the abductors and the hostages have gradually come to like each other. However, an order is given to kill the English captives, as "[t]here were four of our fellows shot in Cork this morning and now [they're] to be shot as a reprisal."[372] In the end, the hostages are shot dead "as a sack of meal"; the two Irish abductors can only feel deep guilt but are powerless to change the situation.

Liam O'Flaherty's "The Mountain Tavern" deals with a tavern hostess who is horrified by two republican soldiers who unexpectedly come across her shabby tavern carrying with them a dying militiaman. She feels disheartened when the soldiers rudely demand free food and medication. It seems to her that republican soldiers have turned into robbers and the Civil War has only brought her misery. Having been similarly robbed many times by republican soldiers, she has nothing left in the tavern; she shouts that they are "daylight robber[s]" who deserve death without mercy. While they argue that many of them have died for her and the nation's benefit, for the sake of a free Ireland, she spits and hisses at them: "Let them die. They didn't die for me. [. . .] Amn't I ruined and wrecked for three long years with yer fightin', goin' back and forth, lootin' and turnin' the honest traveller from my door? For three long years I have kept open house for all of ye and now yer turnin' on one another like dogs after a bitch."[373]

Ironically, the story ends with a real robbery committed by Free State soldiers who later arrive to chase away the three republicans and find one of them just dead. Without any condolences, the Free State official "roughly handl[es]" the corpse of an Irish fellow, saying unsympathetically: "Ha! [. . .] So we got him at last. Eh? Heave him into the lorry, boys."[374]

---

[372] Frank O'Connor, *Guest* 12.
[373] O'Flaherty 27-28.
[374] O'Flaherty 31.

5. The Motif of the Rising

These two anti-war stories show O'Connor's and O'Flaherty's attempts at rewriting the nationalistic experience in Ireland. In particular, they point out that the fantasy of an emancipated Ireland has greatly cheapened the value of the individual, and deepened hatred and misunderstanding between people. By portraying the brutality of militarism, the two writers have, in my view, tried to provide a non-nationalistic, less favourable and more realistic picture of how wars have affected ordinary Irish and English people. It is a hostile picture that patriotic historians would be unlikely to use to impress Irish people of later generations.

5.3. The Lockout Strike and James Plunkett's *Strumpet City* (1969)

I have mentioned in the introduction of this book that prose writing, such as short stories and novels, is always less serviceable to a patriotic canon than poetry, as anthology makers often select poems which salute the rebellion tradition and are easy (for children) to recite. "Revisionist stories," like those set out above, may contain dangerous elements which would subvert the Irish-Ireland ideology. Nevertheless, though prose writing is a less-highlighted genre, some writers have still set out their own statement on early twentieth-century Irish history through novels that scrutinise nationalistic Ireland. I would like to consolidate my argument that no official history is comprehensive enough to include every facet of the "facts." Moreover, at times there are non-linguistic factors determining the outcome of an historical representation, so that reading history is not necessarily a painful experience, but can be thoughtful and entertaining.

To this end, three Irish novels, which deal with three successive events highly relevant to the formation of the Free State, will be examined in order to demonstrate that sophisticated novels may serve as revisionist critiques of history. These novels include *Strumpet City* (1969) by James Plunkett, which is often praised as an epic masterpiece on the lines of *Dr Zhivago*, due to its panoramic and vivid portraits of Dublin before and after the Great Lockout of 1913; and Iris Murdoch's *The Red and the Green* (1965), featuring prohibited love, sex, memory and the politics of 1916 from a philosophical perspective. I will also discuss J.G. Farrell's *Troubles* (1970), which provides a journalistic and rather deconstructive narrative that brings the Anglo-Irish War of 1919 to an ironic but comical level. This novel presents complex interpersonal relations inside and outside a hotel, which is in decline but still run by its Anglo-Indian owner.

Strumpet City is a realistic novel set in Dublin between 1907 and 1914, concerning the strike which led to a lockout of trade union members by a cartel of employers in 1913. The author intended to illustrate the less-documented Irish working class which was exploited by well-to-do employers. However, his works – all written in a realistic style – were not often critically reviewed, in contrast to those of writers who had either tried working with experimental techniques or had gone into exile at some point of their life. As some critics have pointed out, many Irish writers, though not all, who are now given canonical status, were exiles; they were those who, "completely at odds with Ireland, [had] to leave it in order to write."[375] Plunkett was one who stayed home, portraying working-class people as possessing a sense of nobility. His view of Dublin, though perhaps not fully appreciated by critics, is not quite the same as Joyce's vision of "the centre of paralysis." For Plunkett, the city had qualities other than paralysis. In an interview, the author expressed his admiration of Joyce and Sean O'Casey, but felt that only a limited range of Dublin life was addressed in their presentations of the city:

> I wanted to explore what I knew of the city, to get it out of myself and find a shape for my feelings about it. I was a great admirer of O'Casey and Joyce. Thinking that O'Casey had dealt with the submerged, deprived city and Joyce with the seedy genteel, I thought I would try to get the lot in – the company director types, the priests, the decent working men, and the utterly outcast. This is what the city meant to me, along with the smells of it, the feeling of it – those strands I walked as a boy and that are walked in *Strumpet City*.[376]

That is to say that Plunkett intended to broaden the scope of Joyce's and O'Casey's portraits and to scrutinise the labour issue more intensely in *Strumpet City*. Indeed, the novel engages both the bourgeois class and the Catholic Church with the exploited working class, and not only contrasts two extremes of living conditions in Ireland but also explores those factors that made the city appear paralysed. With sections devoted to the life of slum dwellers and the inhabitants of Kingstown, Plunkett intended to give a more objective description of the less-portrayed life of people in

---

[375] Cahalan, "James Plunkett" 9.
[376] Cahalan, "James Plunkett" 10.

5. The Motif of the Rising

the lowest rank of society. Thus, "ashbin children" are described as being "pinched and wiry and usually barefooted, [living] on the cast-offs":

> In the mornings just at the breakfast hour [they] searched diligently in the ashbins of the well-to-do for half-burnt cinders. [. . .] if the well-to-do had stopped casting off for even a little while the children would have gone homeless and fireless and naked. But nobody really thought about that. These things were.[377]

One of the central characters in the novel, Rashers Tierney, is senior among these ashbin people. Plunkett juxtaposes his life with that of King Edward VII, who is paying a visit to Kingstown, when introducing Rashers, who is "r[ising] that morning about the same time as King Edward."[378] Furthermore, although the life of the slum dwellers in the parish of St Brigid and that of the upper-middle class in Kingstown is illustrated in detail, the worlds of the two classes have limited overlap, except through two characters: the condescending priest, Father O'Connor, and kind-hearted Mrs Bradshaw. The former serves at St Brigid but represents employers and the modestly wealthy; he distributes charity donations only to those who do not join the strike, believing that those who take such action deserve hunger as a punishment. Mrs Bradshaw, on the other hand, sends the cast-offs of her family, behind her husband's back, directly to Mary Fitzpatrick, a former maid in her household who married a slum dweller from St Brigid.

With the exception of Mrs Bradshaw and Father O'Connor, who have relations in both areas of Dublin, most characters in the novel only know people of their own social background. However, the reader is still afforded access to the causes and effects of the lockout and other social phenomena, as the author portrays many incidents involving both classes and avoids a narrative which would favour the socially privileged Anglo-Irish and to deals with the issue of human nature through realistic portraits of his working-class characters.

Some critics have acclaimed *Strumpet City* for its significant literary elements which echo parts of Joyce's *Ulysses*. As James M. Cahalan observes, "*Ulysses* certainly exerted no stylistic influence on *Strumpet City*, but Joyce's audacity in writing of Dublin at epic length lurks somewhere in the background of Plunkett's decision to

---

[377] Plunkett 67 and 66-67.
[378] Plunkett 17.

begin writing *Strumpet City*."³⁷⁹ What makes this novel significant is not its depiction of a crucial historical period during the formation of the Free State, but rather the author's refusal to adopt a binary opposition in order to stigmatise the affluent and to honour the working class. On the contrary, he wants to suggest that what really lies behind social problems is the complex issue of human nature shared by people of all orders, religious ones included. A simplistic reading of social phenomena can only serve to worsen situations. Take Father Giffley, for instance, a senior priest in charge of the parish of St Brigid, who discourages young Father O'Connor from organising charity donations in the parish, because he thinks this would only make people in Kingstown more patronising and hypocritical, and would not ultimately solve any problems. He makes it clear that Father O'Connor's charitable scheme "will be a cover for hypocrisy, because you know you can do nothing for these people by throwing them a blanket or giving them a hot meal."³⁸⁰

After serving in the slum of St Brigid for thirty years, the cleric believes that what the Catholic Church can do to help Ireland is to take no side in political and social argument, as "it only serves to inflame the people."³⁸¹ Nevertheless, the Church at the time consisted of many clerics like Father O'Connor, who deemed themselves keepers of the social order and took part in secular campaigns against strikers, revolutionaries, and dangerous nationalists, ignoring the holy duty to be "the comforter of the destitute."³⁸² What should concern a priest, in Father Giffley's view, is to provide the poor with spiritual solace, hope, and peace, and not to take sides for or against anyone. However, Father O'Connor perceives contemporary social conflicts simply as a "battle to be fought [. . .] between Godlessness and God," and acts on this theory in most of his appearances in the novel.³⁸³

Interestingly, Father Giffley can make moderate comments on issues only when he is not drunk. He always appears with a glass of whisky or in the act of pouring one. His addiction to drinking is because he "has to" intoxicate himself against feelings of distress and impotence in the face of the social injustice suffered by his parishioners. Although he would like Father O'Connor to be a "comforter of the destitute," he cannot be one for his own turbulent soul. One day, he gets very drunk and makes a

---

[379] Cahalan, "Making" 95.
[380] Plunkett 98.
[381] Plunkett 98.
[382] Plunkett 98.
[383] Plunkett 359.

5. The Motif of the Rising

horrible scene at a funeral by overturning a coffin and commanding the dead to rise. This performance results from a troubled and restless mind which has experienced no less suffering than those of the slum dwellers at St Brigid in his thirty-year career. Not surprisingly, the Catholic Order he belongs to dismisses him from the parish after the incident, sending him off to an institute in the far west of Ireland to abstain from alcoholism.

The point I would like to suggest using the examples of Father Giffley and Father O'Connor is that issues of social injustice or unbalanced distribution of wealth might have to do with the complexities of human nature, from which even priests are be exempt. That is to say, the Irish Troubles in early twentieth-century Irish society should not be simplistically understood as social problems amongst classes, between the coloniser and the colonised, or of Protestantism versus Catholicism. They are issues stemming from a mixture of common human qualities, such as arrogance, selfishness and greed. What underpins discernible social conflicts, in Plunkett's observation, is the ignorance which exists inside and outside the Church as well as in political entities. Plunkett may have wanted to suggest this point. Therefore, at the end of the novel, when Father Giffley places a note inside an empty whisky bottle and throws it into the sea, the bottle keeps returning with the waves. What Father Giffley writes in the note is "[t]ime takes all away. This was written by a madman on the shores of a mad island." However, time does not eradicate Irish turbulence, as the Northern Troubles proved in the next few decades, and conflicts have endured.

5.4. The Easter Rising and Iris Murdoch's *The Red and the Green* (1965)

Another novel which has an Irish historical event as its backdrop is Iris Murdoch's *The Red and the Green*. Although much of it is set in Easter week of 1916 in Dublin, the author does not detail the Rising as concretely as Plunkett portrays the Lockout in *Strumpet City*. She depicts her characters participating in the Easter Rising in diverse ways in which more than political events can be scrutinised. This is therefore not merely a novel illuminating how an individual reacts against social upheaval, but one which also explores a mixture of human conditions subject to religion, politics, sex, and romance. It is a book that can be read as a historical novel for its portrait of the development of the Rising from a variety of perspectives, and not just that of the armed participants. However, it also deals with philosophical issues.

That *The Red and the Green* can be read as a historical novel is mainly because the author manages to associate her characters with the incidents of the Easter Rising and depicts them arguing on both sides of the political issues. There are times when her characters counter each other with different, often antagonistic, opinions on issues such as Home Rule, the literary revival, and so forth. Although most of the characters are related to each other due to inter-marriage within Anglo-Irish families ("We Anglo-Irish families are so complex, [. . .] We are practically incestuous"), they face the crisis of discovering a national and racial identity while experiencing pressure from contemporary political ideologies.[384] Indeed, most family members pick one identity which they deem suitable and defend it, but in a way they are rewarded with deeper frustration since each shares an unbreakable Anglo-Irish family tie. It is a bond that not only gives them a historical title or label as a specific group of people in Ireland but connects them all as a family. Of the brothers Pat Dumay and Cathal Dumay, for instance, the former is a fervent patriot who supports the Rising but wants to prevent his brother from participating in it. Similarly, the conflict between the cousins Andrew Chase-White and Pat Dumay results less from discrepancies in their political stances than from a shared male competitiveness dating from childhood. Therefore, Andrew chooses to serve in an English cavalry regiment not because he likes horses, but because he had "early impressions of the more patriotic passages of Shakespeare."[385] Last but not least, it is a means to make himself feel superior to his cousin Pat.

One of the climaxes in the novel is that, on Easter Monday morning, Andrew, who was not summoned up for duty, cycles to the Dumays' house in Howth in the hope of hearing Pat's explanation about his (Pat's) relationship with Millie, the aunt with whom Andrew has an affair. His uninvited visit suggests to Pat that Andrew is spying for the English. In order to keep Andrew from informing against him, Pat suggests to Millie that Andrew should be killed if the planned Rising fails. Millie does not agree and proposes that Dumay might just handcuff Andrew with Cathal until the Rising ends. Andrew's reluctance to fight back is not because he is afraid of Pat, but rather because, at the bottom of his heart, he finds it pointless and unnecessary to fight someone and create a bloody scene instead of seeking a peaceful solution. He allows himself to be tied to Cathal without much resistance but voices the opinion that everyone in Ireland suffers from political insanity:

---

[384] Murdoch, *Red* 15.
[385] Murdoch, *Red* 11-12.

5. The Motif of the Rising

'Why did this have to happen? [. . .] It's insane. You can't hold out against the British Army. [. . .] we're the same people, we're brothers, we *can't* fight –' Andrew felt the outrage of it. He wanted to explain that he did not want to fight the Irish, they had done him no harm, there must be some mistake. It could not be that he would have to kill his first man here in Dublin.[386]

Here, Andrew's submission is not because he cannot fight but that he does not want to; he is a trained English cavalryman and should struggle back, or even die, for the honour of his regiment. However, his constant passivity highlights a question which Murdoch may have wanted to stress. Andrew suffers an existential because he finds the Rising and the expected bloodshed melodramatic, while being in Dublin he cannot avoid being involved. The subjectivity of the individual is dismissed as everyone is expected to participate in the melodrama. His acquiescence suggests that he has learnt to take no side in politics as a way of freeing himself: "the realisation that there are people we shall never conquer comes to us as part of the process of growing up."[387]

As for Pat, he begins as a supporter of the Irish Volunteers, but gradually becomes disillusioned and detached from this organisation, as he finds not only that it lacks a clear vision of Ireland's future after a liberation, but also that its leaders are incapable of planning the Rising in an organised manner. Pat genuinely loves Ireland, but in a "nameless" way, while the Irish Volunteers and other politicians dream of an ideological Ireland.[388] His love for Ireland is enough to foster an existentialist viewpoint, which no political or religious propagandists can act on:

[Pat's] patriotism was not of the diffuse and talkative kind, [. . .] he had small use for 'Cathleen ni Houlihan', nor was he interested in Patrick Pearse's archaistic visions of a virtuous manly society whose manners were somehow to be restored. He had never joined the Gaelic League, and though he had attempted to learn Irish he did not think the language important. He was himself a matter-of-fact practising Catholic, but the pattern of his religion, though it remained secure, did not enter into the chief passion

---

[386] Murdoch, *Red* 251.
[387] Murdoch, *Red* 224.
[388] Murdoch, *Red* 77.

of his life. He was not one of those who made their Catholicism into nationalism. [. . .] His Ireland was nameless, a pure Ireland of the mind, to be relentlessly served by a naked sense of justice and a naked self-assertion. There were in his drama only these two characters, Ireland and himself.[389]

One critic of Murdoch's works, Donna Gerstenberger, has commented that *The Red and the Green was* "written as if [the author] has set out to explore the 'Irish Question' without hope of an 'Irish Answer.'"[390] In my opinion, Murdoch was certainly not hoping for an "Irish Answer," but rather was aiming to disclose more questions falling within the Irish Question. Murdoch, as an existentialist philosopher at Oxford in the 1960s, was more interested in the issue of living with or without one's subjectivity, and of how people interact with the external world. She once suggested that we exist because we keep fantasising about who we will be, but not who we are: "we may fail to see the individual because we are completely enclosed in a fantasy world of our own into which we try to draw things from outside, not grasping their reality and independence, making them into dream objects of our own."[391]

In *The Red and the Green*, Pat and Andrew act on external values to some extent, imagining that they are people other than who they are. With the Easter Rising as a backdrop, they go through a difficult inner conflict between the external expectation of a social being in Ireland, and an internal desire to be oneself. But neither of them survives long, they die during 1916-1917. Pat is killed on the Thursday of Easter Week in the Post Office, the day before the rebels surrender; Andrew dies in a battle against the German army in France. Their deaths suggest that, even though both of them have felt aloof from either over-militant Ireland or the English cavalry, they are powerless to resist, and die for the overpowering national mechanism in operation.

Murdoch wrote *The Red and the Green* as an historical novel, in that her characters are situated within the context of the Easter Rising. On the other hand, she did not write as an historian or a journalist, but attempted to call historical representations, or historiography, into question as an existentialist critic. A case in point is Barnabas Drum, a character in the novel who writes a memoir. He is a would-be priest who left the seminary a long time before as he was unable to suppress his lust. He wishes to become a cleric, but cannot resist Millie Dumay's charms. He then marries Kathleen

---

[389] Murdoch, *Red* 77.
[390] Gerstenberg 51.
[391] Murdoch, "Sublime" 52.

5. The Motif of the Rising

Kinnard, a very religious woman who sees herself as "an instrument of [his] salvation."[392] However, lust still dominates his being, so he continues a secret relationship with Millie after his marriage. Having had such a lascivious past, he wishes to write a memoir to let people know, after his death, what kind of person he really was. However, he is incapable of finding a balanced angle from which to write about himself: a man who has looked to religion and women to define who he is, but is much disillusioned. He is neither a "blasphemer," as Millie would have loved, nor a "penitent," as Kathleen expects.[393] He is simply a person "so sunk in [him]self, [he] hardly know[s] that anybody else exists at all."[394] As the writing of his memoir proves, he is incapable of combining his external and internal beings; he then denies this by thinking that what he has written as a confession is in fact a fantasy against his religious wife: "His Memoir, [. . .] was in the end simply a weapon against Kathleen. [. . .] What he wrote in the Memoir was not quite true, and that "not quite" was the stuff of a most wicked lie."[395]

In referring to Barnabas' denial of his own personal history, I contend that the writing of history is itself a process of finding and defining one's own. It is an activity in which historiographers have to come to terms with competing voices in history by self-denial and admission of certain historical explanations and interpretations. Barnabas' difficulty in writing his memoir suggests that history consists of political fantasies. Having said that, *The Red and the Green* is an historical novel which also calls historiography into question, as "[e]ach country tells a selective story creditable to itself. No Frenchman has heard of Agincourt; [n]o Englishman has heard of Fontenoy, if it comes to that," a statement made by one of the characters at the end of the novel.[396] Historiographers with different political concerns, hence, may produce a national history for or against their motherland.

5.5. The Anglo-Irish War and J.G. Farrell's *Troubles* (1970)

Both *Strumpet City* and *The Red and the Green* are novels whose characters are involved in social movements at specific times and locations. Both authors manage to provide a convincing historical background, in which their Irish characters either sur-

---

[392] Murdoch, *Red* 173.
[393] Murdoch, *Red* 97.
[394] Murdoch, *Red* 138.
[395] Murdoch, *Red* 175.
[396] Murdoch, *Red* 276.

vive or die. J.G. Farrell's *Troubles* is different from these two works in that it contains surrealistic and comic elements, and one that traditionalist critics would have to leave out of the canon of Irish historical novels.

This is firstly because the setting is a non-existent town called Kilnalough, a place which the author says is on the east coast of Ireland but which cannot be found on any map. Secondly, although the key character, Edward Spencer, is Anglo-Irish, the decline of his Majestic Hotel is not quite the same as that of traditional Anglo-Irish big houses in Ireland. So-called big house novels tell stories about the latter and were well circulated in Ireland. The fall of the Majestic Hotel, for not conforming to this more popular choice of subject, received limited attention from Irish critics. Thirdly, the inhabitants of the hotel, a group of elderly, sick English ladies, have no influence on contemporary events but are politically and socially marginalised, and feel very anxious they might be murdered by rebels. Fourthly, although the novel does have a set time frame which chronicles the Major's Irish experience during the Anglo-Irish War in 1919, occasionally along with contemporary newspaper extracts about revolutionary events and social unrest in Delhi, Chicago, Poland, and the Middle East, *Troubles* does not exactly conform to the convention of literary realism. Not only are few of the newspaper extracts dated, but Farrell also constantly uses vague phrases such as "in those days," "at that time," "years ago," "a few years later," "one day," "at about the time" throughout the novel. This, like the absence of chapter divisions, in my view gives an elusive sense of time from the beginning of the novel.[397] Moreover, a sense of timelessness is experienced by the senior women lodgers who are very much confined to the hotel due to their age and illness. They know that the rebels are approaching Kilnalough, but can only wait for the outcome of the Anglo-Irish War. These factors might have resulted in the critics' disregard for the novel, because it apparently lacks the realistism of historical novels. Nonetheless, it could be argued that Farrell intends to construct a different version of the year 1919, and raises the question as to what extent historiography can be fictional in nature.

For postmodernist critics, *Troubles* is more than just an engaging historical novel. The author's use of unspecified time, a fictitious location, as well as disjointed newspaper extracts, "unsettle any centred focus" of historical narrative.[398] It is a novel with historical elements transformed and parodied in order, in Farrell's words, "to

---

[397] Farrell 9. These phrases appear on the first page of the novel, and are repeatedly used throughout the story. The loose time frame of *Troubles* is also dealt with in Binns 46.
[398] Crane and Livett 18.

5. The Motif of the Rising

show people 'understanding' history," while the highly fictional components potentially deconstruct the way history used to be seriously understood.[399]

There is evidence to suggest that the author intended to challenge the boundaries between fiction writing and historiography. In terms of technique, the author constantly breaks into descriptive sentences with new perspectives, sceptical comments or dialogues using parentheses. The frequent employment of the latter is rather unusual in classic English writing, but Farrell makes good use of them in order to allow multiple narrators in a single narrative. Although the novel is mainly narrated by one third-person narrator in the past tense, this narrator often presents a second view of a single incident in the same paragraph: one view depicts the factual situation in which the characters find themselves, the other comments on or mocks their ignorance of it, indicates the characters' real thoughts or the game underneath the table. The parenthetic sentences, in many cases, are addressed to the reader only, not to the characters. The effect is likely to create an objective view through which readers can discern both the said and the unsaid:

> Was it true that in London even the horses wore leather shoes? [. . .] The English (that was to say, 'the enemy') were so serious one could never risk making a joke in case they believed you.[400]

> She said that she was going to get married and that she hoped he didn't mind. (Not only did the Major not mind, for a few minutes he could remember nothing about the girl at all; even the circumstances of their meeting escaped him.) But she had waited for him [. . .] she would always think of him, would always remember him with love and affection . . . one can't, after all (why should one want to?), [. . .] pretend that the Past hasn't happened [. . .] the fun they had had together.[401]

> In no time at all the ladies developed a remarkable skill for discerning traces of insulting behaviour in the townspeople. A lack of respect would be

---

[399] Quoted in Bergonzi 58.
[400] Farrell 115.
[401] Farrell 249.

detected (in a turned back, in a 'saucy' smile, in a cheeky 'Good day!') and quick as a flash it would be dealt with.[402]

Parentheses specifying the connotations of words, characters' inner voices, and the embarrassing situations that they get into are numerous. Without these, it could be argued that the narration of the story would be narrowly bound to a single viewpoint. With this unconventional technique Farrell seems to illustrate the complexity of human perspectives not just in interpersonal relations but also in historical terms. Only when readers are allowed to detach themselves from the characters' voices and the narrator's single viewpoint can they understand what is happening at a personalised distance. In this way, they become active participants in the process of reading, especially since there is no central point of view in the author's narration.

The decentralisation of "the Troubles" is also reflected in occurrences at the hotel. Such is the case with Brendan's crush on Sarah: his imperialistic background as an English major is gradually looses significance when he in love with her during his stay in London, the very centre of the Empire.[403] His imagined romance with her awakens him to the wider causes of political and racial unrest in the world, from the colonised in his Empire to the black population in America.[404] His love for Sarah is thus potentially promoted by imperialists. The enlightenment which the romance brings to Brendan is seen in his expectation of Sarah's letter:

[S]he must write and tell him everything that was going on at the Majestic. And she must write immediately. He was on tenterhooks. The thin, starving rats of curiosity were nibbling at his bones. As for London, though it was

---

[402] Farrell 256.

[403] The decentralising effect seems to be more in force with the Major, although he is less aware of it. The Irish around him continue to see him as a foreigner representing English power. The irony lies in the fact that the Major does not seem sensitive to the way the Irish see him; he can be seen simply as an individual who follows his sentimentality and judgment, which are often besotted.

[404] It is worth mentioning that Farrell's *Troubles* is the first novel in a trilogy about the crumbling of the British Empire. The other two are *The Siege of Krishnapur* (1973) and *The Singapore Grip* (1978), both of which concern the defeat of British rule and its influence on India and the Far East, respectively. *Troubles* has inspired Derek Mahon into writing a great modern Irish poem, "A Disused Shed in Co. Wexford," which has been well received in the modern Irish canon. This poem is anthologised in the *Field Day Anthology*, 3:1383-84. I am grateful to Dr. Janet Montefiore for this information.

5. The Motif of the Rising

indeed the centre of the Empire it was no more the centre of 'Life' than, say, Chicago, Amritsar, or Timbuctoo – 'Life' being everywhere equal and coeval.[405]

What Farrell intends to decentralise is not just an imperialistic discourse but also a patriarchal ideology which dominates many social codes at the hotel, including that of gender. The Majestic Hotel used to be "a fashionable place and [it was] considered an honour to be granted accommodation there during the summer season."[406] However, since the Troubles began, there have been fewer and fewer visitors from England, and there remain only long-term residents who pay rent on an irregular basis. As a result, most housekeepers are dismissed; residents have to take care of things which used to be attended to by servants, and women are allowed to enjoy activities which before were available only to men: "A girl [. . .] [was] given a rhinoceros-hide whip for her sixteenth birthday; by the time she was eighteen she could flick a cigar out of a man's lip at twenty paces. [. . .] Young ladies [. . .] would not think twice about barging in here for a smoke and a chat."[407] The "freedom" that is given to the women, though seemingly only available in the hotel, whose lodgers are mostly female, has suggested the possibility of women's emancipation. Moreover, as Edward Spencer pays little attention to the upbringing of his twin daughters, Charity and Faith, they are free to explore their sexuality at the hotel. They play a cross-dressing game with another friend, Padraig, and plan a "rape trip" to Dublin. The cross-dressing game ends painfully when Padraig, dressed in women's clothes, is discovered while dancing with the Auxiliaries. He is thrown into a swimming-pool and almost drowns. The fantasy of being raped results from the girls' overhearing of old ladies' conversations about what respectable ladies can do in Dublin. Therefore, when "they were bored, [they] ask[ed] everyone for money – so that they could run away to Dublin and get raped like everyone else."[408] In the event, they do not go, but have an unpleasant one-night stand with two soldiers from the Auxiliaries.

The novel ends with a fire at the Majestic Hotel, when all the elderly ladies are asked to leave by local policemen, since the rebels are approaching the town. The arsonist, however, is actually an elderly Irish retainer, Sean Murphy, whose life is al-

---

[405] Farrell 120.
[406] Farrell 10.
[407] Farrell 216-17.
[408] Farrell 301.

most entirely controlled by, though not devoted to, the Protestant Anglo-Irish hotel owner. Refusing to be transported with the elderly lodgers to a safe place and feeling that he has no place to go, yet full of hatred against his master/owner, he starts a fire and dies in the process. The Majestic Hotel is completely razed; the only thing "strangely undamaged" is a statue of Venus in the residents' lounge.[409]

The burning of the Majestic Hotel is, in my opinion, a key act of decentralisation. It demonstrates that the "central" territory where the characters' memories are based is not indestructible. Other locations in the novel, such as London and Dublin, take on different meanings for various characters when they are free from imperialistic or anti-colonial discourses. The "strangely undamaged" statue of Venus, which has quietly witnessed the fuss inside and outside the hotel, might represent love, which remains beyond time and is the only solution to human troubles.

As I mentioned earlier, the author of *Troubles* does not follow the convention of historical novels in which a significant national event is explored. He tends to decentralise historical narratives and imperialistic ideology when he invents the highly fictional Majestic Hotel in Kilnalough and subsequently destroys it by fire. He does not treat the Anglo-Irish War and other world events as seriously as his fellow historians and writers but rather with a degree of amusement. However, his approach to history is not simply a comic one but one which questions the idea of the "reference source" in historiography. In his view, the over-emphasis on "my/our history" is the underlying cause of unrest throughout the world, since some people use history as a political weapon. With this novel, Farrell may have intended to play down "the human as centre" in historiography. He has Dr Ryan, an old Irish doctor devastated about the bloodshed in Ireland, constantly murmur on different occasions the following words which are never heard properly until the last few pages of the novel: "People are insubstantial. They never last. All this fuss, it's all fuss about nothing. We're here for a while and then we're gone. People are insubstantial. They never last at all."[410]

To sum up, I would like to return to my original argument about the use of historical stories for the purpose of understanding history. Despite some historians' suspiciousness regarding emplotment in stories used as historical sources, their preference for historical monographs is open to doubt as well, because many historians have to select memorable incidents from amongst others when giving an historical

---

[409] Farrell 446.
[410] Farrell 441-42.

5. The Motif of the Rising

account. History itself is far more complex than monographs can reveal. As a result, the presentation of history, whether illustrated in a dramatic or non-dramatic way, should be credited for the perspectives it demonstrates. For an understanding of history, readers should be encouraged to read historical novels, stories and monographs as widely as possible.

I have already referred to Gibbons' statement that "[what] speech possesses [. . .] is historically bounded" to illustrate that history is not entirely re-writable due to its linguistic limits. This might only partially apply to novelists, because despite language's historical boundedness their intercultural experiences help provide new and unconventional standpoints on history which might expand linguistic limits. Writers with the experience of "sitting between two (cultural) stools" may present a broader-historical perspective.

Iris Murdoch, born in Dublin in 1919 and raised in London, developed a detached view of Ireland as an exile: "I feel as I grow older that we were wanderers, and I've only recently realised that I'm a kind of exile, a displaced person. I identify with exiles."[411] Farrell was born to an English father and an Irish mother and had some childhood experience of India and the Far East due to his father's work there. Like those of Anglo-Irish stock, "he remarked later in life that he was always treated as English when in Ireland, but regarded as Irish in England."[412] The ambiguity of his nationality enables him to see Irish history unrestricted by either an English or an Irish perspective, but to interpret it with a sense of amusement and irony. However, Murdoch's and Farrell's alternative treatments of history from intercultural experiences were not much appreciated and their works attracted limited notice in Ireland and England when published. As for Plunkett, he was an Irishman from a Catholic working class family who grew up in Dublin. Nevertheless, he developed a "cross-class" viewpoint when he lived in a peculiar part of Dublin during childhood, an experience which nourished his comprehension of social issues, which is well reflected in *Strumpet City*. He remarked on this cross-class experience in an interview, and his belief in its significance parallels that of Murdoch's and Farrell's cross-cultural backgrounds: "I was born in Irishtown, halfway between Ringsend and Sandymount – Sandymount highly respectable and Ringsend poor. When I came out

---

[411] Quoted in Conradi 10.
[412] McLeod.

the door, if I turned left I was going into opulence and if I turned right I was headed down into poverty."[413]

This chapter has illustrated a number of presentations of the historical events in Ireland in the 1900s and 1910s. But what do these war stories signify to readers around the globe in the twenty-first century? There is no clear answer to this, but reading them may equip people with a new social conscience and enable them to see the vulnerability of peace, freedom, and love. George Lukács has said: "the past [. . .] [i]s the prehistory of the present."[414] What has happened in history cannot be presented entirely without bias, but reading historical novels, stories, biographies, and academic monographs can broaden one's perspective as opposed to glorifying certain communities. The canon that features historical events would consequently be reformulated and diversified along with readers' own responses, instead of being directed only by historians or government-funded institutions. The formulation of canons will be an activity open to writers and readers who approach history from different angles and with their individual interests. It is a renewable canon that does not necessarily keep presenting evidence of the most destructive elements of our history, but still manages to engage contemporary readers with the past, since they may choose to highlight the prospect of history, rather than a historical scar.

---

[413] Cahalan, "James Plunkett" 9.
[414] Lukács 53.

6. The Awakening of Irish Private Conscience: Mary Lavin, Her Texts, and the Canon

> If one is a woman one is often surprised by a sudden splitting off of consciousness, say in walking down Whitehall, when from being the natural inheritor of that civilisation, she becomes, on the contrary, outside of it, alien and critical.[415]

> [E]ither she could write as a woman, in which case she created a limited art, or she could write as a man, in which case she created an inauthentic art.[416]

Mary Lavin was born in 1912 in East Walpole, Massachusetts, USA, of Irish parentage, emigrating to Ireland at the age of ten with her mother, and first settling in Athenry. This medieval town, situated in the middle of county Galway, was isolated from the urban turbulence of early twentieth-century Ireland. Unlike most writers of her generation – who often dealt with the (de)colonial issues of their time – the young Lavin was more struck by the cultural differences between Ireland and the USA.[417] It is fair to say that Lavin, as a woman writer who often saw Ireland from an outsider's angle, produced different perspectives on Ireland, and that contributed to her dissimilar choices of subjects for presenting the nation: non-patriotic and non-religious. Her efforts in depicting various aspects of Ireland, therefore, demonstrated the possibilities of seeing Ireland from broader, inter-cultural points of view, not necessarily from an insular, political, or specifically Irish Catholic outlook.

The border-crossing experience provided Lavin with an individualistic observation of different facets of Irish life, and a view that was tempered by distance. It could be conjectured that the overwhelming "cultural shock" that Lavin experienced during her childhood underpinned her later exploration of diverse human conditions in adulthood. Lavin's scrutiny of human conditions in general, though to a great extent portraying Irish townsfolk in the background, did not prevent her works from being studied across many countries for their universality. Compared with other writers of

---

[415] Woolf 96.
[416] Sharon O'Brien 96.
[417] Recent studies of Lavin's works often link her name to male predecessors and contemporaries, such as Sean O'Faoláin, Frank O'Connor and Liam O'Flaherty, though, unlike these writers, her subject matter rarely deals with Irish politics or the Troubles.

her generation who paid much attention to Irish historical or political matters, Lavin, whose subjects centred on more humanistic concerns and could be read outside of an Irish context, attracted a wider international readership; many of her stories have been translated into other languages.[418]

However, Lavin was not a well-reviewed writer in Ireland until the 1970s, even though she had started her career in 1939 with a debut short story in *Dublin Magazine*. Before that, she, like many Irish writers, had to survive with overseas opportunities for publication and foreign sponsorship to maintain her writing career. Although her short-story collections and novels were circulated in Ireland, they did not always receive critical attention and were often criticised for a lack of patriotic elements. In particular, the awards and sponsorships given to her were mainly from British or American organisations, such as the 1943 James Tait Black Memorial Prize from the University of Edinburgh, the 1959 and 1961 fellowships from the John Simon Guggenheim Memorial Foundation in New York, the 1971 Ella Lynam Cabot Award from Harvard University, and the 1974 Éire Society of Boston Gold Medal. Her first Irish award was as late as 1975 with the Gregory Medal from the Irish Academy of Letters.[419]

The factors behind the neglect of Lavin's works in Ireland could be listed as follows. Firstly, her depiction of rural and middle-class Ireland did not always contain a perceivable or distinct Irishness, so that some critics considered her portraits of Ireland as less than authentic. Secondly, her stories often contained critical messages in regard to the problems arising from the Catholic domination in Ireland, resulting in little support from local or Catholic critics. Thirdly, her heroes or heroines did not always come up to the exacting expectations that Irish patriots had of Irish people. Therefore, her stories were of little use for the nationalistic state. However, I would argue that these readings involved false assumptions about Mary Lavin, or stereotypes directed at Irish women writers in general. To illustrate these observations, this chapter will be rereading those of her works that received mixed reviews.

Regarding the first issue, it can be argued that Lavin's Irishness was fabricated in a peculiar way overtly different from that of many of her predecessors and contem-

---

[418] Some of Lavin's stories have been translated for publication in Dutch, German, Hebrew, Walloon, French, Italian, Polish, Russian, and Japanese. Critical studies and bibliographies have appeared in English as well as in other languages.

[419] She was conferred with an honorary degree of Doctor of Letters by the National University of Ireland in 1968.

6. Mary Lavin

poraries. Her Irishness was not particularly political, but encapsulated different cultural, ethnic, and religious facets of Ireland. More specifically, as her early border-crossing experience had equipped her with a detached spirit, she was later adept at making critical observations of the "paralysed" Irish psyche, as her predecessor James Joyce asserted. This sensibility was further strengthened when she experienced a marked contrast in social ethos between Athenry in Ireland and East Walpole in Massachusetts. The former was a small, almost insular, town where "religion [. . .] was all pervasive," but in the latter "there were transgressions, but there were not sins and people did not go burrowing into your conscience."[420] In other words, in Athenry, she was more "bowled over" by the religious differences:

> When I came to Ireland the religious thing bowled me over. Catholicism was much different from what I had known. I saw a whole new concept of sin in my aunts who were scrupulous and harrowed. My mother's family were at the mercy of what we now call superstition. They did not think for themselves; they accepted everything they were told, and I am sure often misinterpreted it. In America there were transgressions, but no sins and people did not go burrowing into your conscience.[421]

However, such differences did not, turn Lavin towards disillusionment, neither did they motivate her into exile, as with some Irish male writers. She remained in Ireland, continuing with her attempts to picture the weaknesses of Irish culture and Catholic materialism with an independent eye. Although her persistence in retaining independent judgments did, at times, disturb some of her critics, her writing still managed to convey deep compassion for suffering. It may be reasonably assumed that her early border-crossing experience was so critical in her development that Lavin was thus able to penetrate the preoccupations and predicaments of Irishmen and women at a later stage. Besides, her overseas experience provided Lavin with a broader perspective, so that she could attract readers, both within and outside Ireland, to empathise with those labouring under various human conditions.

It is interesting to note the differences between Lavin and James Joyce, whose writing career preceded hers by almost four decades.[422] Unlike Joyce, who put much

---
[420] Levenson 29.
[421] Maurice Harmon 291. The interview was conducted in 1979 with Catherine Murphy and reprinted in a special issue dedicated to Lavin in 1997.
[422] James Joyce started to write prose sketches in 1900 in the form either of dramatic vi-

emphasis on urban residents, Lavin observed rural life, events, and people in great detail. She widened Joyce's scope of Irish paralysis to cover not only urban life but also conditions in the country, displaying how the symptoms of paralysis affected the entire country. In this connection, her first collection of short stories, *Tales from Bective Bridge*, published in 1942 – almost three decades after Joyce's *Dubliners* came out in 1914 – suggests that the Irish psyche remained the same before and after the establishment of the Irish Free State. Political independence did not contribute to a deparalysed Irish psyche, but further promoted Irish insularism with religious and patriotic ideologies. The widespread mental paralysis could have seemed to her a more crucial matter for examination, because its consequences had a more direct impact upon individuals in their everyday lives than fervent, political movements could ever achieve.

Lavin's examination of Irish paralysis provoked controversy in regard to whether she portrayed authentic Irishness. In addition to this debate, some critics have found it an uneasy task to accommodate her portraits of diverse female experiences with patriarchal expectations. It could be contended that such critics' wariness was due to their insufficient exposure to female voices in a patriarchal society where Irishwomen were expected to be onlookers or "angels in the house." Notably, Lavin's portraits of various kinds of Irishwomen, such as single mothers, rebellious teenage girls, young and lonely widows, spinsters, women suffering as a result of domestic violence, sterile women, and disowned daughters, disturbed her critics to a great extent. This was largely because such depictions either transgressed the fundamentalist Catholic rule, or dwelt too deeply on the margins of society. It is fair to assume that her portraits of Irishwomen were so realistic that critics, mostly male, found them difficult and unsettling to deal with.

Another reason behind the late recognition of Lavin's literary contribution at home in her native Ireland was the fact that women writers had historically been ignored or marginalised in the canon of modern Irish literature. As discussed earlier in Chapter Two, the constitution of the Irish canon included a limited female input and tended to conform to mainstream values such as patriotism and Puritanism. Any consideration of female contributions would therefore be subject to patriarchal points of view. Under such circumstances, Lavin's portraits of women's lives could hardly be

---

gnettes or prose poems. These writings were first circulated in manuscript. See Welch 174-76.

6. Mary Lavin

expected to attract much attention, let alone give rise to any discussion on artistic elements in her works.

This chapter will focus on those determinants that resulted in the mixed reviews of Lavin's works, and her late admission into the modern Irish canon. Close readings of some of her short stories and the novel, *The House in Clewe Street* (1945), will illustrate relevant issues such as the writer's attempt to examine mental paralysis under the social codes of Irish insularism, patriarchy and Catholic teaching at the time; and the ways in which she skirted the censorship that had banned many of her contemporaries' works. Last but not least, this chapter will explore to what extent this author may be rightly considered ahead of her time in commenting on questions related to gender, social injustice, class, religious control and individualism.

6.1. Repositioning Mary Lavin

There can be nothing more discouraging for a writer than to be introduced as an amateur who had "an obtuse approach to her people,"[423] particularly after (s)he thought (s)he had produced a novel with "a great deal of care and concentration."[424] Nevertheless, Lavin's first novel, *The House in Clewe Street*, was described by W.J. Igoe in the *Catholic Herald* in these terms, as he regarded the novel as lacking proper moral teaching but focusing instead on the portraits of "infantile morality."[425] It is evident to say that many critics, like Igoe, did not pay much attention to the scrupulous portraits of Irishwomen and their problems that Lavin intended to bring to light with "a great deal of care and concentration." They tended to evaluate Lavin's works based simply on the choice of her subject matter rather than the way in which she dealt with it – particularly from a woman's point of view.

It might be surmised that Igoe's criticism was not without personal bias, given that Lavin's works really offered little by way of moralist teaching. However, the different perceptions separating Lavin from her critics might suggest a conceptual gap between what was written and how it was read. That is to say, readers might be subject to external forces as to how to read or evaluate a work by existing standards,

---

[423] Igoe 3.
[424] Quoted in Peterson 44. Peterson spotted an unpublished article in which Lavin defended her novel(s) as being unfairly reviewed. She recollected that she did write her two novels "with a great deal of care and concentration." The article is now filed with the Mary Lavin Collection at Southern Illinois University, Carbondale.
[425] Igoe 3.

while writers might have intended to question the standards that critics and readers held in accord with rigid religious ethics or political sentiments. Unable to prescribe a suitable reading for works that would provoke a response from the readership, writers would then be censored, or find themselves unfavourably reviewed. The fact that Lavin's works were labelled as amateurish was a means of frustrating the writer, and of discouraging readers from reading her works seriously.

On the other hand, what gave rise to the perception gap between Lavin and her critics might be predominantly traced to the following facts. Firstly, some critics, who contributed to mainstream newspapers or magazines, might be expected to conform to community values and interests, particularly in the case of Christian publications. It might be true to say that Irish Catholic critics who worked in a puritanical environment would be particularly concerned about whether Irish novelists had incorporated religious lessons into their works. Although Lavin was a Catholic writer who demonstrated a marked understanding of Catholic teaching in her works, some Catholic critics did not think that she presented moral issues as unambiguously as they expected. They largely neglected Lavin's possible intention of directing her readers to rethink social and moral issues from different angles. Evidently, Lavin's attempts at portraying insular Irishness, the materialistic Irish middle class, superstitious Irishmen, and the exploited, among other aspects of Ireland, did not merit any comment on their part. It is noteworthy that Lavin's being neglected could have had much to do with her presentations of Ireland not always favouring the dominant position of the Catholic Church, and her often giving a voice to those struggling on the margins of society.

Secondly, the labelling of Lavin as amateurish reflects the general underestimation of Irish women writers of her time. As Frank O'Connor pointed out, "[an Irish] woman cannot afford to caricature herself as a man may do, and if she does, she is made to pay for it. It is a drawback to the Irish woman writer."[426] This general devaluation of women writers and artists might have been to blame for Lavin not receiving the critical attention she deserved. Critics might have assumed that an "amateurish" woman writer would not have written anything very substantial. On the other hand, the fact that Lavin did not write much about political emergencies that had recently happened, or were happening, but instead concentrated on women's lives, probably gave rise to the notion that her writing bore no relevance to her age.

---

[426] Frank O'Connor, "Girl" 30.

6. Mary Lavin

It is worth noting that, despite the negative environment for women writers at home, Lavin still continued writing with her private conscience as the criterion as to what she thought significant, not changing subjects to make herself more welcome and popular. Lavin stated in an interview that the most faithful critic for a writer is actually the writer himself/herself, and she went on to add that "[w]riters should read and re-read what they have written to find out what it is that they are trying to say."[427] Consequently, her avoidance of fashionable topics, such as the Great Lockout of 1913, the Easter Rising, the Black-and-Tan War, and the Civil War, is understandable. She might have wanted to suggest that there were other relevant facets of Ireland worth exploring outside of the political arena. Her second novel, *Mary O'Grady* (1950), set against the backdrop of the 1910s, was a work that referred to few contemporary events, despite the fact that this was a crucial period leading towards Irish independence. Her refusal to write specifically for nationalistic causes may suggest her silent protest against the patriarchal tradition, as this novel focused extensively on how domestic women survive strict social codes. The fact that the social upheavals of the 1910s did not impinge on her characters' consciousness implied how Lavin insisted upon observing Irish life from a non-political angle.

Another factor explaining Lavin's lack of critical attention in the mid-twentieth century is the ambiguity of the feminist statements in her works. That is, her works, though not always written in line with patriarchal and patriotic values, did not appear to side with a feminist school. Lavin, as a critic of her own writing, was more concerned about human conditions in general. Notably, even though she had depicted women's predicaments in many of her works, she also expressed her sympathy for males who were blind to their own mistakes and weaknesses. She was not apt to pass any form of judgment on to her readers, while she was more likely to waken their private conscience "in a sober, occasionally grim, and wholly unsentimental tone."[428] Although she did write a large number of stories about women in trouble, she did not seem to join nor endorse any feminist social campaign throughout her lifetime. Her efforts in revealing genuine human dilemmas with little display of sympathy for any sort of political correctness, as a result, made her works attractive to readers outside Ireland.

---

[427] Quoted in Boylan 15.
[428] "Irish Eyes Unsmiling" 721.

Some might contend that Lavin's neglect in Ireland had much to do with her realistic portraits of the clergy, as some of her stories did not appear to display much respect towards them, which resulted in unfavourable reviews. However, what is more noteworthy is that she tended to see the clergy as being as human as ordinary people, experiencing all sorts of feelings and weaknesses. Conscious, perhaps, of Catholic critics' antipathy towards her, she openly defended her approach to the clergy in an interview. She emphasised that her works were by no means anti-clerical, but rather aimed to reveal what appeared to be true about clerical life. She said:

> I see priests and nuns as just the same as the rest of us, victims of curial despotism. Sometimes I have portrayed clergymen as less than they ought to be or as downright destructive, but that is not anti-clericalism. It only means that when a man acts according to his nature, he sometimes behaves in a way that is contrary to the accepted purpose of his calling.[429]
>
> I have never to my knowledge written an anticlerical story, although I have written about priests and nuns who were weak and human, because when they fall their fall is more tragic than that of other men and women.[430]

It could be argued that the manner in which Lavin viewed and portrayed clerical life was consonant with her approach to the life of people in general. In other words, not only did she think that the clergy should not be privileged to the degree that they were exempt from any scrutiny of their life, but a similar approach was also applied to her examination of the lives of Irishwomen and men. To her, "real life is a veil," and the task of writers was to reveal what lurked behind the curtain, according to writers' own private conscience.[431]

It could also be claimed that Lavin's emphasis on individual private conscience had gone through an academic inquiry. That is, before she took up her career as a creative writer, she had begun writing a doctoral thesis on Virginia Woolf following an M.A. dissertation on Jane Austen. The academic training she received at University College Dublin provided her with a critical understanding of the role a writer should play in his/her work. According to Richard F. Peterson, Lavin had demonstrated in her dissertation the importance for a writer to be omniscient, so that (s)he

---

[429] Harmon 289.
[430] Murphy 224.
[431] Quoted in Pritchett x.

6. Mary Lavin

could maintain an objective narrative against subjective reading and writing. Her point in relation to the importance of omniscience can be summarised as: "[in case of] the dangers of a laid-on morality, [. . .] the best method of the novelist is to make his views part of the texture of the story. The novelist needs to remember that omniscience is a privilege rather than a weapon."[432] The omniscience she referred to could well indicate the demonstration of an independent conscience with which a writer could make more thorough observations on the various facets of incidents, before (s)he put pen to paper.

Lavin's debut short story, "Miss Holland," was written during an early stage of writing-up her doctoral thesis on Virginia Woolf in 1939. Her academic study of Jane Austen and Virginia Woolf for her M.A and doctoral theses, respectively, afforded her insights into women's potential predicaments in a patriarchal environment. The success of this story confirmed her interest in creative writing, so she "immediately abandoned" her doctoral thesis.[433] The significance of studying Jane Austen was the author's knowledge of "a woman's worth," even though "there [wa]s no overt feminist doctrine in [her] novels."[434] It could be suggested that Austen's novels had a relevant impact on Lavin and directed her attention towards women's frustrations. In addition, her academic observations on pre-Victorian characters prepared Lavin to some degree for proper objectivity with which to scrutinise Irishwomen and men.

Apart from the fact that Lavin did not particularly write for religious and male interests, she often came under criticism for not exploring a more diverse range of subjects, as well as for confining her characters to rustic and middle-class Ireland. One uncomplimentary review, critical of the narrow scope of her subjects, typifies the type of criticism she experienced. The reviewer deemed Lavin to be "emotionally hemmed in by rural Ireland, and few of [her] stories dig [. . .] deep. They rarely reach beyond the particular to any kind of universality. [. . .] Her story [. . .] is essentially anecdotal, and the same may be said of other pieces."[435] This view oversimplifies Lavin's close observations of various facets of Irish life. In fact, Lavin delineated not only the comedies and tragedies that occur in everyday life, but also the uniqueness

---

[432] Peterson 45.
[433] Quoted in Kelly 11. In her Preface to *Selected Stories* (New York, 1959), she described the abandonment of the thesis on Woolf as immediately following her attempts at writing a creative story.
[434] Quoted in Kaplan 24.
[435] "Irish Eyes Unsmiling" 13.

Irish Literary Canon

of ordinary individuals. In particular, she often managed to display the power and weakness of the Irish psyche through a third-person, objective narrative, expressing her deep compassion for the people, even when she had to raise questions and produce satire. It is perhaps true to say that she intended to attract people's attention to "the present" through giving illustrations of the feelings and thoughts of ordinary characters. Her depictions of Irish life might, at times, appear anecdotal or trivial, but what is worth noting is that she could find significance in simple incidents. It can be conjectured that her interest in the present was the reason why she did not attempt the sort of romantic or mythic subjects that her predecessors had characterised.[436]

It is also necessary to look at issues that do not appear to bear any direct relation to Lavin's works, but which have contributed to their neglect in Ireland. Apart from the fact that she wrote little in relation to nationalistic Ireland, the general disregard for the achievement of short story writers had a negative effect on Lavin's recognition in Ireland, even though she had been a prolific story writer. It could be contended that dramatists and poets in Ireland had been over-stressed from the early twentieth century, and there had been limited discussion on the achievements of short story writers as well as their ideas and ideals of nation formation. Some might argue that the short story was not really a disregarded genre in the making of the Irish nation, as many Irish revivalists had addressed both middle-class and rustic populations with revised tales from the oral tradition. But such tales, according to John Wilson Foster, promoted an unrealistic expectation centred on "the past and the future," rather then the present.[437] Ernest Boyd also maintained that the stress placed on poetry and drama caused "fiction and narrative prose" to be "the weak point of the Revival."[438] The enduring effects include the decrease of opportunities for modern Irish novelists to publish their books in their own land. As Tim Pat Coogan indicates: "from [the Rising] until 1951, when the Dolmen Press was set up, there was no Irish publishing com-

---

[436] Some of her predecessors had highlighted mythic or romantic Irish (female) figures in their works, or even seen them as the maternal symbol of Ireland, such as W.B. Yeats' "Kathleen ni Houlihan," and James C. Mangan's "Dark Rosaleen." Nevertheless, Lavin wrote very little about these mythic characters.

[437] John Wilson Foster argues that revivalists' emphasis on drama and poetry directed people's interest to the past and the future: "[they] are the dimensions in which the Irish tend to live, which might explain a certain lack of enthusiasm for realism in art and explain (or be explained by) there having been no important middle-class stories dedicated to the present with all its immediate fulfillment." Quoted in Cronin 17.

[438] Boyd 374.

6. Mary Lavin

pany devoted to issuing imaginative literature on a commercial scale."[439] Owing to limited opportunities for publication in Ireland, "[m]ost Irish writers at this time had to seek publication either in London or New York."[440]

Mary Lavin, as a writer surviving under these circumstances, was not exempt from the difficult situation that prose writers experienced at home. Like many of her contemporaries, both male and female, she had to seek foreign recognition before being acknowledged as a talented writer, and even then some critics still deemed her to be amateurish. Many of her short stories first appeared in American and English magazines, and her novel, *The House in Clewe Street*, was serialised in the *Atlantic Monthly* in Boston. It is true to say that her reputation as a writer, and a loyal readership, were built up more stably overseas than at home. Constant support from overseas publishers afforded Lavin the opportunity to demonstrate her talents, allowing her to avoid any local demands for nationalistic and puritanical stories.

It could be contended that Lavin was aware of the lack of critical attention to the short story in Ireland. She might also have been conscious of some negative attitudes towards this genre, which led people to think that this form of writing, due to the limitations of length, could not produce profound moral significances. Nevertheless, in order to clarify this judgment, and from the standpoint of having written in prose, she contended that the power of a short story lay in its refined texture, as did that of poetry:

> I don't think the short story has – or should have any limits. [. . .] What lies ahead for the short story? Not, I think, a great change in technique. It need only readers to accept that it is already a powerful medium in which anything, anything, anything that is to be said can be said, as in poetry. The short stories of Conrad, Thomas Mann, D. H. Lawrence, Hemingway, Faulkner, even Tolstoy are not really dwarfed by their great novels.[441]

Here, she suggests that literary conventions, if not arbitrary, should be more flexible in their scope, while at the same time arguing that the short story is not necessarily less complex in essence than a novel or a novella or poetry. In other words, as a practised writer, she did not think that writing a short story took any less effort and con-

---

[439] Quoted in Cronin 14.
[440] Cronin 14.
[441] Lavin, "Afterword" 222.

centration than writing a novel or poem. What mattered, according to her, was whether writers of different genres could present a refined medium through which their most profound concerns for life could be presented and heard properly. This refined medium, furthermore, had to be free from political considerations as well as open to accommodate various subjects and issues for scrutiny. Incidents which took place within family and rustic settings were therefore appropriate for discussion. Moreover, by calling literary conventions into question, Lavin also demonstrated her unwillingness to remain ignored in Ireland, as her intention was to represent her personal Irish experience, an experience accumulated through close observations of female predicaments and male powerlessness. This counteracted the traditional, male-privileged canon in Ireland.

In the next two sections, I will consider some of her short stories and the novel, *The House in Clewe Street*, to discuss the ways in which Lavin probed into the mindset of people, and to determine who eventually had or had not been "hemmed" into the state of complacence. Her portraits of Ireland were not always entertaining or peaceful, but were rather grim when the paralysis of the psyche was put under a microscope.

6.2. Stories in Perspective

It may be observed that a large number of Mary Lavin's heroes and heroines are closely related to, or come from, middle-class or rustic Ireland, or from labouring backgrounds. People interact with each other in an environment that superficially looks peaceful but is troubled in different ways. Lavin, as a writer who had had close contact with the countryside since childhood, tended to see these characters with deep compassion, due to her familiarity with their nature and the dilemmas they faced. Her depictions of Ireland, unlike those of some overseas critics and anthologists who were apt to see the country in a nostalgic or romantic way, are unsettling. Although her stories often involved appealing descriptions of nature in Western Ireland, behind the surface there were always striking lessons that readers could hardly be indifferent to.

Lavin's 1939 debut short story, "Miss Holland," for instance, features a well-bred, but over-protected heroine's disillusionment with urban citizens: Agnes Holland is a forty-five year old, properly educated, middle-class woman who has newly arrived in the city and found lodgings in a boarding house following the death of her father and the sale of the home property. Before leaving the country, she had no real knowledge

6. Mary Lavin

of the ways in which urban people talked and behaved, particularly those from the labouring class. Her old-fashioned, bourgeois upbringing in the country brings with it a sense of superiority over the other lodgers which makes her feel like "civilising" them. One day, when she is sitting at the dining table with the rest of the lodgers, she is about to express for the first time how fond she is of the cat, when she overhears from the conversation that it has been attacked with a shotgun by one of the lodgers. This comes just as she is thinking of the most appropriate and elegant words to use to describe the cat. She is greatly shocked and feels utterly disillusioned.

Lavin does not specify how Miss Holland manages to cope with the shock of this incident but refers to the laughs that the lodgers enjoy with one another in general. These lodgers simply ignore Miss Holland's distress when she hears about the cat, and pay no attention to her departure for the door. However, Lavin creates a clue in this story to a mixture of social problems that keep Miss Holland – an unmarried, middle-aged countrywoman with old-fashioned upbringing – from actively interacting with the other lodgers whom she newly met in the city. In particular, the different perceptions of the value of a cat to people with varying educational backgrounds and from different classes foreshadows some kind of social class tension in that people in the same community have no genuine understanding of, or concern for, each other. The lodgers that Miss Holland finds hard to befriend are not even aware of their narrow-mindedness, and have not even a little sympathy for the cat. In other words, what appears to be a crisis in "Miss Holland" mirrors the wider crisis of Ireland, where people of different ethnic origins, political beliefs, and religious denominations have found no ways to accommodate one another peacefully. Although Lavin does not address these issues so explicitly in this story, the boarding house which she depicts suggests the writer's observation on the irresoluble conflicts of values amongst different social classes in Ireland. To some extent, this debut story demonstrated Lavin's interest in social issues and female predicaments in a patriarchal and hierarchical society.

It is also noteworthy that the main protagonist could be held to be neither Miss Holland nor the lodgers, but the voiceless cat which entertains lodgers in different ways: Miss Holland is enthralled by its liveliness, while others appear to be indifferent to it. It might be appropriate to judge that to kill a cat, which cannot not defend itself, might suggest that Irish society has not yet become sufficiently tolerant to consider the interests of the "Other." The killing of the cat might therefore imply Lavin's concerns for those deprived people on the social margin, although this point is only made rather implicitly in her narrative.

If "Miss Holland" was Lavin's critique of Irish society in general, another short story, "Sunday Brings Sunday," contains a commentary on the moral guardianship assumed by the Catholic Church in Ireland. This story concerns a teenage heroine, Mona, a devoted girl who believes whatever the priests say without a second thought: "[she] drinks in every word the priest utters. [. . .] I believe in my heart that if the priest told [her] to cut off her right hand she'd do it without thinking another thought," as her mother says.[442] Mona prays whenever she can, because a parish priest declares that "prayer is an efficacious thing," and "it is a good thing [. . .] to go down on our knees and humble ourselves by prayer."[443] Mona does pray, but as she grows older, she begins to experience feelings toward boys. She befriends one boy, and after a brief courtship they go to bed. Mona soon develops a strong sense of guilt for having lost her virginity, but being considered a good girl by the clergy, she does not have the courage or strength to go to confession. All she can do is to pray privately for God's forgiveness, even when walking in the street. One day, on her way back from school to home, she accidentally slips into a ditch during such a moment of prayer and drowns, and people wonder how that was possible in such a shallow ditch.

Lavin tells the story as a third-person narrative, making no reference to why it was a fatal slip for Mona. To the narrator, Mona's death is more likely due to her excessive sense of guilt. Mona's religious upbringing might have given her a stronger sense of morality than other people in the community would have had. She was overwhelmed, since her childhood, by priests' sermons on the consequences of committing mortal sins, including not raising hats when passing by a priest. Mona is profoundly affected by the repeated priestly warnings. As with the young Stephen Dedalus in James Joyce's *A Portrait of the Artist as a Young Man*, Mona becomes obsessed with thoughts of the unredeemable life in Hell, here depicted by the clergy in similarly threatening language. Unlike Stephen, Mona does not grow old enough to retrieve her private conscience to see what went wrong. It could be said that she is metaphorically crucified by the weight of the guilt prescribed by the clergy.

---

[442] Lavin, "Sunday" 73.
[443] Lavin, "Sunday" 63.

6. Mary Lavin

Mona's death could be seen as a misfortune for which the whole community should also be held responsible, since Mona's strong sense of guilt is also caused by tremendous pressure from a society which conforms to strict religious codes. That is why her fear of being found out as morally deviant could have resulted in the fatal slip into the ditch. In other words, pressure from the community has restrained her from making sensible judgments. I would argue that Lavin's observations on the teachings of the Irish Catholic Church had much to do with her childhood experience in America. She was not adverse to Catholicism *per se*, but felt aware that "religion was another peculiar twist in the minds of [people in these small Irish towns]."[444] She herself had gone through what Mona experienced as a child. In a 1979 interview, she recollected how she was brought up: "As a child I was not allowed to judge by my own private conscience. I remember resenting that anybody would think or decide for me. [. . .] It is almost impossible for people to know what is right and what is wrong."[445]

While "Sunday Brings Sunday" is a story that addresses the consequences of suspending independent judgment, Lavin was not always pessimistic. She wrote "My Vocation" in order to demonstrate the possibility of retrieving one's private conscience. The story is narrated by a mature woman who recalls how she received the call to join a religious order at the age of thirteen, and how she realised that this vocation was mixed with her childish expectation of a religious profession. In the story, the unnamed heroine grew up in a poor family in Dorset Street in Dublin and developed a kind of admiration for nuns who appear serene, beautiful, and angelic in church, in contrast to the women in her shabby neighbourhood: "You'd see them inside in a kind of golden cage, back of the altar. [. . .] They were like angels; honest to God".[446] The narrator responded to an advertisement placed by a convent to recruit postulants; no dowry or higher education are expected. Soon there were sisters calling upon the family to check if the heroine met the requirements to join the order. Their home visit was a great disappointment to the narrator, because the nuns behaved condescendingly to poor families like hers. Moreover, they made a terrible scene in front of the house when they departed: they fell out of a carriage when the horse bolted unexpectedly and used foul language. Closer observation of the nuns brought the revelation that their angelic image was an illusion; they could be as arrogant, rude,

---

[444] Lavin, *House* 182.
[445] Harmon 290.
[446] Lavin, "My Vocation" 270.

and embarrassing as ordinary people. The narrator decided not to join the order after their visit.

The purpose of the story is evidently not to ridicule religious sisters, but to present them as human. Lavin also gives a voice to nuns, who were traditionally supposed to be silent and submissive to the instructions of the Church. The discouraging words from the heroine's mother to her "nun-to-be" daughter were that nuns had unequal status in the Church, pointing out that "[t]hey [are] not allowed a hot water bottle in their beds [. . .], they have to sit at the back of the chapel with no red plush on their kneeler. [. . .] it's a queer thing to see the Church making distinction."[447] The mother, though not directly against the heroine's idea of entering a convent, was aware that her daughter might have been swayed by the obsession of the angelic illusion. She referred to neighbours' comment on nuns to suggest that life in the convent could be harsher than the heroine imagined: "[nuns] can eat things out in the world that they can't eat in the convent. As long as you don't ask them! Don't say will you or won't you! Just set it in front of them."[448] Although this might be a stereotypical comment on nuns, it does make a contrast with the angelic image that had haunted the heroine.

Another noteworthy fact in "My Vocation" is that Lavin also criticises the way in which the Catholic order operated its missions. In particular, the reason why no dowry or higher education were needed was that the Order could send postulants to look after lepers or teach people in foreign lands: "you don't have need to be too highly educated to teach savages."[449] Those who had dowry and education presumably had more possibility of serving in their home country. As they had more understanding of the ways in which the order organised its missions, all the heroine's parents could do, besides the mild discouragement mentioned earlier, was to borrow some luxuries, including a piano, to decorate the house, so as to avoid their daughter being looked down on by the order. However, the expected pecuniary contribution was still quite a concern for the father: "what will I do for money [. . .] when they come looking for your dowry? If you haven't an education you have to have money going to those convents."[450] The teenage heroine, nonetheless, did not realise the trouble that she might bring to her poor family when she applied to become a postulant: she did not listen to her parents before the visiting sisters disappointed and dis-

---

[447] Lavin, "My Vocation" 271.
[448] Lavin, "My Vocation" 273.
[449] Lavin, "My Vocation" 273.
[450] Lavin, "My Vocation" 272.

illusioned her themselves. Lavin's presentation of nuns as arrogant shows that they also suffer from the same human weaknesses as ordinary people. She once claimed that "priests and nuns are just the same as the rest of us, victims of curial despotism."[451]

Lavin wrote numerous stories, like "My Vocation," which were not particularly biased against the Catholic Church, but her picture of the clergy at times irritated religious critics. A critic from the *Catholic Herald* remarked that Lavin wrote "without adequate knowledge" of Catholicism, and her stories "show[ed] frivolity in the writer."[452] This critique foreshadowed Lavin's omission from the modern Irish canon until the 1970s, even though she claimed that "I have never to my knowledge written an anticlerical story."[453] The concerns that she constantly expressed about how people survived, or failed to survive, the rigidity of Catholic teaching at the time formes a major theme in her stories.

It could be claimed that Lavin was susceptible to gender bias against females, but in many of her short stories she is reluctant to portray women as victims or helpless. She often features women as independent beings, not necessarily set against patriarchy, but able to overcome human weaknesses such as loneliness and seduction. It may well be the case that when she produced works featuring Irishwomen's lives and thoughts, she did not intend to endorse a feminist political statement. She presented the fate of women and their possible life choices according to her personal understanding of female predicaments in a patriarchal environment.

To illustrate this point, "In the Middle of the Fields" may serve as an example. The young widow, Faith Vera, who runs a farm by herself and lives alone in a house surrounded and cut off by fields, is introduced by an elderly servant, Ned, to one of her late husband's friends, Bartley Crossen, for his services of mowing the meadows in the farm. However, having agreed to do the job the next day, Crossen then decides to put it off for another week and prioritise jobs for other people. He visits Faith again at night for this – without an appointment, which allows her little time to properly compose herself before she opens the door. Although Faith is reluctant to receive any visitor after dark, being polite, she still lets Crossen in. Before this late night visit, Faith was told by Ned about Crossen's moving romance with his late first wife, Bridie, whom Crossen courted years ago in the same house where Faith lived now. As

---

[451] Harmon 291.
[452] Burdeti 3.
[453] Murphy 224.

a widow who sympathises with Crossen for losing a loving life partner, Faith is concerned whether he will ever forget Bridie: "[w]hen the tree falls, how can the shadow stand?"[454]

Feeling irritated by Crossen's postponement of the job, she successfully resists his idea "crossly," "sharply," "impatiently," "angrily," "raising her voice."[455] Faith here appears to be a demanding character who wants to avoid being taken advantage of in any way; her manners are not stereotypical, as might be expected of a young woman. The story then moves on to Crossen's attempt to seduce Faith who, with her bare feet and disarranged hair, looks like "a young girl" in Crossen's eyes.[456] He assumes that this lonely widow has a similar sexual interest as he. Faith, on the contrary, has been very annoyed by this unexpected visitor. After asking her if the children have gone to bed and making other small talk, Crossen makes his first attempt to broach the subject of sex with a drastic change of topic. He "asks suddenly: Aren't you never lonely here at night?"[457] Not getting a positive answer from Faith, Crossen makes a second, third, and fourth move by whispering suggestively to Faith: "Are you never lonely – at all?"; "Is there nobody could stay here with you – at night even?"; "What about a little kiss?"[458] To convince Faith that it is all right to make love to him, Crossen even begins a long story in which he explains that he does not love his second wife, Mona; he married her initially because he expected her to look after his child (who was Bridie's). To Faith's disappointment, Crossen not only has no respect for Mona but has forgotten Bridie and wants to seduce her in the same house where he courted his first wife. Faith certainly does understand Crossen's intention in asking these questions and telling this story, but she either corrects his words "coldly and quickly" or pretends to be deaf to his suggestions.[459] Unable to take advantage of Faith, Crossen, with frustration, utters his last question which greatly angers her as she takes it as an insult: "You're not blaming yourself [for being a beautiful, lonely widow], surely?"[460]

---

[454] Lavin, "In the Middle" 1203. This is a comment from Ned meant to encourage Faith to move on in life after the loss of her husband, but it sounds somehow irritating to her ears.
[455] Lavin, "In the Middle" 1204-06.
[456] Lavin, "In the Middle" 1204.
[457] Lavin, "In the Middle" 1206.
[458] Lavin, "In the Middle" 1206.
[459] Lavin, "In the Middle" 1206.
[460] Lavin, "In the Middle" 1208.

6. Mary Lavin

Crossen's final attempt irritates Faith tremendously because he underrates women's integrity. In particular, his questions are not only offensive to a woman but they also involve the patriarchal stereotype of young, beautiful widows who are supposed to be lonely, discontented, and unfaithful to late husbands. Unable to tolerate Crossen's discourteous and insulting questions any longer, she interrupts his conversation by observing that if anyone is to be blamed, then Crossen should have blamed his late wife: "Arrah, what you are blaming any of us for! [. . .] It's got nothing to do with any of us – with you, or me, or the woman at home waiting for you. It was the other one! That girl – your first wife – Bridie! It was her! Blame her!"[461] In the end, she says with some degree of cynicism to Crossen that she is glad for Bridie that this kind of husband is no longer her earthly husband: "You thought you could forget her, [. . .] but see what she did to you when she got the chance."[462]

Lavin does not feature Faith as a stereotypical widow or a victimised woman in a patriarchal society. She does not apply the word "widow" to introduce Faith, nor portray her as helpless and solitary. On the contrary, Faith is mentally equipped and articulate enough to defend herself from being taken advantage of. She acts as an independent being who insists on not relying on her late husband's family, but rather on living alone "in the middle of the fields." Her four refusals of Crossen, ranging from the polite to the furious, suggest a strong determination against being viewed as a desired object of men. It could be contended that she finds herself self-contained outside a romance or remarriage. Her rejection of Crossen is therefore unlikely to be motivated by any desire to defend her chastity for her late husband's sake, as expected by society. It could also be argued that her self-containment lies in the fact that she knows what she would and would not do. The inappropriate questions Crossen asks disgrace himself while at the same time they testify to Faith's non-compliant personality. Nevertheless, contemporary feminists at the time of the story's publication might not have found it political enough to demonstrate the social inequality between males and females, as Crossen might not seem to feminists to have suffered any form of moral condemnation. However, it is worth remarking that Lavin is unlikely to have composed this story to impress feminists but rather intends to leave readers with an open and rather ambiguous conclusion, so that they could evaluate the whole event from a more objective angle.

---

[461] Lavin, "In the Middle" 1208.
[462] Lavin, "In the Middle" 1208.

"In the Middle of the Fields" is like many of Lavin's short stories that appear to be episodes of Irish life, as the writer tended to demonstrate that "real life is a veil."[463] In general, she managed to sift Irish cultural elements from casual incidents, thus commenting on Irish politics, Catholic rule, gender stereotypes, and, last but not least, human frailty. Although her works seldom appeared to be acrimonious about the nationalistic and Catholic authorities, they contained the writer's profound and critical concerns for Ireland. Her endeavour to explore various aspects of the countryside suggests that she aimed to be more than a ruralist writer, or an amateur, namely someone who wrote professionally and with genuine affection for the people of the land. Her critique of different facets of Irish society can be found in her novel, *The House in Clewe Street*, in which she expands on her observations from glimpses of life to a greater, more coherent span of incidents across three generations. The next section will explore the consequences of the tragedy and comedy in Irish life that Lavin presents in this novel.

6.3. Class and Patriarchy in *The House in Clewe Street* (1945)

The study of Lavin's short stories has demonstrated that she wanted to unveil the real life that Irish countrymen and women led, and to do this from an onlooker's perspective, an approach which enabled the writer to describe in a more realistic manner the successes and failures of people in a morally, religiously, and/or politically confined society. Her long novel, *The House in Clewe Street*, showed how a variety of social forces determined her characters' happiness, anger and despair, even though they were not involved with (anti-)colonial politics.

What is striking about the unconventionality of *Clewe Street* is that the writer portrayed different generations of the Coniffe family over a very long span of time.[464] This device enables readers not only to detect the social circumstances which nourish a hero(ine), but also to observe a series of causes and effects which lead to his/her

---

[463] Pritchett x.
[464] Some critics disliked this aspect of the novel. A reviewer from *The Catholic Herald* described *Clewe Street* as a "monstrously long novel." A critic from *The Washington Post* remarked: "Long, it still gets nowhere. [. . .] Beautifully written in its individual parts, it still lacks structure." I would argue that the length of a novel does not necessarily affect its narrative intensity and quality but can be an essential element for a social history. See "Humor" 13 and Igoe 3.

6. Mary Lavin

suffering and joyfulness. It could be argued that by placing Irish protagonists in a more complex social context over a longer period, rather than within the framework of a limited space and time to which most short stories had to conform, Lavin offered a more thoughtful critique of social, cultural and human weaknesses. The novel, about the rise and fall of the Coniffes, might serve as a social history recording middle-class life in an insular Irish town, and the treatment of women in particular. Although characters in the novel do not experience any of the anti-colonial turbulence in the Irish society of the time, they are affected by other important social determinants. In *Clewe Street*, Lavin presents various factors other than the political that might have significant influence on people's outlook on life. Lavin's indifference to political issues was arguably intentional, as a protest, albeit mild, against the over-emphases placed on history, nationalism, and other matters that were more relevant to male concerns and contributions. *Clewe Street*, whose setting is a mixture of domestic and public spheres in the country and the city, gives a better picture of Irish life outside its political arena.

In addition to being a record of middle-class life, this novel provides access to an understanding of Irishwomen, whose ideas and feelings had been neglected in comparison to male voices in political campaigns, although the contribution of women had important effects on the other half of the population. Lavin describes different types of women and made them speak from various social positions; some were economically privileged, and some greatly deprived. In this novel, Lavin also features interactions among women at home as well as those driven out of home. More significantly, she reveals how they survive or fail to overcome social restrictions imposed on them by different social classes.

The incidents that occur in *Clewe Street* mostly concern the Coniffes, a landed family which has settled in the town of Castlerampart for many generations. As successive misfortunes cost the lives of its senior male members, the three Coniffe daughters, Theresa, Sara, and Lily, are given temporary custodianship of the Coniffe properties, before Lily's only son, Gabriel Coniffe, reaches the age of twenty-five years. Theresa, the eldest sister of the three, consequentially gains the highest authority over the family and tenants at Castlerampart. What is noteworthy is that her role as a demanding landlady and senior figure in the household put her in direct and indirect contact with people of different classes within the town. Moreover, as she is aware that the role she has taken over from her father and grandfather is supported by patriarchal hierarchy, she intentionally reassumes the patriarchal codes within the community of people who live there and work for the Coniffes. The patriarchal ethos is therefore in no way diminished under her leadership, but is in fact reinforced.

It is interesting to look at how women on different levels of the social hierarchy in *Clewe Street* are treated, including those whose appearances are minor. Examples include Mary Ellen, Doss Dolan, Agnes Finnerty and Onny Soraghan. They are often forced into silence and victims of middle-class hypocrisy and snobbery. In the novel, the Coniffes are at the centre of these middle-class lapses. Mary Ellen, for instance, is a senior housemaid discharged by Theresa, who thinks that Ellen is "too old to work" and "getting in [everyone's] way" in the house.[465] Her hardship does not end after she is turned out. To make the most use of her, Theresa puts her into a spare cottage, giving her a few hens to feed in expectation of fresh eggs every morning. Theresa's arrangement for Ellen apparently rests not on genuine sympathy but, as she says, is so that they would not "look badly in the eyes of the town."[466] The fact that Ellen worked for the Coniffes throughout her entire lifetime left her with no opportunity to nurture a family of her own. There is no retirement for women of her labouring class. Furthermore, not only her labour, but also her dignity is demeaned to maintain the social privileges of the Coniffes.

Doss Dolan is another figure whose role in the novel is as minor as Ellen's, but whose appearance is nevertheless an important one which attests to the life of those people who are marginalised in the community of Castlerampart. She never utters a word in the novel, but "everyone in the town knew that [her facial] disfigurement was the result of an accident in infancy."[467] A rat attacked her face and the doctor accidentally cauterised it during an operation. She was cast out to survive in one of the rampart hovels, even before the townspeople knew of her existence. As a fearful and humiliated "creature," she could only venture out for food and necessities when darkness had fallen. The kind, but in practical terms useless regards from townspeople are only motivated by their desire for "a special reward" in another world.[468] There is no actual helping hand proffered to her, only derision from youngsters. Her very presence, though only occasional in the novel, is real evidence of the townspeople's "falseness and hypocrisy."[469] The location of her dwelling reveals that she has

---

[465] Lavin, *Clewe* 216.
[466] Lavin, *Clewe* 216.
[467] Lavin, *Clewe* 207.
[468] Lavin, *Clewe* 209.
[469] Lavin, *Clewe* 209.

been assigned, from her infancy, to the most marginalised social rank in a highly patriarchal and hierarchical society. She has no women compeers and no children are allowed to approach her. Her appearance in the novel also marks the stark contrast between the well-to-do life of the Coniffes and hers in the rampart hovels.

Another pair of contrasting female characters consists of Gabriel's two potential fiancées: Agnes Finnerty and Onny Soraghan. Agnes is an obedient young Catholic girl intended by Theresa to marry Gabriel. That she would be "chosen" by Theresa as the ideal wife for Gabriel, and her future niece by marriage, is largely because of Agnes' submissive nature and her middle-class Catholic upbringing. Her submission would complement Theresa's dominance in domestic matters and public issues with townspeople and tenants. Although Agnes appears to be "a saint" with all the qualities that came to represent Catholic expectations of women, her "air of mystery and remoteness" does not count as an attraction for young Gabriel.[470] On the contrary, he falls for Onny, a servant girl substituted for Mary Ellen, not only for her looks, but for her unmannerly but unaffected conduct. Through her, Gabriel finds an outlet for his rebellious leanings against Theresa's detailed manipulation of his life since childhood. These leanings are suppressed by Theresa and the god-fearing sentiments he acquires at Church. His empathy for Onny for also being under Theresa's unrelenting dominion is a key factor in the development of their relationship.

Belonging to a somewhat higher class than Doss Dolan's, the young Onny replaces Mary Ellen as someone who would be of use to the landed Coniffes. In order to secure her humble wages and realising the "shoes" that she has been put into as a member of the labouring class, she quickly learns to perform her duty as a diligent, silent, and submissive maid in the Coniffe household. She grasps that her only way to survive the risk of being turned out like Mary Ellen is to demonstrate her ability to give a good "performance" whenever she is in the Coniffe house. As her performance as a hard-working servant girl is successful, her rebellious nature is well concealed; only when she attends Sunday Mass alone does this part of her reveal itself. Her reluctance to go into the church to kneel and confess, to which she prefers wandering in the graveyard, suggests her keenness to liberate her undisciplined nature. Interestingly, Gabriel and Onny find that escape to the graveyard is a relief from the Coniffe house that they have common, and there they begin their acquaintance and troubled relationship. This also suggests that their escape might only come with death.

---

[470] Lavin, *Clewe* 224.

Although Gabriel has been brought up in the Coniffe house by three women – his mother, Lily, and his two aunts, Theresa and Sara – he is immensely affected by Theresa, who has an uncompassionate and demanding character; his mother and the other aunt are timid in front of her. The young Gabriel, due to lack of a genuine paternal figure to identify with at home, gradually came under the influence of Theresa's controlling personality. Hence, after setting up a love relationship with Onny, he learns to take charge of her, as she is supposed to be socially inferior to him because of her class and gender. Nonetheless, Onny is never a vulnerable or submissive character who craves or needs Gabriel's protection. Differently from other female figures in the novel, she has the chance to live up to her individuality. Her later conversations with Gabriel, after they elope to Dublin, show her eager expression of her subjectivity: "I'll tell you one thing I don't like. I don't like being corrected! [. . .] I don't belong to you!"[471] "[Y]ou think you'll marry me, and then you'll be able to order me about. You'll say you have legal right over me. Oh, I know your game!"[472] Unfortunately, she does not outlive those who intend to control her, but dies miserably on her way to, or back from, an abortionist. Her death may be read as an escape to "another world," where she is be unlikely to suffer the deprivations resulting from her labour. On the other hand, Onny's death suggests her silent protest against the patriarchy and hierarchy that prevent women of her class from claiming their place in social history.

This novel can be read as a *bildungsroman* in which Lavin presents in detail how young protagonists explore and counteract the obstacles of life and a depiction of the rise and fall of the Coniffes. The hardships the characters endure are accompanied by social expectations determining who they are and how they should behave. Lavin, nevertheless, passed little moral or religious judgment on her characters, but depicts the events in an objective way and sometimes with a humorous tone. It could be claimed that through her narration of the characters' development, readers might develop an understanding of, and sympathy for, these figures who fight against various kinds of discrimination, community pressures, and religious judgments. To be more specific, these characters all have to manage to survive with limited choices in their lives, conforming to the social codes which have been assigned to them.

---

[471] Lavin, *Clewe* 329.
[472] Lavin, *Clewe* 437.

6. Mary Lavin

Theresa, for example, is the oldest among her siblings, and has no choice but to accept the obligations handed down by her forebears: to look after the landed business of the Coniffes in Castlerampart. On the one hand, as people in this patriarchal society are doubtful about women's ability, it is understandable that she has to demonstrate and assume a stronger personality to ensure that things are done as she wants. In particular, she is never an uncompassionate person as a child, but a change in her personality comes about in her 30s. She misses out on a gentleman caller who is expected to marry her rather than her little sister, Lily. The event progressively reduces the possibilities of her marrying someone else, since she is no longer, according to patriarchal standards, at the prime age for marriage. After this, she develops a degree of jealousy and enmity towards Lily. Theresa's mixed emotions for her sister, therefore, push her to emulate their authoritarian father. Her two siblings and her nephew, Gabriel, consequently come under her control after the sisters' father dies. However, Lavin's portrait of Theresa's development shows that she is actually pathetic in the way that she is never able to claim her female individuality. As the head of the Coniffe household and having no husband, she has no choices but follows the instructions that her late father gave. Notably, in a similar way to Onny, she is also a victim who fails patriarchal codes: her father's over-protection put off many opportunities for her to get married, and Lily's younger and more appealing looks attract the attention of Theresa's gentleman callers. These things all contribute to turning her into an unappealing person.

As for Gabriel, he also suffers a twist of personality at Castlerampart. It could be contended that the two authorities of family and Church have produced overwhelming effects on his perception of the world from a young age. His perspectives on the family are coloured by Theresa, who has monitored Gabriel's every move since childhood. His elopement with Onny, therefore, represents his confrontation with her authority, while it does not help to alter the patriarchal mindset that he inherited from the Coniffes. On the other hand, as there are no other male members in the Coniffe household, Theresa, who took up his grandfather's position and appears to be a controlling person, becomes a chief source for Gabriel's learning to take responsibility over his social inferiors. In particular, Theresa's authoritative attitudes towards her two acquiescent siblings, Sara and Lily, influence Gabriel's perceptions of the female, the weak and the powerless. His constant arguments with Onny, who comes from an inferior class, are owing to his unconscious mimicry of Theresa. He often claims ownership over Onny, suggesting that he has come to assume Theresa's domineering character: "You cannot leave me. Married or not you belong to me."[473] Nevertheless, his imitation of Theresa leads both of them towards tragedy, as not only is he unable to keep Onny under his command, but he also indirectly causes her death.

Religious authority has also had decisive effects on Gabriel since childhood. Take one of his deliberate absences from Sunday Mass, for instance. His mistaking the juice of blood oranges, bought from a vendor when wandering outside the church, for God's blood, followed by a strong sense of guilt and physical discomfort, suggests that his independent judgment has been threatened. This is because religious authority has given him a deep dread of committing mortal sins. His dread of falling from a state of grace becomes clear in his argument with Onny about how to dispose of an old broken picture of the Virgin Mary. It is a picture which Onny used to aid her prayers for the ending of a short thunderstorm, while Gabriel thought it was simply a natural phenomenon and that her prayer was unnecessary and superstitious. Hearing Gabriel's remark, Onny therefore tears the pictures into pieces and uses them to fix the holes in her shoes. Knowing the holy picture is disposed of in such a way, Gabriel angrily accuses her of a lack of respect. His argument with Onny suggests that his religious upbringing at Castlerampart was an overwhelming influence on him, so that he can hardly tell the difference between genuine and superstitious beliefs. In other words, there is little difference between burning a picture of the Virgin Mary or tearing it into pieces, in terms of violating a superstition.

Compared with the authority of Theresa that he has challenged by eloping with Onny, religious authority seems to exercise greater domination over his emotions, reactions, and outlook on life. Onny, by contrast, is less obedient in complying with these authorities. As a maid from the less-advantaged class, she is less bound to traditional ethics, which explains why she is more than pleased to be offered a job as a paid model. It may be observed that she is the most courageous figure in *Clewe Street* in fighting against various social powers that threaten to discipline and change her personality. She is also the most outspoken one in defending her female individuality. In particular, her intentional absence from mass, insistence on having an abortion, and making a living by being a model all suggest her tenacity in keeping her individuality intact from patriarchal control. As a whole, through Onny and other female characters, Lavin demonstrates how rigid social codes have made Irishwomen's lives routine and inescapable. Their attempts to escape are often destined to be tragic.

---

[473] Lavin, *Clewe* 438.

6. Mary Lavin

In conclusion, it seems that the female figures in *Clewe Street* represent different prototypes of women, no matter whether they were silenced or vociferous, in a patriarchal and hierarchical society. Lavin provides pictures of their troubled lives so as to suggest that they are miserable in different ways. One of their shared difficulties is that few of them can successfully claim their individuality as independent beings, but surrender to different sorts of prejudice against them. In other words, there are no women who could claim to be winners, including Theresa, who holds on to patriarchal and hierarchical values when dealing with women inferior to her. She may remain snobbish after Onny's death and Gabriel's return to Castlerampart, but she can hardly claim that Onny's blood is not on her hands. If she does have a sense of guilt, it is probably brought forth by the patriarchal society that governs her attitudes. Onny's dignified protest through death is a backlash against this society in general.

However, Lavin's critique of the pitfalls of male-privileged society was not much appreciated. Many of her contemporary critics tended to sit in moral and religious judgment on her hero(ines): "They forget about their families back in Castlerampart, they forget to go to church as they were brought up to do, they entirely forget to be married. And, really, life is not amusing for long."[474] Some critics assumed "[Lavin's] acceptance of the conventional bourgeois attitudes she depicts."[475] Seamus Deane tackled the issue of her technique: "[Lavin] is not, in any technical sense, an innovator," as she was swamped with "[t]he poverty of Irish intellectual life."[476] These criticisms foreshadowed the lack of any profound and accurate analyses of Lavin's texts, even though the writer had unveiled key causes which led to women's suffering and consequential social tragedies.

What is worth attention about Lavin's repositioning in the modern Irish canon is that during the 1970s, when attention was starting to be paid to the achievements of Irish women writers, Lavin was exemplified by Deane as an author who could not stand comparison with those in Eastern Europe and the United States, as the latter produced "a literature of alienation."[477] Lavin and her contemporaries, according to him, lacked experimentation in both subject matter and technique, and proved that

---

[474] "Smalltown" 18.

[475] Rachael 336.

[476] He named three of Lavin's contemporaries who suffered similarly from the poverty of Irish intellectual life: Frank O'Connor, Sean O'Faolain or Liam O'Flaherty. See Deane, "Mary Lavin" 244.

[477] Deane, "Mary Lavin" 244.

"[s]ociety and literature retain their intimacy in Ireland to such a degree that our best literature is still, [. . .] social."[478] Although Deane did not really mean that the "literature of alienation" outshone the type of Irish literature that openly embraced social issues, it could be argued that some critics might have thought that the latter remained conventional and should be more open to non-traditional subject matters. Nevertheless, I would contend that both literatures had their own significance. In addition, the value of a work may vary in different political, religious or cultural contexts, so it could never be appropriate to value one more highly than another developed in a dissimilar environment. What really makes one writer outshine another, in my view, is whether (s)he writes to testify to his or her private conscience, rather than to echo mainstream values. It could be judged that Lavin had fully expressed her independent conscience in her writings and thus provided her readership, across the continents, with abundant food for thought. This is the reason why Lavin wrote prolifically without worrying about her position in a present or future Irish canon.

---

[478] Deane, "Mary Lavin" 244.

7. Divinity and Humanity: The Heterodox Writings of Kate O'Brien

Eibhear Walshe, the chief editor of *Ordinary People Dancing*, a collection of essays dedicated to Kate O'Brien published in 1993, introduced this author as a "deeply problematic" Irish woman writer.[479] In Walshe's opinion, O'Brien was a writer whose "problematic" nature coincided with that of James Joyce and Samuel Beckett, while there was a lack of understanding regarding how deeply, or disturbingly, she had written about Ireland. The three writers all undertook efforts to picture the psychological weakness of the Irish under the influences of Catholicism and nationalism, but only the two male authors were given relevant attention in the international study of Irish literature in English. As for O'Brien, she did not appear to merit much mention in most monographs or discussions about Irish modern literature until the 1980s, even though she had been a prolific playwright, journalist, literary critic, columnist, and novelist. It could be contended that the problematic nature of her writing lies in her portraits of insular and xenophobic Ireland. However, it could also be due to the nature of the Irish canon itself being so problematic that O'Brien's works could not be adequately accommodated within its framework. As her works often involved provocative elements challenging the Irish Catholic Church's puritanical doctrines with regard to extramarital love and homosexuality, "Catholic paternalism [had] attempted to outlaw her."[480] Two of her works, *Mary Lavelle* (1936) and *The Land of Spices* (1941), which touched upon these two particular issues, were banned by the Irish Censorship Board to prevent them from "falling into the hands of very young people."[481]

Faced with stringent censorship at home in Ireland, like many of her Irish contemporaries, O'Brien had to seek overseas publication. She moved to England in 1920 and worked for *The Manchester Guardian* as a freelance journalist after graduating from University College Dublin in 1919. She initially established herself as a playwright and had a long-running play in the West End of London, before publishing her debut novel, *Without My Cloak*, in 1931.[482] The novel won her the Hawthornden

---

[479] Walshe 1.
[480] Walshe 8.
[481] Quoted in Terence Brown 196. This comment of the censors specifically referred to *The Land of Spices*.
[482] She wrote four plays before publishing her first novel: *Distinguished Villa* (1926), *The Silver Roan* (1927), *Set in Platinum* (1927), and *The Bridge* (1927). *Distinguished Villa*

and James Tait Black Prizes. Her major works, which mostly had Ireland as their background, were published during her years of exile in England.

Although O'Brien was a prize-winning writer with several bestsellers during the 1930s, most of her works suffered from a lack of recognition in Ireland before she died in 1978. Her ten novels were out of print up until the late 1980s, when Arlen House in Dublin and Virago Press in London reprinted some of them. The reason why her works were so neglected in Ireland, in addition to their being banned by the Censorship Board, might have been her daring portraits of aberrant love set against traditional moral values, and sceptical observations on nationalistic and Catholic rule in Ireland. This resulted in what could be termed an unofficial censorship against her: many Irish bookshops would not stock her books, and librarians would not order her works. Because of their suspected anti-Catholic and anti-nationalistic nature and tone, her works received little positive notice from local critics. Despite this unfriendly reception in Ireland, she still tenaciously determined to demonstrate what her private conscience conceived of the moral and religious conflicts that formed the experience of Irishmen's everyday lives. She once explained that her insistence on the exploration of moral issues stemmed from this fact: "I am a moralist, in that I see no story unless there is a moral conflict."[483] This suggests that by not writing in line with fundamental Catholic doctrine, she tended to unveil the problems that were apparent to her in the moral teachings of the traditionally-minded Irish Catholic Church.

This chapter will be rereading some of O'Brien's novels and critical essays to see how she exercised her conscience in order to examine an Ireland that was constrained by religious and nationalistic bounds. I propose interpreting her works with reference to the historical and social contexts in which her hero(ine)s do or do not survive. This textual analysis will suggest how the writer explicitly voiced her views against Church-State relations and questioned puritanical morality. Last but not least, I suggest that reading her fictional and non-fictional works will provide a more precise understanding of not only her deep concerns about the devastating effects of Irish parochialism, but also her attempt to introduce alternative cultural perspectives to Irish readers whose perspectives were limited by censorship.

---

won particular acclaim and had a long run in London's West End in 1926.
[483] Mercier, "Kate O'Brien" 98.

7. Kate O'Brien

7.1. *The Land of Spices* (1941): Irish Nationalism, Homosexuality, and Private Conscience

Before this chapter discusses the unsettling nature of O'Brien's works, it is important to note the special historical context in which she grew up. She was born in Limerick in 1897, at a time in which the country had been suffering from political instability following the disgrace of Charles Stewart Parnell in 1889. The fall of Parnell, a prominent Protestant nationalist MP, was due to the public and political reaction to his adultery with his colleague's wife, Katherine O'Shea. His fall from power initiated a split within the Irish Parliamentary Party, intensifying the sectarian divisions between Catholics, Protestants, and different shades of nationalists. One of the consequences was that people with varying nationalistic perspectives and denominational backgrounds had feelings that were too bitter to allow them to seek reconciliation and to work together for solutions to the issues relating to Home Rule.[484]

However, O'Brien, who was educated at Laurel Hill Convent School, a French-run institute in Limerick, developed a rather detached attitude towards the Irish Question. She expressed her foreign perspective in *The Land of Spices* (1941), addressing issues relating to the making of Ireland as a nation. In the novel, Helen Archer, an English character with a French religious name, Mère Marie-Hélène, is the head of the French order and its school, the *Compagnie de la Sainte Famille*, in "Mellick," a fictional town (based on Limerick). Due to her English nationality, she is distrusted by the local Irish clergy, who do not deem her competent in providing nationalistic education and accuse her of "training Irish girls as suitable wives for English Majors and Colonial Governors."[485]

The accusation is untenable in the Reverend Mother's eyes, as it is known that "foreign teaching orders [were] not subject to the authority of the local church hierarchy," and participating in local political campaigns is not the tradition of the *Sainte*

---

[484] Some Irish nationalists insisted on overthrowing the British government in a revolution while others proposed maintaining the subsidiary relation to the English Crown after Ireland obtained political independence under the Home Rule Bill. Some aimed to revive Irish culture and language through education without a political agenda, such as the early stage of the Gaelic League. These views conflicted with each other to differing degrees, and sometimes different religious sentiments and ethnic backgrounds engendered further antagonism amongst the Irish themselves.

[485] Kate O'Brien, *Land* 92.

Famille.[486] However, preconceiving that "Irish national life is bound up with its religion [. . .] and not a foreign tradition," local clergymen often call upon the Reverend Mother, urging her to modify the curricula in more nationalistic terms. Having more concern for spiritual needs than patriotic sentiments in the curricula, she reasons with the Irish clergy that nuns at *Sainte Famille "are not* a nation," so the curricula are not necessarily concerned "with national matters."[487] Emphasising that *Sainte Famille* belongs to a religious order whose charitable operations had reached countries far beyond Ireland, she suggests to visiting clerics, including a nationalistic bishop, that they should develop a broader vision that is not confined to "local incidents."[488] It could be contended that she is reserved about the over-secularism of the local order, whose clerics appear to have confused their spiritual mission with political matters. In her eyes, a Catholic order – no matter whether it is of Irish, English, or French origin – should avoid pleasing politicians but should serve the needs of people across geographical and ideological boundaries. But her suggestion is not taken to by the Irish clergy who misunderstand her attitude as representing support for the English coloniser. In fact, she represents neither English Protestants nor Irish nationalistic Catholics; her ambiguous identities – an English Catholic heading the Irish branch of a French *Sainte Famille* order – allowed her a broad perspective towards the nature of the Catholic mission.

That the author made the Reverend Mother observe the Irish clergy's involvement with nationalism might be to suggest the inappropriateness for a religious body to act on political causes. Moreover, the author might have intended to bring to light gender inequality within the Catholic hierarchy – from the view and experience of a senior member of a religious order. That is, although the Reverend Mother might be exempted from being subject to male clerics in her disputes as the head of a foreign order in Ireland, most women were virtually subjugated to males within Catholic communities regardless of their rank. Displeased about the insularity of the Irish clergy, the Reverend Mother still has to conform to clerical codes and to voice her opinions in the modest manner that is expected of a nun. For instance, she waits on visiting priests: "Reverend Mother smiled as she replenished Father Conroy's cup"; "she withdrew again to her post by the coffee-pots."[489] Nevertheless, I would argue that

---

[486] Breen 178.
[487] Kate O'Brien, *Land* 15.
[488] Kate O'Brien, *Land* 168.
[489] Kate O'Brien, *Land* 14.

7. Kate O'Brien

this behaviour is tactical, while she takes advantage of the privileges given to her foreign order to defend her educational views. Declining Father Conroy's request that she adopt a more nationalistic curriculum, she confronts him as follows:

> [Father Conroy] spoke angrily [. . .] '[o]ur young girls must be educated *nationally* now, Reverend Mother – to be the wives of *Irishmen* and to meet the changing times!'
> '[B]ut if the 'changing times' you are so sure of are to have no place for Christian discipline and common politeness, I can only say I'm glad I shall not see very much of them.'
> She spoke very coldly, and offered the young man some cakes.
> 'No, thank you, Reverend Mother,' he said, 'It's a terror the way you won't see what I mean at all.'
> 'I do see what you mean, Father – and I find you are rude, and officious. But you are, after all, very young.'[490]

Faced with increasing pressure from the visiting clergy, Reverend Mother does make a slight concession in the curricula of *Sainte Famille*.[491] She approves of an optional course of the Irish language conducted by an Irish nun of her order, but counters at the same time that this is not part of the "mission of her order."[492] It could be contended that this minor concession testifies to her shrewdness in two respects. Firstly, the European-styled curricula remain unchanged, while they meet nationalistic expectations to some (formalistic) degree with the inclusion of an optional course. Secondly, her views are expressed firmly but gracefully, even though they are not particularly agreeable to Irish nationalistic clerics. More specifically, following her argument with Father Conroy, she apologises to him for "having spoken unjustly," but also makes the unmistakable though implicit criticism that there are some "people want[ing] to make a political weapon of the education of children."[493] She does not soften her critical views while making an apology, and makes further comments regarding the nationalist issue.

What is also noteworthy about the Reverend Mother in *The Land of Spices* is that she remains a Catholic woman with unconventional qualities. This unconventionality

---

[490] Kate O'Brien, *Land* 92-93.
[491] Breen 178.
[492] Kate O'Brien, *Land* 168. This nun is Mother Mary David.
[493] Kate O'Brien, *Land* 96-97.

lies in her outspokenness against the questionable values of the Irish Church at her time, but is not necessarily related to her English nationality or the extraterritorial privileges granted to foreign orders in Ireland. She is also a broad-minded Catholic educationalist set firmly against parochial Irish clerics. Her reservation about Irish nationalistic education is not because she has little understanding of anti-colonial causes, but rather due to her reluctance to politicise education or to turn pupils into potential patriots. As an educationalist, she does exercise "power in [her] hands" in educational matters, as Father Conroy states, while she refraines from manipulating this power to adapt the school to be "politically correct" in the context of the Irish nationalistic campaign. Compared with Irish clerics, she apparently has more regard for whether education provided by religious orders "train[s] girls, for their own sakes and for the glory of God, to be Christians and to be civilised" or just makes them fulfil "the needs of Gaelic Leaguer or British officer."[494] She further appears to have a genuine concern about the quality of teaching that pupils receive. In her eyes, the chief contribution that *Sainte Famille* makes to Irish pupils is to allow them to acquire different cultures. However, radical nationalists might insist that Irish education should be free from foreign influences and should prepare pupils to have a sense of patriotism.

That the Reverend Mother's concern about the objective of *Sainte Famille*'s education has little to do with her own English origin can be seen from the following fact. Not only does she insist that the curricula be European in outlook, but also that the school should maintain French as the language used between nuns and pupils on many occasions.[495] With the French ambiance at *Sainte Famille*, she provides students with an alternative choice of cultures: "There was a good French smell of coffee. At every footfall in the room the chandeliers tinkled prettily."[496] It could be conjectured that, on the one hand, the presence of *Sainte Famille* as a European establishment in Ireland with a non-nationalistic educational aim indirectly unsettles the bonding between the Irish Church and anti-colonial campaigns. On the other hand, the Reverend Mother's maintenance of a European outlook towards education, albeit

---

[494] Kate O'Brien, *Land* 168.
[495] Kate O'Brien, *Land* 15. In the syllabi of *Sainte Famille*, subjects included authors with English, French, Spanish, and German origins. Non-English/French authors included the German playwright, Friedrich Schiller (1759–1805), and the Spanish poet, Fray Luis de León (1527–1591).
[496] Kate O'Brien, *Land* 7.

7. Kate O'Brien

with an optional course on the Gaelic language, suggests a reminder from the author to her Irish countrymen that national education does not necessarily have to be nationalistic, and that education should aim to broaden pupils' horizons and enrich their intellectual aspirations, but not to train girls in a pragmatic manner in order to become someone's wife or a parochial citizen.

As for the novel's historiography, it could also be argued that the novel documents the experiences of a few middle-class Irish Catholic families at the turn of the twentieth century, since the author was schooled in Limerick at a similar institution to *Sainte Famille*. These families are able to afford their children to enter a boarding convent school, and are not too concerned about whether the school provides Gaelic courses, as I demonstrated in Chapter One. Their sending children to *Sainte Famille* might suggest their approval of a teaching that favours a European outlook and disagreement with what the clergy labels "a truly nation[alistic] education."[497] However, from the end of the nineteenth century, the voices and experiences of the Catholic middle-class were often a neglected subject for writers and historians. Many of the renowned (Anglo-)Irish writers' portraits of the Irish were limited to those of two social classes: either the Protestant Ascendancy or the poor and peasantry sections of the populace.[498] As to historians, it is evident that they placed more emphasis on revolutionary events and did not consequently explore much of the life of the emerging Catholic middle class. It could therefore be contended that O'Brien, unlike other writers and historians of her generation or in the recent past, contributed to depicting an ignored element in the written portrayal of Irish life: "The Irish Literary Revival might never have happened as far as the nuns and girls of *Sainte Famille* are concerned," as one critic commented on the novel.[499]

The significance of *The Land of Spices*, in addition to being an historical presentation of a sector of the middle-class community largely neglected by historians, lies in the author's critical observations on the politics of early twentieth-century Ireland.

---

[497] Kate O'Brien, *Land* 15.

[498] These include the Banim brothers, William Carleton, Lady Morgan, W.B. Yeats, Lady Gregory, and J.M. Synge. The Banim brothers and William Carleton focused on the endurance of the Catholic peasantry; Lady Morgan produced romances of historical figures; W.B. Yeats and Lady Gregory as revivalists in the twentieth century were keen to rewrite mythic and fairy tales; Synge dealt with the comedies and tragedies of peasants in the west of Ireland.

[499] Breen 183.

The novel might be read as political, as the English protagonist, the Reverend Mother, engages in several confrontations with Irish clerics. Their conversations demonstrate the impending (anti-)colonial crisis outside the school, even though the Reverend Mother does not appear to represent any ready or identifiable political ideology (her institute is French in its essence, and she does not speak in favour of the English at any point in the novel). Some might argue that she represents a hard-line traditionalist standpoint in pedagogical matters, in that she disagrees with the appeal of Irish nationalists for an improved, de-Anglicised Ireland. However, in my opinion, her disagreement has little to do with colonial causes and is more likely the result of her perception of a mixture of prejudices towards social minorities within the context of the nationalistic discourse. This point is illustrated in the Reverend Mother's irritation when visiting clerics belittle nuns as mere "trainers" of Irish girls for uxorial purposes. Such disparaging remarks might have been based on reality, as the author was indirectly exposed to a similar accusation during her schooldays at Laurel Hill. In her memoir, "Memories of a Catholic Education," she mentions that the school was accused by the *The Leader*, a nationalistic weekly in Dublin, for "educating Irish girls to be [. . .] wives for bank managers and British colonial governors."[500] O'Brien, however, assumed that its Superior "might have winced about the bank managers, as they would have been a very low social target."[501] My intention in specifying the episode was to suggest that the discourse of Irish Nationalism might have indicated to the fictional and the real Reverend Mother that Irish women's education was derogated by fundamentalist politicians who assumed that because of it girls would lean towards materialism as the wives of bank managers and betrayers of Irish nationalism. These irrational charges against the non-nationalistic education at *Sainte Famille* seems to suggest to the Reverend Mother that there is little difference between Irish nationalists and English colonisers, as both have little respect for others, including those with dissenting views on education. The Reverend Mother, taking a rather detached stance about local politics, consequently comments that Irish nationalism is an inconsistent discourse exhibiting the cultural weaknesses of both England and Ireland: "How odd were these Irish, who believed themselves implacably at war in the spirit with England, yet hugged as their own her dreariest daily habits."[502]

---

[500] Kate O'Brien, "Memories" 28.
[501] Kate O'Brien, "Memories" 28.
[502] Kate O'Brien, *Land* 54-55.

7. Kate O'Brien

It should be noted that the mixture of prejudices against women's education that the Reverend Mother detects is appreciable not only in Irish clerics' unfair remarks about the ultimate purpose of girls' education, but also in the middle-class community's patriarchal values, which is set against girls' intellectual development. As a woman who had been liberally educated before entering the religious life, the Superior displays a greater concern for girls' equal opportunities with boys with respect to university education. Her fight for Anna Murphy against her authoritarian grandmother, who strongly disapproves of Anna's entering a university, even with a scholarship, is a striking example of this in the novel. This struggle further underpins her views about female education being free of any agenda with a domestic or wifely end. Nevertheless, the general expectation of Irish girls, at the time of the Reverend Mother, was their "practical usefulness" after graduation.[503] They were confined to the choice of serviceable roles as wives or bank clerks, as Anna's pragmatic grandmother had pre-arranged for her granddaughter. In a word, higher education for girls was often conceived as a waste of money, an attitude not merely confined to the grandmother, but reflecting a general sentiment in a typical patriarchal society.[504]

Another unconventionality of the English Superior is that she is a highly self-conscious figure with her own individualistic views on current affairs, compared to those religious sisters and brothers who mostly take a ready-made side in Irish colonial politics in *The Land of Spices*. This self-awareness can be discerned from her insistence upon one's independent opinions, even under great pressure from Irish priests: "I was only speaking for myself."[505] More specifically, the issue she is personally addressing is the objective of Catholic education: "We [at *Sainte Famille*] educate our children in the Christian virtues and graces," whereas those visiting clerics appear less concerned about the values of "Christian discipline and common politeness" but more interested in educating Irish girls "nationally [. . .] to be the wives of Irishmen," as they claim explicitly.[506] Their leaning towards nationalistic education with patriarchal sentiments greatly irritates her, which leads her to remark openly that "I can only say I'm glad I shall not see very much of [your ideas]."[507] It could be argued that her stress on the pronoun "I," even amid antagonistic political discourses,

---

[503] Kate O'Brien, *Land* 256.
[504] Kate O'Brien, *Land* 256.
[505] Kate O'Brien, *Land* 97.
[506] Kate O'Brien, *Land* 92-93.
[507] Kate O'Brien, *Land* 93.

reveals her efforts to maintain intellectual autonomy under ideological confrontations. Her self-awareness, in my observation, is an acquired characteristic rather than a naturally inherent trait. It is her homosexual father who provides the most liberal education during her childhood and adolescence: "she was free to read anything" and was taken on journeys "in pursuit of art and architecture and history" to Belgium, Holland, the Rhineland, Normandy, and Brittany.[508] They enjoy a close father/daughter companionship until she accidentally discovers her father's homosexual affair with a former student.

Although she abruptly abandons her father "with a merciless heart," entering religious life as a way, she thinks, of punishing him for being a sinner who "fell into some offence against society, some stupid sin," the influence of the liberal education she received proves to be unerasable.[509] This influence deepens in the convent along with the solidification of her theological knowledge, as well as a growing affection for one of her pupils, Anna Murphy. She realises that her arrogance with its moralistic biases displayed towards her loving father might constitute a greater religious sin than his being a homosexual. Nevertheless, only when she knows that her father is dying on a lonely bed does she realise how she wrongly sat in moral judgment over his sexual orientation. More specifically, she still "held him to be a sinner" with "no casuistry," "but [. . .] saw her own sin of arrogant judgment as the greater."[510] His death leads her to repent that her hostility towards her homosexual father was, theologically speaking, "not merely against God but against His Creature."[511] The sexuality of her father is therefore no longer a despicable sin in her eyes, but rather contributes to God's "Land of Spices" mentioned in a sonnet which comes to her mind almost at the end of the novel.[512] With regret for her own sin, Reverend Mother implores her beloved Anna, before she sets off for university studies in Dublin, to "be the judge of your own soul; but never for a second, I implore you, set up as judge of

---

[508] Kate O'Brien, *Land* 147.

[509] Kate O'Brien, *Land of* 144 and 160. The "sin" here refers, in the eyes of young Helen Archer, to her father's homosexuality and infidelity, with her later understanding, as a mature woman, of why her father chose to live abroad as an exile.

[510] Kate O'Brien, *Land* 160.

[511] Kate O'Brien, *Land* 160.

[512] "The Land of Spices" is from a sonnet written by George Herbert (1593–1633). The stanza from which the phrase was taken is: "Church-bells beyond the stars heard, the soul's blood / The land of spices; something understood."

another. Commentator, annotator, if you like, but never judge."[513] Her plea arises from her concern for the unknown, perhaps difficult, circumstances that Anna is going to encounter. She is genuinely remorseful for having been merciless to her own father, whose love for her was genuine and who, though he sinned against Christian morality for being an homosexual, insisted on giving her the most liberal education, which was to prove helpful to her in cultivating a non-materialistic vision of human issues.

It could be maintained that Reverend Mother's sentiments towards her father, which metamorphose from negation to acceptance, and her subsequent confrontation with local nationalistic priests, hint at real experiences in this area, as it is common for people to behave irrationally when confronted with (sexual or political) heterodoxy, a position that is invariably due to ignorance. That her father was discharged from his Cambridge teaching post owing to his sexuality is an example of such human irrationalism. However, in the Reverend Mother's theological understanding, not irrationalism is the most knotty human issue, but the lack of love and respect for God's other creatures. Some people are therefore wrongly labelled as sinners, traitors, or pagans. In her view, this classification does not conform to God's teaching and suggests the refusal of private judgment. History has demonstrated that, under some circumstances, people are apt to throw stones, perhaps illogically, at those who appear to be morally transgressive. It might therefore be justifiable to say that *The Land of Spices* is more than a novel concerning sexual deviance or political stance; rather it testifies to a more complex human condition. Earlier, I mentioned the split within the Irish Nationalistic Party and other social consequences due to the fall of Parnell; although these issues are not specifically addressed in the novel, they arose largely from the same irrationalism which O'Brien observed as a shared feature of any society. This irrationalism is often the cause of conflicts, from the personal and social to the international level.

7.2. *Mary Lavelle* (1936): Forbidden Desires versus Catholic Teaching

The issue surrounding the deprivation of one's intellectual autonomy is an important theme in many of O'Brien's novels. The author explores the causes and effects of the loss of one's independent conscience in *Mary Lavelle*, in which the Irish protagonist goes through a great deal of struggle to free herself from the bondage of religious and

---

[513] Kate O'Brien, *Land* 284.

moral ideologies and formulate her own private judgment with regard to love. In the novel, the author again tackles a fundamental Christian taboo, namely homosexuality and extramarital love, in order to testify how people are excessively dominated by the influence of fundamentalist religious teaching and ignore the importance of relying on their private conscience.

Mary Lavelle is set in 1922, the year in which the Irish Free State is established after decades of sometimes bloody, anti-colonial campaigns against England. However, this political triumph, at least in the view of traditional Irish historians, rarely enters the narrative of the novel. Instead, the rarely-depicted life of a group of unmarried Irishwomen who, mostly for financial reasons, leave for Spain to become governesses is extensively and realistically depicted. The dramatic events in Ireland do not affect their lives at all, while some of them ware able to enjoy a more liberal lifestyle. The author's choice of date is significant not only because of the alternative picture of the year 1922 that the author provides about the life of Irishwomen in exile, but also because of her perception as a female writer that nationalistic events might be over-emphasised. More importantly, she herself is living in Bilbao, Spain, like one of these governesses, in that very same year of 1922. Although *Mary Lavelle* is not necessarily her own story, it could be implied that O'Brien attempted to construct, or retell, the history of Irish women emigrants who, like many of these governesses, never returned to Ireland. It could be argued that this novel, published in 1936, was one of the earliest works by an Irish writer to deal with the neglected community of Irishwomen in Spain.

The novel's protagonist, Mary Lavelle, is a young Irish lady who has been engaged to a gentleman in her hometown of Mellick, before setting off for Altorno, Spain, to become a governess. Unlike most other Irish governesses who are compelled to work abroad for financial reasons, Lavelle simply wants to experience living overseas for a year before getting married. Nonetheless, this year marks a turning-point in her life, as she is able to observe the insularity in Irish culture from both geographical and moral perspectives; she develops a personal knowledge of love by experiencing religiously forbidden love with both genders. This year overseas awakenes her dormant conscience, while it is also an emotionally turbulent year for people who fell in love with Mary.

In particular, two important characters romantically entangled with Mary in Spain, Juanito Areavaga and Agatha Conlon, are also mentally plagued by what, according to their Catholic upbringing, are sins. Juanito, a married Catholic Spaniard, the son of

7. Kate O'Brien

the family Mary worked for, and "a Spanish [renowned] patriot and 'one of Spain's great men'," though truly in love with Mary, runs the risk of ruining his promising political career if their love affair is ever found out.[514] Agatha, a lesbian governess, admiring Mary more than affectionately, is tormented by the unspeakable desire of her unorthodox sexuality. She chooses to keep her distance from other Irish governesses to avoid being questioned or gossiped about in matters concerning her romantic life.

The passion between Mary and Juanito develops from their first glimpse of each other at the Areavaha's, and before too long they develop an intimate relationship which could be regarded as adulterous from a religious point of view; Mary has a fiancé and Juanito a wife. Before their affair is discovered by a local priest, they experience scruples from their own Catholic consciences. They both know their relationship could be construed as disgraceful, while their strong feeling of attachment is undeniably genuine. The tortured relationship enables Mary to have some sympathy for Agatha, who confesses to feeling forbidden, lesbian desires towards her. Although Mary does not return Agatha's passion, her "sin" about being Juanito's mistress makes her conceive that "everything [could be] a sin" for the Catholic Church. She not only comfortes Agatha by saying that lesbian desire isn't "rot" but in friendship "reache[s] for Agatha's hand" – several times during their conversation.[515] She remarks compassionately to Agatha: "You take one kind of impossible fancy, I take another."[516] For her, lesbian love is no longer a sinful desire, but rather a human feeling as much as the love she experienced for Juanito.

The sympathetic portrayal of the troubled emotions experienced by the three characters might suggest possible weaknesses in Catholic moral teachings, although the depiction of forbidden desires does not necessarily imply that the author is an anti-Catholic or anti-moralist. It is likely that by introducing moral conflicts the author might be generating a reconsideration of traditional Catholic dogmatism. The fallen characters in some way or other still justify Catholic moralism, while their experiences reactivate a private conscience in examining what had hitherto been taken for granted. They consequently form a more sympathetic understanding of religious doctrine.

---

[514] Kate O'Brien, *Mary Lavelle* 254.
[515] Kate O'Brien, *Mary Lavelle* 285, 297.
[516] Kate O'Brien, *Mary Lavelle* 297.

An example of this is Juanito and Mary's love affair. Although they could be accused of an adulterous romance by fundamental moralists, Juanito still acknowledges that "the only possible spiritual rule of thumb is the Christian, the Catholic."[517] His high regard for Catholic teachings does not stem from guilt provoked by the extramarital affair, but rather from his realisation that "every single human situation differs from every other."[518] It is hence inappropriate to apply one moralistic principle to all human situations. To put his comprehension of the nature of love into practice, he resolves to promote the legalisation of divorce in Spain, once he becomes the Premier in the future: "there is no such thing as legislation for happiness," he remarks.[519] As for political issues, his awakened, private conscience leads him to see himself as an upholder of Communism "very different from Lenin's," in that "the spiritual basis of life must be left alone," so as to maintain the substantial values of life.[520] Therefore, it could be maintained that, through the character of Juanito, the author presents a moral character who, on the one hand, respects Catholic values, but at the same time makes moral judgments with compassion. As for homosexuality as a sin, Agatha's being able to comment on fundamental Catholic teachings with the remark that "hard cases make bad law" is presumably the result of the bitter struggle between her inner self and her religious upbringing in Ireland.[521] Although constantly aware of the religious negation of her sexuality, her private judgment has led her to distinguish between internal, precious emotions, and external moral theology. Abiding by her awakened private conscience, she chooses not to return to Ireland, where the religious ethos concerning sexuality is dogmatic. She prefers to settle in Spain in old age, jesting that she will not regret becoming "the sort of muttering hag children throw stones at."[522] What is ironic is that only by being exiled from Ireland can she maintain her most independent conscience and individuality.

A more thorough exploration of lesbianism with regard to Catholic teachings can be found in *As Music and Splendour* (1958), in which the author explicitly elaborates the way in which patriarchal and moral sentiments discriminate against homosexual desire as an expression of human sentiment. The author also proposes an al-

---

[517] Kate O'Brien, *Mary Lavelle* 260.
[518] Kate O'Brien, *Mary Lavelle* 260.
[519] Kate O'Brien, *Mary Lavelle* 260.
[520] Kate O'Brien, *Mary Lavelle* 260.
[521] Kate O'Brien, *Mary Lavelle* 298.
[522] Kate O'Brien, *Mary Lavelle* 297.

ternative perspective which provides a theological apologia for lesbianism. These issues will be considered in the following section in order to examine how traditional Catholic moralism, in O'Brien's view, is inconsistent with the diversity of human emotions and experiences.

7.3. *As Music and Splendour* (1958): Leading towards Lesbian Liberation

Although homosexuality is a recurring theme in O'Brien's novels, *The Land of Spices* and *Mary Lavelle* only demonstrate O'Brien's early attempts to explore this prohibited moral issue. Homosexual desire is not developed further than a subplot in both novels, whereas her last novel, *As Music and Splendour* (1958), presents a more sophisticated exploration. Somewhat surprisingly, this novel is largely ignored by lesbian critics, since, according to Emma Donoghue, such critics "know of no context of 'Irish lesbian fiction' in which to place [the author]"; it therefore "fall[s] down the gaps between traditions."[523] The novel, however, is "the climax of all her novels," displaying lesbians' "sexual self-determination."[524] I would argue that O'Brien makes greater efforts in this last novel to depict all facets of human romance through lesbian and heterosexual figures, without making any moral judgment.

The work is set in the late nineteenth century, at the time of the Land War (1879–1882) in Ireland. The mention of the Land War is very brief in the novel – no more than one sentence – but is significant enough to suggest an important historic moment that the Irish heroine's hometown is experiencing.[525] As in *Mary Lavelle*, the author once again refers to historical events only in passing, focusing instead on two Irish girls who are sent to Italy and France in order to learn professional singing. It could be suggested that the author intends to draw her readers' attention to the ignored experiences of overseas Irish women, as their financial contribution to Ireland is the least discussed or recorded topic by historians. Many contemporary Irishmen and women, for one reason or other, laboured overseas in the hope of sending money home. The two Irish heroines, Clare Halvey and Rose Lennance, are no exception to this widespread phenomenon, belonging to neglected and peripheral communities in written Irish historiography.

---

[523] Donoghue 37.
[524] Donoghue 39.
[525] Kate O'Brien, *As Music* 114. The brief mention of the Land War only appears on this page, when Irish characters allude to it during a toast in the context of a dinner party.

Clare and Rose are two of the Irish girls sent to Europe at a very young age because of their promising voices. They are trained by vocal coaches in Italy for a few years, then begin careers as professional opera singers touring around Europe. However, this profession causes unhappiness. They are financially deprived by their agents and suffer from the pain of unstable loving relationships. Although they seem to have access to echelons of upper-class society, the singers can not decide at will where and when to work. They have to follow the agents' touring arrangements to play assigned roles on stage over and over again and sing the same songs which might be contrary to their frames of mind. To some extent, their exile has the same cause as that of the Irish overseas manual workers, because they labour primarily for money and are subject to agents. However, as the number of these Irish singers was limited, and they could not freely express their emotions but only entertain well-to-do audiences, the exile they experienced was too easily overlooked by historians.

Life behind the scenes for these touring Irish singers was tough in many respects, not least financially, as they had to pay back the high tuition fees needed to train them for the stage. They might have earned some money but it was handled by agents who passed much of it to the singers' former teachers, families, and home communities which had financed their overseas training. Under contracts with agents, they were not at liberty to decline any performances, even when under the weather. They had to rely on the patronage of the upper-class, but could hardly earn enough to afford visits to their homeland. These singers were destined to entertain others, but did not find any satisfaction in their own lives.

As touring singers, their lifestyle was very different from the parochial one at home. Moreover, being far away from puritanical Ireland, they were less bound to the dogmatic teachings of the Church and had encountered a highly artistic and bohemian lifestyle. They had opportunities to explore various human experiences, not least of which were romantic encounters with people with different sexual orientations. Nonetheless, the author does not detail their sensual life but rather examines the nature of love from theological and philosophical perspectives. Characters involved in their successes and failures in love were subject to private judgments, illustrating that conventional Catholic teachings were no longer able to explain the consequences of (aberrant) love.

It could be argued that, as well as to depict the largely ignored life of Irish women as touring singers, the novel's aim is to demonstrate weaknesses in the Church's traditional moral teachings, and to stimulate greater debate on non-heterosexual love.

7. Kate O'Brien

Such relationships are presented, to differing degrees, as varying from individual to individual, and the people affected are portrayed as being in need of religious support and friendship. The author daringly presents courtships between students and teachers, sex before marriage, romance between a former priest and a singer, and lesbian love, while she avoids passing any moral judgment. The love affairs between these bohemian characters conflictes with Catholic morality, but they realistic situations that many people might directly or indirectly encounter. While these lovers are presented as violators of existing religious norms, they are not posited as aggressively non-conformist in religion. In particular, with individual reinterpretations of Catholic doctrines based on personal experience, some characters develop an awareness of the limits and potentiality of love, and therefore broaden their perception outside the dogmatic sphere.

The character of Clare illustrates this. She is a lesbian Irish singer brought up as a Catholic who falls in love with Luisa Carriage after they first meet in the residence of their Italian coach. Although Luisa's turning her affections to her heterosexual agent saddens Clare, she comes to realise that love does not mean owning someone as a property, nor for use as a weapon against a betrayer. Love is rather to be used to free oneself from resentment or jealousy. She applies this interpretation of love to those around her who, in one form or another, cannot conform to religious teachings on prohibited love. She figures that, in terms of Catholic doctrine, everyone is born as a sinner, no matter what their sexual orientation is. She confronts Thomas Evans, one of her male, heterosexual admirers who despise lesbianism, by saying: "You can argue as you like against my loving Luisa. But I can argue back all your unbridled sins. We all know the Christian rule – and every indulgence of the flesh which does not conform to it is wrong. All right. We are all sinners. You and I and Rose and Antonio and Rene and Mariana – and all our friends."[526]

In her view, who is or is not a sinner is for God to decide. What mortals should concern themselves with is whether people behave in an honest manner towards themselves and their loved ones. Thomas, who has a disreputable history of dealings with women, hence appears to Clare as a person in need of reform. She knows that her being lesbian is a personal choice, not one due to loneliness, otherwise "nothing would be easier on this earth than to kiss you, dear Thomas."[527] Compared to her be-

---

[526] Kate O'Brien, *As Music* 208.
[527] Kate O'Brien, *As Music* 210.

ing unable to choose a career, her choice of coming to terms with her lesbianism is an act faithful to her own conscience rather than a rebellion against Catholic teachings. Faced with Thomas' insulting remark on her "unnatural, appalling" behaviour, she counteracts him firmly with reference to an individual understanding of the Catholic rule:[528] "I am a sinner in the argument of my Church. But so would I be if I were your lover. [. . .] I know perfectly well what [I'm] doing. [I am] so well instructed that [I] can decide for [myself]. There's no vagueness in Catholic instruction."[529]

Apparently, Clare is judging her own conduct according to what she understands of Catholic instruction, instead of acting as a moral judge like Thomas, who unsympathetically accuses Louisa of being "promiscuous [. . .] and a whore."[530] That is to say, after several years of travelling abroad on the European mainland with experiences of ups and downs in relationships, she has learnt that Catholic teachings should not be justified as moral weapons against "sinners" but should form the foundation on which one decides for oneself, rather than forming opinions about others. What contributes to Clare's liberal understanding of Catholic teaching, leaving aside her years of observation of the bohemian life in metropolitan cities, is the freedom given by her former coach, Mère Marie Brunel, during her early study at an Irish convent school. The reason why Mère Marie Brunel would not be strict with Clare and Rose is because she knows it is the way to "keep up [singers'] morale more efficiently than too much discipline would have done."[531] On the other hand, as she was a touring singer herself and foresaw that Clare and Rose would inevitably encounter turbulent love affairs after leaving puritanical Ireland, she intentionally prepares the ground for them to cultivate a private conscience even though they are still underage. In other words, Mère Marie Brunel clearly knows that an independent conscience – not necessarily against Catholic principles but conforming to individual circumstances – will be the way in which her pupils master their lives behind the stage.[532]

It could be contended that Clare's individual interpretation of Catholic instruction implies the intention of being a non-conformist Catholic. Nonetheless, having been brought up as a Catholic means that she unavoidably went through a process of struggle before she could lay claim to her own views against Catholic conventional-

---

[528] Kate O'Brien, *As Music* 211.
[529] Kate O'Brien, *As Music* 207.
[530] Kate O'Brien, *As Music* 211.
[531] Kate O'Brien, *As Music* 33.
[532] Kate O'Brien, *As Music* 33.

7. Kate O'Brien

ism. In an argument with Louisa about confession, she articulates her views on spiritual absolution: "I'd find it hard – if I ran into serious moral conflict – I'd find it hard to decide that I was right and the Eternal Church wrong!."[533] However, as she repeatedly emphasises her self ("I") in her statement, it could be contended that her inner being is emerging with questions concerning the teachings of the Eternal Church, so that she refuses to be a "slave of the Penny Catechism."[534] It could therefore be assumed that her Catholicism means more than an external, formalistic concept and has become intellectualised. She does not come to a negative judgment on the value of Catholic codes due to her unorthodox sexual orientation, but defends it generously as follows: "I'm not a fervent believer, I never was, even as a small child. But Confession and all the rest – it's a discipline. I suppose that I have in spite of myself what Grandmother calls 'The Faith.' If I have, I'm glad. I imagine I'd be lonely without it."[535] The irony, however, is that the Irish Catholic Church apparently fails to accommodate Clare's lesbianism with the same generosity

Clare's finding an independent conscience is largely due to the benefit of her years of exile to the European mainland, while her fellow Irishmen and women at home, particularly those in Ballykerin, are not as fortunate as her in developing a personal concept of religion. The teaching and practice of the catechism remains an important part of the everyday life of people in Ballykerin. The marked contrast in religious perceptions is manifested when Clare is finally able to make her first home visit, after touring overseas for more than a decade. For several years she longed to come home, but is disillusioned by the primitive life there. She finds herself unable to adapt to this and has to continue her exile in Europe:[536] "Clare spent a lonely summer, cold and lonely, in Ballykerin. She was shocked at how difficult she found the primitive life of her own people, and it saddened her to realise that, *prima donna* or not, she could not ever live now the simple, clean, courageous and uncomforted life."[537]

What leads Clare to find the life in Ballykerin "primitive" seems not to be the absence of cultural diversities in her hometown – of which she was aware before leaving it – but the "simple, clean, courageous and uncomforted life." It is the kind of life which came to be the preference of the Irish Catholic Church, but prevented its disci-

---

[533] Kate O'Brien, *As Music* 144.
[534] Kate O'Brien, *As Music* 144.
[535] Kate O'Brien, *As Music* 144.
[536] Kate O'Brien, *As Music* 343.
[537] Kate O'Brien, *As Music* 343.

ples from being discerning about its teachings; nor could they recognise why a simple life might be "uncomforted," or unpleasant, to one's soul. Clare's disappointment in her hometown therefore reveals the author's awareness of the cultural gap between Ireland and the European Continent. Although Clare's comments on the aridity of Irish cultural life might sound condescending to some local ears, the contrast she depicts between the highly exquisite life she came across on the European mainland and the rather simplistic one in Ballykerin is honest. The latter life, though seemingly untroubled and serene, keeps Irish people from being critical and makes them complacent about the insipidity of Irish life. In other words, the lack of stimulation from other cultures has, in Clare's observation, resulted in "[a] tendency of my race [. . .] to become nuns and priests."[538] The Irish culture is not significantly variegated but remains "primitive" and too self-content.

As Music and Splendour is a work that portrays the neglected lives and voices of Irish women living overseas in the late nineteenth century. It is also a novel that demonstrates the cultural parochialism which undermines independent conscience and relies overmuch on the Christian guidelines. The work was published in 1958, and mirrors the conservative ethos that prevailed at that time, as Irish literary censorship had been rigorously enacted for several decades. The enactment of censorship, as is seen in the works of many of O'Brien's contemporaries, evidently reinforced the consequences of cultural tribalism. This novel might have been written as a reminder of the cultural incoherence between Ireland and other European countries. It also provided a liberal perspective on homosexuality – proposed by a Catholic heroine – which might be provocative to traditional moralists but relevant to awakening the concept of a dormant, private conscience.

7.4. *Pray for the Wanderer* (1938): An Irish Artist's Protest

To underpin my reading of O'Brien's concern for the cultural insularity and other consequences of Irish censorship, it is useful to refer to one of her highly controversial novels, *Pray for the Wanderer* (1938). In this work, O'Brien demonstrates how Ireland was a parochial state under the dominant rule of the Catholic Church at the time. The novel was published only five months after *Mary Lavelle* was banned by the Irish Censorship Board in 1937. As with O'Brien's other novels, the protagonist, Matt Costello, is an Irish exile, returning to Ireland as a writer with critical views on

---

[538] Kate O'Brien, *As Music* 210.

7. Kate O'Brien

the cultural destitution of the land of his birth. He is known as "Mellick's returned celebrity," but his works have been banned within the Free State.[539]

Through Matt Costello's outspoken criticisms of the cultural weaknesses of Ireland, the author provides a vivid picture of how the nation has culturally drifted away from the highly cultivated western European countries where artists are more respected. Matt's attitude upsets local clerics as well as his conservative family and more than likely reflects O'Brien's own experience as a banned writer in Ireland. Matt knows that the questions he asks of locals will not soften the antagonism that the Church displays towards him as a writer with unorthodox views, yet he still chooses to unreservedly vent his frustration and anger, so as to trigger a rethinking of Irish literary policy.

The novel begins with Matt Costello's arrival in Mellick. His arrival is not welcomed by the local clergy, as his works are manifestly not in line with fundamental Catholic values. Father Malachi, who represents the local church and community, accordingly calls upon him and his family several times to express his concern, because members of his congregation assume the writer will promote "neo-paganism [. . .] to us here in Ireland."[540] His conversation with Matt is rarely friendly and often hostile, and is always delivered with a measure of cynicism about his ambition to be a writer. On one of his visits to Matt, for example, he confronts Matt about his purpose for the return visit with a degree of innuendo: "[h]ave you come back, like Saint Patrick, 'to dwell amongst us'?"[541] His comparison between Matt and Saint Patrick is not likely to be intended as a compliment and implies that the writer is meant a counterattack on Saint Patrick. His visit, as a representative of the local church, suggests that clerics are acting as moral guardians of their parishes. Matt's presence in Mellick, as a banned writer returning from England is therefore conceived as a danger to Mellick, which is permeated with a puritanical ethos.

On some occasions, Father Malachi and Matt argue about different approaches to literature. Father Malachi, as a fervent and patriotic Catholic, believes that literature should only be read if one agrees with the writer's denominational background and political stance. As Matt's works are alleged not to conform to Irish Catholic values, Father Malachi assumes that Matt is writing in agreement with Protestant causes and interests: "[you] invent[ed] a sentimental sort of Protestant conscience to take the

---

[539] Kate O'Brien, *Pray* 118.
[540] Kate O'Brien, *Pray* 118.
[541] Kate O'Brien, *Pray* 118.

place of the orthodox one he was given at baptism."[542] His approach to literature is obviously based upon dichotomous biases from which only works with a moralistic, pure, and patriotic nature can be endorsed by the Church; those deemed to contain impure, immoral, or traitorous elements consequently have to be banned.

It is striking that the community Father Malachi represents is hostile not only towards Matt Costello but also to his family and friends: they are "getting [themselves] talked about in the town in connection with this Costello fellow!"[543] The hostility almost verges on the irrational: "[Matt should] count himself lucky that his return wasn't celebrated by a public demonstration and the public burning of all available copies of his works in front of the Father Mathew Memorial!"[544] These unfriendly remarks suggest that there is an ongoing conflict between conservatism and individualism, Puritanism and artistic freedom. Father Malachi's visits to Matt personify a community's intervention in the presentation of the arts, while Matt strongly believes that "politics are death to the creative artists" and refuses to be subject to any political discipline.[545]

Although Matt is frustrated by the hostility that he is shown at home, he does not moderate his critique of the cultural dreariness of Ireland. On the contrary, he unrelentingly points out that Irish life has been, under the domination of the Church, not only artless but also culturally backward by European standards; Piccaso, he notices, is still unknown to locals in Mellick.[546] Frustrated at being banned in Ireland and angry about the country's cultural position, he attributes Irishmen's ignorance to the Church whose "dominance has never sat naturally and humanly on us."[547] As a result, "[Irish people] don't understand painting, good, bad or indifferent. No sculptors, and none coming. Absolutely no composers of music."[548] He is particularly concerned about the consequences of censorship which deny Irish people access to the diversity of cultures to be found outside of Ireland. In the presence of Father Malachi, he scathingly observes that

---

[542] Kate O'Brien, *Pray* 124.
[543] Kate O'Brien, *Pray* 168.
[544] Kate O'Brien, *Pray* 168.
[545] Kate O'Brien, *Pray* 119.
[546] Kate O'Brien, *Pray* 46.
[547] Kate O'Brien, *Pray* 46.
[548] Kate O'Brien, *Pray* 46.

7. Kate O'Brien

[censorship] is a confession of failure. It is a denial of human judgment and understanding, and a gross intrusion on liberty. [. . .] Too many negative regulations are a symptom of weakness in any authority. [. . .] I'm not prepared to be saved on Ireland's dictated terms.[549]

The mention of "Ireland's dictated terms" suggests a cultural and moralistic dictatorship through which the Church decides how the Irish should behave. These terms have far-reaching effects on the psyche of Irish people, as the Catholic Church, which was granted a special position in the 1937 Constitution – before the novel came out – morally and lawfully circumscribes the perception of Irishmen. O'Brien illustrates this morbid climate through portrayals of family members of Weir House, who host Matt in Mellick. The head of Weir House is Matt's married brother, Will Costello, who is a devout Catholic farmer; a "family man [. . .] save[d] [. . .] under the mysterious imperative of the religious life."[550] His wife, Una, is expecting their sixth child, and has been confined to home since the time of their marriage. Their family appears to conform to the stereotype promoted by the Irish Catholic Church and the state, while Matt regrets that it is only a consequence of Catholic propaganda.[551]

In Matt's observation, a family man like his brother is so parochial that he is unable to "see, even to grasp at [. . .] even to combat [. . .] the Western world"; he cannot not realise that "life might fruitfully be a lonely track or a jealously personal adventure," nor see "where the frightened world had got to."[552] What his brother knows best is the simple farm life and a religion that "circumvents [his] blood emotions" and produces "emotional aridity."[553] As for Una, the hostess with already five children, although amiable, she is no less conservative than her husband. She expects Matt not to prolong his stay at Weir House, as he could be "a downright bad influence" to children and "[turn] them into absolute little cadges" for gifts and

---

[549] Kate O'Brien, *Pray* 124.
[550] Kate O'Brien, *Pray* 6.
[551] Eamon de Valera, President of the Executive Council (prime minister) of the Irish Free State, granted a new Constitution in 1937. The Constitution recognised the "special position" of the Roman Catholic Church and the Family as the natural primary and fundamental unit group of Society. Will Costello's family apparently complies with the expectations of the Church and the State, in which Catholic doctrine is the moral guide to the Family as the foundation of the country.
[552] Kate O'Brien, Pray 6.
[553] Kate O'Brien, *Pray* 6 and 16.

children and "[turn] them into absolute little cadges" for gifts and pleasure.[554] She is afraid that if Matt extends his stay, her family will have difficulty in returning to the "normal farmhouse life" after his departure.[555] I would argue that Una's concerns and Father Malachi's constant visits imply a problematic mindset according to which people can only feel safe and content within the context of an unvarying life of this kind. The "normal" family life that Una prefers is one that discourages certain kinds of "pleasure-seeking" activities.[556] The problem with this mindset is, in Matt's eyes, openly enacted under "[De Valera's] tricky constitution" of 1937.[557] This "subtle, but dictatorial and obstinate" constitution over-emphasises the importance of the "family as social unit," and ignores alternative lifestyles.[558] A constitution based upon fundamental Catholic values is a threat to creativity in arts, and Matt wonders:

> Could [an artist] live in De Valera's Ireland, where the artistic conscience is ignored. [. . .] Could he live here because [. . .] here was a morality that scorned and banished hers and his, a pious, Christian island where noise and applause and passion [. . .] would never thrill the quiet? Could he live here, turning over a new leaf?[559]

Apart from Matt's unrelenting criticism of the morbidity of Irish life under the Church's discipline, another controversy caused by *Pray for the Wanderer* was the courtship of Louise Lafleur, an actress whose husband, Adam Wolfe, is sexually impotent. Matt daringly urges Louise to divorce Wolfe and marry him, for he has long adored Louise before leaving Ireland, seeing her as the muse who inspires his works. With Louisa, he relies on his instinct for love rather than on traditional moral values. He cannot understand how Louise can willingly stay married to Adam, whose love has been platonic rather than physical for some eight years. Matt's ideal of love is utterly different from Louise's and essentially romantic: "Love is an hour we give and take, a need we fulfil in each other, a mood, a release, a perception. [. . .] We do not *own* the instrument of [love] – we use and bless and love it."[560]

---

[554] Kate O'Brien, *Pray* 133.
[555] Kate O'Brien, *Pray* 133.
[556] Kate O'Brien, *Pray* 133.
[557] Kate O'Brien, *Pray* 30.
[558] Kate O'Brien, *Pray* 41.
[559] Kate O'Brien, *Pray* 98.
[560] Kate O'Brien, *Pray* 90.

7. Kate O'Brien

Nevertheless, what underpins this flowery definition of love is Matt's "delusion" about Louise. He loves her because of the charisma she produces on stage. He idolises her but does not recognise that she "[feeds her] fans their illusion" of "a bloody good actress."[561] In reality, she, as she describes herself, is no better than "an ordinary, good-natured, quiet woman" who is "ignorant" and "miserable."[562] She opts to remain married to Adam since they understand each other, a knowledge which goes beyond the momentary passion that Matt is seeking. She declines Matt's courtship, knowing that his love is mixed up with romantic delusions. As she directly points out to him: "You swept me up on your marvellous, fantastic admiration to be something better than myself. You simply forced me to be your dream, your Muse and your illusion."[563] Although Louisa's refusal to divorce Wolfe could be claimed as an ideal example matching Catholic expectations, she at least reacts more soberly and temperately than Matt in the matter of love. In other words, Matt's love is ardent, but it is of a sort that could jeopardise a relationship more severely than platonic love.

O'Brien's treatment of Matt's failure in love suggests that he is presented as a humane and vulnerable person. He is cynical, as a renowned writer, about the issues of Irish censorship and parochialism, while he has his blind spots about private matters such as relationships with women. He might be incisive about the aridity of Irish life under the rule of the Irish Church, but he still cannot distinguish faultlessly between delusion and reality when under the influence of romantic emotions. In other words, the author allows readers to discover the kind of person Matt is and his function within the novel. In my view, he is not a kind of tragic hero who insists on writing provocative but banned works. Instead, he is introduced as someone courageous enough to express his emotions and ideas. His courage is simply what most Irish people lack in response to the relentless censorship on artists at the time that O'Brien published the novel in 1938.

Pray for the Wanderer was not banned in Ireland, though it contains some explicit criticisms of government policies. This could be because, in the end, Matt chooses to continue his exile; Weir House remains an integrated "social unit" guided by Catholic principles, and Father Malachi's role as a moral guardian is not affected. Moreover, Matt's liberal, possibly dangerous, foreign ideas do not pollute puritanical Mellick.

---

[561] Kate O'Brien, *Pray* 91.
[562] Kate O'Brien, *Pray* 90.
[563] Kate O'Brien, *Pray* 90.

Irish censors thus did not bother to ban the novel, because it seemingly upheld the three Irish key values: family, faith, and farming.

However, the author was not completely innocent in her depiction of Irish conservatism. On the contrary, she examined puritanical Mellick through the eyes of both Matt and herself. Matt's flaws might derive from his romantic illusions regarding the external world. On the other hand, they also suggest a wider social crisis with respect to intellectual freedom and cultural refinement. In particular, artists who promoted liberalism were regarded as "myth-creating, anti-social, and unnecessary," and could only see people helplessly "[g]oing back alone into the places of doom and panic and despair."[564] Matt's frustration was, therefore, not only personal but also a national one in that Ireland was turning into a "smug, obstinate and pertinacious little island" under "the authority of [. . .] the 'sea-green incorruptible!'" Ironically, many writers possessing an "artistic conscience," like Matt, were compelled – whether directly or indirectly – to go into exile due to their heterodoxy against the prevailing influence of the Church. They were not blessed by their communities but feared, and had to opt for exile to maintain their individual conscience. O'Brien, as one of the banned Irish writers, might be regarded as sympathetic to the suffering of her exiled contemporaries, calling for a "prayer for these wanderer(s)." Matt's exile could consequently be read as a protest against those forces that disciplined Ireland with rigid dogma.

7.5. Kate O'Brien: A Cultural and Literary Critic ahead of Her Time

The early part of this chapter mentioned that O'Brien was prolific not only as a novelist but also as a literary and cultural critic, while recent research has placed more emphasis on her creative works. Her non-fictional writings, particularly those written for magazines, academic journals and newspapers, have not been sufficiently explored to date. In order to evaluate O'Brien's legacy, it is necessary to study her critical essays, for it is in these media that she elaborated her dissenting ideas more explicitly, particularly those on the insularity of Irish culture. These essays were written mostly during the period when she resided overseas, reviewing new fictional works or stage plays that she encountered abroad. At times she commented on contemporary political or religious issues. All in all, her newspaper and journal articles reveal that the writer endeavoured to introduce fresh perspectives to Irish readers.[565]

---

[564] Kate O'Brien, *Pray* 119 and 183.
[565] She often contributed articles to *Hibernia*, *Irish Digest*, and *University Review*, and she

7. Kate O'Brien

In her non-fictional works, it is evident that O'Brien was as critical about the religious life of Irish people as in her novels. She was particularly interested in reviewing religious concepts taken for granted by the Irish. In one critique for *Hibernia* magazine in 1965, for instance, she argued that St Patrick, who had been worshipped by the Irish for centuries, was more likely to have been an intellectual than a missionary. She suggested that his contribution did not only consist of the introduction of Christian culture, but also extended to bringing a new variety of knowledge to Ireland. He also instigated an active economic interaction between Ireland and other parts of Europe which involved immigration and emigration across the centuries.[566] However, Irish people during the twentieth century, perhaps under the influence of the prevailing dictates of the Irish Catholic Church, largely saw him as a religious patron of Ireland. She therefore proposed an alternative, perhaps even subversive, reading of St Patrick from a broader, cultural perspective. This interpretation, which follows, might appear iconoclastic to the ears of conformist Catholics, but she objectively examined how St Patrick culturally connected Ireland with other European areas:

> If Saint Patrick was a gentleman he was a foreign gentleman. [. . .] I think we feel much sympathy and fraternity towards most of his kind and kith in Europe. If there were for our better fortune, [. . .] two Saint Patricks entirely devoted within one century to the task of making us into Christians, gentlemen and European intellectuals, then all the more did they involve us with the sources of Christian culture, for it is certain that they were respectively a French and an Italian gentleman; and one of them appears to have been an intellectual, the other a mystic poet, and a man of imagination.[567]

---

was a regular columnist of *The Spectator* and *The Irish Times* for many years. In *The Spectator*, O'Brien maintained a column reviewing newly-published fiction from 1937 to 1956. She also contributed a column entitled "Long Distance" in *The Irish Times* from 1967 to 1971, during which period she resided in England and France, writing the articles from abroad.

[566] According to tradition, St Patrick came to Ireland in 432 A.D. At the time there had been ongoing immigration to Ireland from the lands that are now known as Scotland and England, as well as northern and southern Europe, including the Mediterranean and the Iberian peninsula.

[567] Kate O'Brien, "Irish Writers" 15. As there is still a lack of known detail of St Patrick's life, O'Brien's confident assertion that he was a "foreign gentleman" can hardly be proved or disproved. Nevertheless, O'Brien's reassessment of St Patrick's identity was

To O'Brien, the cultural, intellectual, and religious significance of St. Patrick's arrival in Ireland should be given an equal emphasis to its religious dimension. In other words, to evaluate St Patrick from only an Irish Catholic perspective would not comprehensively assess his significance to Irish history. He introduced not only the Christian faith but also the concept of a wider European culture, on top of the already existing pre-Christian culture whose Ogham inscriptions, the oldest form of Celtic Gaelic, still survive. This pioneering figure also skilfully "combine[d] Christian doctrine with native [Druid] legend," so that Irish Christianity could "c[o]me down through the centuries with a distinctive local flavour."[568] The religion he brought to Ireland was a "Latin brand of Christianity."[569] Nevertheless, the historical backdrop to his mission was largely ignored by both Roman Catholics and Protestants in Ireland, who tended to highlight St Patrick's miraculous acts, such as raising people from the dead and driving the snake population from Ireland. In O'Brien's opinion, the centuries old veneration of St Patrick did not contribute to the amelioration of the country's culture. She argued, in the rest of her article, that the narrow function of St Patrick as a religious icon suggests a "terrible loss" which turned Ireland "back into parochialism."[570] Ironically, O'Brien's opinion would have little impact on her contemporaries, as the dominant Irish Church and the Censorship Board had actually driven away many writers who "dwelled upon us," like St Patrick from Ireland, her metaphorical description of Matt in *Pray for the Wanderer*.

I believe that by drawing readers' attention to the controversy surrounding St Patrick, O'Brien encouraged the questioning of the iconic, singular use of this national saint for purely religious purposes, calling for closer attention to the European intellectualism that he represented. He was a successful missionary, while in terms of cultural archaeology he was an able Latin scholar well acquainted with druidical and Christian traditions and able to symbolise both. This had not, however, been adequately investigated at the time that O'Brien wrote this article.

---

likely to emphasise his cultural significance for Ireland, since he had long been regarded narrowly as a religious icon for both Irish Catholics and Protestants. The current view on St Patrick's identity is that he might have been a Romano-Briton born somewhere on the west coast of the British mainland. I am in Prof. Norman Vance's debt for this information.

[568] Blanshard 14.
[569] Blanshard 16.
[570] O'Brien, "Irish Writers" 15.

7. Kate O'Brien

Another role that O'Brien assumed, other than as a cultural commentator, was that of a literary critic who took a special interest in the issues relating to female writing. As an "unfashionable" Irish woman writer who knew there was "nothing I [could] do about [my unpopularity]," O'Brien was conscious of the existence of a strong male literary tradition that hindered female writers from being properly received.[571] She believed that one of the principal ways to enhance the visibility of women writers would be to reassess the traditional canon to reveal why they were rejected and how women could be more justly repositioned.

O'Brien's regard for the status of women writers in the canon can be seen from her essay "English Diaries and Journals," written in 1947, by which time she had published seven novels with themes of female predicaments in patriarchal environments.[572] This essay criticised male domination in the production of literary history, and examined how the majority of women were excluded from the mainstream literary forum due to the lack of a formal education and confined to the domestic sphere. But such difficulties did not mellow women to submit to the role of silent participants in social activities. Some Irishwomen still gave vent to their feelings and ideas by keeping a diary. With sympathy for her women predecessors who were not able to express themselves freely and creatively, O'Brien argued that their diaries should be treated seriously as documentation with historical and literary merit, because they recorded social observations from a female perspective. She firstly referred to the misconception that traditional critics held about women diarists: "the best English diaries have been written by bores. [. . .] A bore has been excellently defined as 'a person who mentions everything.'"[573] Here, "everything" holds a negative implication as to the unselective contents of female diaries, but O'Brien proposed a different approach, for "everything [could be] a light, a lamp, a gentle, accidental resurrector [. . .] for what had been cold and dead."[574] That is to say, what now appears to be "cold and dead" might well contain significant historical value, and picture an accu-

---

[571] Michael O'Toole 128.

[572] O'Brien's call for attention towards women's diary writing is quite pioneering. Before her, and even many decades after she wrote this article, women's diary writing was still not recognised for its literary and historical values. A more comprehensive collection of Irish women's diaries to date is the recent fourth and fifth volumes of the *Field Day Anthology of Irish Writing*.

[573] Kate O'Brien, "English Diaries" 195. This essay mainly deals with female diarists, although O'Brien does not specify that it is only women bores that keep diaries.

[574] Kate O'Brien, "English Diaries" 185.

rate glimpse of life within specific social contexts. Women's diaries might be written without the solid structure of novels or short stories, but nevertheless they could still tackle issues on both domestic and social levels. For such women, diary-keeping could represent a private channel through which to express their views, while testifying to their writing capabilities and creativity. After surveying a number of their writings, O'Brien firmly demonstrated that women diarists could be professional storywriters in the way they turned trivialities into coherent plots, if they were not denied a public career: "they very likely would not have been diarists if they could have been something more directly self-expressive. They are diarists *faute de mieux*, whether they knew it or not."[575]

That O'Brien paid attention to diary writing suggests two relevant issues with regard to canon formation of. Firstly, the denial of women diarists implies the negation of women's experiences in writing, particularly of those incidents directly documented by women themselves. Male writers might write sympathetically about feminine dilemmas, but are evidently not able to reflect in a convincing and genuine manner the way in which women understand these issues. The traditional canon, as a result, appeared to be questionable for not providing enough of women's own voices. Secondly, the constitution of the traditional canon became problematic under O'Brien's examination, for male writers were usually given credit for the majority of genres, while the diary was regarded as a form of *ennui* writing. The biases against women diarists, in O'Brien's opinion, related to a general depreciation of women which was not immediately remediable by simply accommodating the diary into the traditional literary canon. As a result, she contended that there should be a new approach to the study of diaries; an approach free of existing or conventional literary standards, as women diarists did not initially write for accomplished readers and critics. The merit of their writings came from their unprofessional but individualistic artistry: "A good diary is not necessarily literature; for of its nature it must be free of most of the disciplines and tests of a work of art."[576] In other words, women's diaries are not just a form of literary writing but rather works decipherable by sociologists, historians, psychologists, and feminists.

It should be appropriate to say that, ahead of her time, O'Brien viewed Irish culture as a social text for criticism. As a banned writer who lived overseas for years, she

---

[575] Kate O'Brien, "English Diaries" 226.
[576] Kate O'Brien, "English Diaries" 186.

7. Kate O'Brien

often targeted Irish conservatism in her articles. She usually examined cultural issues accompanied by literary examples, to suggest that the prevailing conservative discourse had unavoidably affected how Irish writers were perceived in their own country. Needless to say, the depreciation of women writers was one such consequence.

In a 1977 essay entitled "Imaginative Prose by the Irish 1820–1970," she reviewed a number of prose writers, particularly canonical but possibly over- or underestimated authors, arguing that patriarchal, hierarchical sentiments hindered proper re-evaluation of women writers. As she pointed out in this article, deep-seated reservations about the contribution of female writers lingered on from the colonial era to the Free State: "although we were free now to go to Mass and to confess our sins, we had a Hierarchy to reckon with, a great body of bishops rightly more sure of its authority over us than England or Westminster could ever be."[577] Irish people therefore remained submissive and unable to challenge the authorities in any effective manner. In the realm of literature, they were obliged to accept critics' conventional views but could not judge or question works as independent readers. She exemplified four Irish writers: James Joyce, Samuel Beckett, and Somerville and Ross, contending that they should be reviewed more appropriately by Irish critics and readers.

As for Joyce, the lack of fair discussion of his works in Ireland, she figured, was because there was "a kind of revolt against [his] greatness" in Ireland, even though he "ha[d] [. . .] strong and formative [influences] in Europe, but not markedly so in Irish letters."[578] The "revolt" was a result of Catholic moralism implanted in the psyche of the Irish, so that they could hardly face the Dublin that Joyce recreated "out of the deep shadows" with "a new and special kind of morality of imagination."[579] It could therefore be contended that many Irishmen, under the moral guidance of the dominant Catholic Church, had not been able to approach literature in a more sensible way and to accept critical views on Ireland.

Despite their gender, O'Brien did not sympathise much with Somerville and Ross, two Protestant Anglo-Irish women writers who produced "amusing witnesses to Irish life [. . .] which made us laugh."[580] Although she acknowledged that their *The Real Charlotte* was "one truly good novel," many of their short stories could not be "read

---

[577] Kate O'Brien, "Imaginative" 309. This article was published posthumously; O'Brien died in 1974.
[578] Kate O'Brien, "Imaginative" 313.
[579] Kate O'Brien, "Imaginative" 309.
[580] Kate O'Brien, "Imaginative" 313.

[. . .] with complete peace of conscience," in spite of the fact that they contained "irresistible fun." To her, Somerville and Ross "[wrote] from too far outside their [rural] subjects," which made her pictures of Irish life – of the colonised Irish at least – somewhat out of focus.[581] Although they might deserve a place in the Irish canon for "[having] an ear for our rural idioms," O'Brien stated that their approach to characters lacked the "professional detachment" of Flaubert and Mary Lavin.[582] Their works could hardly outshine those by Irish writers who wrote in line with "the savagery of Swift, the contempt of Joyce, the desolate queries of Samuel Beckett."[583]

Beckett was another author highlighted by O'Brien. She gave him particular credit for his courage in questioning the existence of God in *Waiting for Godot* and other works. The question he asked, in O'Brien's view, was simply but significantly whether there stands an authority (omnipotent or otherwise) to which we should morally and spiritually submit, and "who am I" if no such authority exists. To O'Brien, "[h]e is indeed a man of sorrow, acquainted with grief [but] not [a] total pessimist," because he opened an important theological debate for both Christians and non-Christians, while not providing any definitive answer.[584] Nevertheless, Beckett, like Joyce, was banned in Ireland. Irish people, under the control of the religious hierarchy, still had limited access to such liberal views, even after the political liberation of Ireland from her former coloniser.

This chapter has demonstrated that Kate O'Brien was an active figure intervening in the (re-)creation of modern Irish literature as a novelist and critic and presented views beyond the constrictions of her culture and time. However, her writing has not received much critical attention in Ireland. Until the 1980s she was almost absent from discussions or curricula on modern Irish literature; the study of her works still remains to be explored in a far-reaching and profound manner. Some critics conjec-

---

[581] Kate O'Brien, "Imaginative" 313.

[582] Kate O'Brien, "Imaginative" 313-14. In this article, although acknowledging that Somerville and Ross were "gifted" writers, O'Brien still regarded them as amateurs for often writing in a tone of "the from-above amusement of the jokey, look-how-clever-I-am writer" (313-14). This criticism of Somerville and Ross can be seen as radical in some sense, but it cannot be denied that the two writers wrote largely about and from the perspective of their own class, the gentry. Their portraits of Irish people are often comical, which has incurred criticisms of their potential reproduction of "stage Irishmen."

[583] Kate O'Brien, "Imaginative" 313.

[584] Kate O'Brien, "Imaginative" 315.

7. Kate O'Brien

ture that this neglect is because "the cult of [male Irish writers] was grotesquely overdeveloped" in the Free State, and "questions of national identity were regarded as the only serious critical question."[585] However, I would argue that the situation is more complex. The neglect of this author is a likely result of the lack of a suitable categorisation of particular features of her works. Her works disrupted conventionalism in Irish culture, but was not simplistically anti-Catholic. Such ignorance was possibly intentional, as traditionalists resented O'Brien's encouragement of her readership to practise their individual judgments against the influences of "the penny catechism."[586] Her undermining of the parochial image of St Patrick, in addition to her sympathetic portraits of lesbianism, also unsettled orthodox readers who thought highly of the moral function of literary works; her demonstration of the value of largely ignored women diarists may also represent a challenge to traditional literary critics. These causes all contributed to her neglect in Ireland.

In conclusion, I would contend that Kate O'Brien was an unconventional Catholic woman writer who applied her individual interpretation of Christian theology to disclose the tribalism of Catholic Ireland in the past. She also courageously tackled the issue of canon, one of the most complex issues in Irish cultural ideology, in order to redress the unfair perception of women writers. More importantly, her unfailing enthusiasm for dealing with religious, artistic and romantic topics in her novels suggests a genuine concern for an independent conscience. She might therefore well have agreed with Eavan Boland, a contemporary Irish poet and feminist critic, on the need for a critical attitude towards any existing, agreed understanding of society and literature as a way of refusing the disciplines of the dominant, patriarchal literary tradition: "It is an Irish fault that we are inclined to see our literary past as solid, as a monolith. [. . .] Napoleon said that history is an agreed lie; I certainly believe that literary tradition is an agreed fiction."[587]

---

[585] Meaney 79.
[586] Kate O'Brien, *As Music* 144.
[587] Boland 3.

Conclusion

By exploring the inclusions and exclusions in the Irish literary canon in the mid-twentieth century, as well as the various factors that underlay its formulation, this book sought to demonstrate that canons are not just a collection of literary works but the representation of a dominant culture. In post-Treaty Ireland, as the social ethos was largely dominated by nationalism and Catholicism, the making of Irish canons was unavoidably influenced by the two forces. To ensure that future generations and the public would properly be de-Anglicised and learn a "correct" sense of Catholic Irishness, some members of the Education Board, textbook editors and censors endeavoured to re-create a canon which conformed to the mainstream values of the time – under the supervision of the Catholic government. (The 1937 Constitution had legalised the special position of the Irish Catholic Church over most domestic issues.) Although these officials and social élites – as named above – had not necessarily met to discuss the making of an Irish canon, they collaborated to produce a national discourse by exemplifying literary works in line with the interests of Catholic nationalists. This book, by scrutinising the ways in which they influenced the public's perception of Irish literary canons, has attempted to demonstrate how political, religious and other relevant social forces were involved in canon formation. In general, these forces, though not all compatible with each other, mostly aimed to strengthen a nationalistic discourse exclusively for Southern Ireland. Put another way, how Irish canons were formulated could be seen as mirroring the making of Ireland as a nation. Education in particular – which this book has dwelt on in the first three chapters – demonstrated the ways in which English and Irish canons were systematically re-introduced, reinforced and/or deconstructed through different measures at various levels of post-Treaty schooling.

By observing how Irish canons were (re-)formulated during those decades in which the Irish nation gradually found its feet, this book has also demonstrated that the making of Irish canons could be subject to changes of social ethos, even though some were initially tinged with glamorous, patriotic sentiments. More specifically, what makes literary works "canonical" and worth teaching or reprinting year after year, is not always that they have inherent, "universal" merits, but that they directly or indirectly conform to the mainstream social values of the times. In the case of Ireland, the social values were at times under the surveillance of the political and religious bodies in power, and did not always remain unchallengeable. In *pre*-Treaty Ireland, for instance, Irish culture had been to a great extent Anglicised since 1830 through national education and other means. Although the purpose of English national education in Ireland was to "civilise" the next generation of Great Britain, it also aimed to turn Irish pupils into "happy English child[ren]" and educate/Anglicise them in a way that the English expected.[588] As English cultural influences had become so deeply rooted in Irish culture by the early twentieth century, the changes of political sovereignty – from Britain to Ireland – could not prompt Ireland to become (re-)Gaelicised as quickly as some Gaelic Leaguers wished. Chapter One has shown that educationists such as Patrick Pearse at his St Enda's school had to provide a bilingual education as well as run courses for Irish pupils who wished to sit for the Intermediate Examinations in English, at the request of parents.[589] Apart from this, the teaching of literature at Irish secondary schools, even during the 1920s to 1940s after Ireland had become a Free State, was not to be effectively de-Anglicised but, for one reason or another, placed Anglo-Irish literature in a subsidiary position to the traditional English canon. Although there was an increasing number of texts by Irish writers selected for inclusion in textbooks, the making of Irish canons, as Chapter Two demonstrates, would hardly be free from the inerasable English cultural influences that existed historically in Ireland.

Chapter Three, which observes how Irish canons were received and modified by university faculties in the 1930s, has delineated how Irish-centred historiography fitted into the curricula of higher education. As the Emerald Isle used to accommodate a mixture of cultural and denominational influences, the antagonism between faculty members (with different political aspirations) towards the making of an Irish canon was intense. The examination papers and syllabi to some extent formed the battlefield on which these academics propounded their various ideologies. This chapter has shown that, amongst other causes, the chairpersons' political leanings and educational backgrounds could influence the canons and what should be included and excluded in

---

[588] To turn every Irish pupil into a "happy English child" was first proposed by the Protestant Archbishop Richard Whately (1787-1863), one of the earliest Commissioners at the National Board of Education in Ireland. The Anglicising aim of English national education in Ireland has been discussed in Chapter One. Quoted in Lyons, *Culture* 9.

[589] It should be noted that although the Intermediate Examinations were conducted in English, this examination system did not take place in England but only in Ireland for Irish children. At the request of parents, St Enda's still needed to provide relevant courses in order for these children to compete with those from national schools, to secure a passport – an Intermediate Certificate – to proper jobs or further education.

Conclusion

syllabi. Nevertheless, any change in the canon – at the academic level – could be difficult, in that the universities, whether the Protestant-based TCD or the Catholic-orientated UCD, were often acting as the fortresses guarding the integrity of traditional values. The struggle towards making an Irish canon to be taught in university classrooms – of various humanities departments – also reflected how Irish society in the mid-twentieth century experienced the change from a state politically affiliated to the United Kingdom to an independent one. Notably, individual faculty members' attempts to make an Irish canon with themes and subjects different from those already in the English one had, to some extent, facilitated the de-Anglicisation of Ireland. That is, what graduates learnt about Irish literature and history had consequentially contributed to the making of an Irish identity at both the cultural and political levels. As these graduates would probably be the future dominant (upper-)middle classes and school teachers, the sense of Irishness with which they were nourished at the universities would produce significant influences on their families, friends, and colleagues.

Apart from the educational factors relevant to the emergence of Irish canons, this book has also explored various grounds on which Irish anthologists and creative writers presented their own favoured varieties of Irishness. The various kinds of Irishness they constructed through anthologies, or featured in their own creative writings, demonstrated that Irish canons could potentially be somewhat variegated. However, as the social ethos of the newly independent Free State was generally nationalistic, and the Irish Catholic Church was widely recognised as the moral guardian of the state, the making of Irish canons was expected to comply with the expectations of the Church and the nation. Chapter Four has elaborated that anthologists would, perhaps under the strong influences of the two unified bodies, privilege those works that either caricatured Englishmen or presented the "clean" country life of the west of Ireland with nostalgia. Some anthologists would even re-edit the works they selected – probably without the consent of the writers – in order to endorse the Gaelic Revival. It could therefore be observed that there were more political and social considerations, aside from aesthetic ones, to be taken into consideration in attempting to underpin a nationalistic canon. What is interesting is that, outside Ireland, British cultural imperialism was so powerful that Irish independence had little impact on the perception of the English canon overseas – at least in the first half of the twentieth century. Some anthologists in the US, for instance, were cautious about describing Irish-themed works (in English) as a separate element of the British canon. That a series of anthologies of English literature – published in Boston and New York in the

1930s – did not always specify the nationality of Irish-born writers might, on the one hand, suggest the difficulty of cultural decolonialism. On the other hand, it might have shown how editors, such as Edward O'Brien, intended to keep contemporary politics away from the editing of literary anthologies. Having compared anthologies compiled over a long span of time in Ireland and overseas, this chapter intended to elaborate on how people perceived Irish and English canons differently from one period to another. In other words, the canonicity of literary works would at times more easily be decided by colonial and decolonial sentiments than by aesthetic criteria.

The works of Mary Lavin and Kate O'Brien studied in Chapters Five and Six show how Irish women writers could be as critical of cultural insularism in mid-twentieth century Ireland as their male compeers. Nonetheless, the two writers' literary contributions did not seem to receive much attention before the 1970s. The lack of discussion of Lavin and O'Brien was due, on the one hand, to the patriarchal tradition in which male perspectives and interests were often given prominence. On the other hand, as the union of the Irish Catholic Church and the nationalistic government greatly dominated the social ethos of post-Treaty Ireland, literary works which called Catholic moral teaching and patriotic ideology into question could rarely be evaluated as canonical. As for Lavin, the fact that her works were not highly appreciated in Ireland was in part because some critics did not judge her writing techniques to be innovative enough, and she seemed to have held on tightly to middle-class values. Chapter Six, however, illustrated that these criticisms were not justified, as Lavin had in fact made good use of literary realism as well as her feminine sensitivity to reveal how Irish women of different classes were deprived of their individuality in a male-centred society. Notably, she had delineated carefully the ways in which these women survived – at times tragically – the prejudices against them in a highly patriarchal and hierarchical environment. Her questions about Church-dominated Irish society and the lack of emphasis on Irish patriotism in her works resulted in her being neglected by local critics. Her short stories and novels were evidently better received outside Ireland and have been translated into many languages.

Kate O'Brien was as prolific as Mary Lavin in her writings since the 1930s, and some of her works were censored in Ireland for dealing with "immoral" issues. Differently from Lavin, her questions about the puritanical ethos of mid-twentieth century Ireland were more striking and unrelenting, which kept her from being appreciated as a recognisable Irish writer; nor could she be placed in the canon. What should

Conclusion

be noted is that O'Brien not only thought ahead of her time about female autonomy, but she also had great concerns about the inadequate presence of women in the canon. Apart from illuminating in Chapter Seven how O'Brien's unconventional choice of subjects from homosexuality to anti-censorship made her an unacceptable writer in Ireland, this chapter has also demonstrated the writer's disappointment about the underestimation of women's writing in general. She, writing as a literary critic, had endeavoured to reassess the literary merits of women's diaries, as she believed that women had honestly recorded, by this means, their feelings, thoughts and imaginations at times when society greatly discouraged women from being outspoken and required them to be submissive. Her remarks about how women writers were under-represented in the canon or the literary forum of her time were a challenge to the male-privileged tradition. Being more than a novelist, she also worked as a historian who reappraised St Patrick's contribution towards Ireland, arguing that he might have been an overprized figure in Catholic terms. The questions and issues she raised in relation to the insularity of Irish life and literary phenomena were substantial for the reconstruction of canons. Nevertheless, not until the late 1970s were her works granted more accommodation by Irish critics. It might hence be safe to judge that she has, in one way or another, depicted a fuller understanding of Irishness – from a woman's viewpoint – without strictly conforming to Catholic moralism and Irish nationalism.

Bill Readings has argued in his article "Canon and on: From Concept to Figure" that the significance of canons lies in the social context in which they are valued. He contends that "[t]he literary canon does not contain value, it contains texts which in some sense demand to be read again, which are in that sense literary."[590] He also admits that when canons are studied as a matter of knowledge, they would be "indefensible against the claim that [their] inclusiveness must necessarily exclude someone."[591] This book, which discusses the selection of works in the making of Irish canons, has attempted not only to demonstrate how external forces have dominated the outcome of canonisation, but also to delineate the circumstances under which some literary works were praised as having greater value than others. The study of canon formation, as performed by this book, has served as a window through which one can observe the *zeitgeist* of different historical moments in Ireland.

---

[590] Readings, "Canon" 168.
[591] Readings, "Canon" 168.

Bibliography

Akenson, Donald Harman. *A Mirror to Kathleen's Face*. Montreal: McGill-Queen's UP. 1975.

Altbach, Philip G. "Education and Neocolonialism." *The Post-Colonial Studies Reader*. Ed. Bill Ashcroft, Gareth Griffiths, and Helen Tiffin. London: Routledge, 199. 452-56.

Altieri, Charles. "An Idea and Ideal of a Literary Canon." *Critical Inquiry* 10.1 (1983): 37-64.

Anyon, Jean. "Ideology and United States History Textbooks." *Harvard Educational Review* 49.3 (1979): 361-86.

Arnold, Matthew. *Culture and Anarchy*. 1869. Cambridge: The University Press, 1932.

Ashcroft, Bill. "Introduction to "Part XI: History." Ashcroft, Griffiths, and Tiffin 355-57.

Ashcroft, Bill, Gareth Griffiths, and Helen Tiffin. *The Postcolonial Studies Reader*. London: Routledge, 1995.

Bailey, Kenneth C. *A History of Trinity College Dublin 1892-1945*. Dublin: The University Press, 1947.

Bergonzi, Bernard. "Fictions of History." *The Contemporary English Novel*. Ed. Malcolm Bradbury and David Palmer. London: Edward Arnold, 1979. 42-65.

Binns, Ronald. *J.G. Farrell*. London: Methuen, 1986.

Birmingham, George A. Introduction. *Irish Short Stories*. Ed. Birmingham. London: Faber & Faber, 1932. 9-17.

Blanchard, Paul. *The Irish and Catholic Power: An American Interpretation*. Boston: Beacon, 1953.

Boland, Eavan. "The Legacy of Kate O'Brien." *With Warmest Love: Lectures for Kate O'Brien 1984-1993*. Ed. John Logan. Limerick: Mellick, 1994.

Boyce, D. George. "1916, Interpreting the Rising." *The Making of Modern Irish History: Revisionism and the Revisionist Controversy*. Ed. D. George Boyce and Alan O'Day. London: Routledge, 1997. 163-87.

Boyd, Ernest. *Ireland's Literary Renaissance*. 1916. Dublin: Figgis, 1968.

Boylan, Clare. "Ruralist Writer Who Shone amid Dublin's Bright Lights." *Guardian* 27 Mar. 1996: 15.

Breen, Mary. "Something Understood? Kate O'Brien and The Land of Spices." *Ordinary People Dancing: Essays on Kate O'Brien*. Ed. Eibhear Walshe. Cork: Cork UP, 1993. 167-90.

Bressler, Charles E. *Literary Criticism: An Introduction to Theory and Practice*. London: Prentice Hall, 1994.

Brown, Merele, E. "The Idea of Fiction as Fictive or Fictitious." *Stand* 15 (1973): 38-46.

Brown, Terence. *Ireland: A Social and Cultural History 1922-1985*. London: Fontana, 1985.
Bryk, Anthony S. *Catholic Schools and the Common Good*. Cambridge, Mass.: Harvard UP, 1993.
Burdeti, Francis. "Ireland Inspires Two Novelists." *Catholic Herald* 3 Dec. 1943: 3.
Cahalan, James. "James Plunkett: an Interview." *Irish Literary Supplement* 5 (1986): 9-12.
_____. "The Making of Strumpet City: James Plunkett's Historical Vision." *Eire-Ireland* 13.4 (1978): 81-100.
"Canon." *The Concise Oxford Dictionary of Current English*. 9th ed. 1995.
"Canon." *Easton's 1897 Bible Dictionary*. Ed. M.G. Easton. *ChristWeb*. 28 Oct. 2004 <http://www.christweb.com/cgi-bible/dictionary.pl?Word=canon&Define=Yes>.
Carey, James J. Introduction. *New Senior Prose: Matriculation and Leaving Certificate Prose*. Ed. by Carey. Dublin: M.H. Gill and Son, 1955. xi-xiii.
_____. *Exploring English 2: An Anthology of Prose for Intermediate Certificate*. Ed. Carey. Dublin: Gill and Son, 1967. iii-xi.
_____. Introduction. *Leaving Certificate Poetry: Interim Anthology*. Ed. Carey. Dublin: Educational Company of Ireland, 1969. 1-3.
Carleton, William. Preface to the First Series. *Tales and Stories of the Irish Peasantry*. Ed. D.J. O'Donoghue. Vol. 1. 1830. London: J.M. Dent, 1896. 5-6.
"Carleton, William." *Concise Oxford Companion to Irish Literature*. Ed. Robert Welch. 1996. Oxford: Oxford UP, 2000.
Carter, Paul. "Spatial History." Ashcroft, Griffiths, and Tiffin 375-77.
Clifford, James. "On Ethnographic Allegory." *Writing Culture: The Poetics and Politics of Ethnography*. Ed. James Clifford and George E. Marcus. Berkeley: U of California P, 1986. 98-122.
Coleman, Michael. "Representations of Americans and the Irish in Education Reports, 1850s-1920s." *Irish Historical Studies* 3.4 (2002): 33-51.
_____. "'Eyes Big as Bowls with Fear and Wonder': Children's Responses to the Irish Nation Schools, 1850-1922." *Proceedings of the Royal Irish Academy* 5 (1998): 177-202.
Collier, D.A. *Irish Without Worry for Everyone*. Dublin: House of Retreat, O.M.I, 1959.
Collins, John Churton. *The Study of English Literature: A Plea for its Recognition and Organization at the Universities*. London: Macmillan, 1891.
Conradi, Peter J. *Iris Murdoch: The Saint and the Artist*. London: Macmillan, 1986.
Coolahan, John. *Irish Education: Its History and Structure*. Dublin: Institute of Public Administration, 1981.
_____. "The Irish and Others in Irish Nineteenth-Century Textbooks." *The Imperial Curriculum: Racial Images and Education in the British Colonial Experience*. Ed. J.A. Mangan. London: Routledge, 1993. 54-63.

Bibliography

Corkery, Daniel. "The Ember." *The Hounds of Banba*. By Corkery. Cork: Talbot, 1920. 5-15.
Crane, Ralph J., and Jennifer Livett. Introduction. *Troubled Pleasures: The Fiction of J.G. Farrell*. Dublin: Four Courts, 1997. 5-18.
Cronin, John. Introduction. *Irish Fiction 1900-1940*. Belfast: Appletree, 1992. 11-21.
Cullen, Louis. *The Hidden Ireland: Reassessment of a Concept*. Mullingar: Lilliput, 1988.
Cullen, Mary. Introduction. *Girls Don't Do Honours: Irish Women in Education in the 19th and 20th Centuries*. Ed. Cullen. Dublin: Women's Education Bureau, 1987. 1-6.
Culler, Jonathan. *Structuralist Poetics: Structuralism, Linguistics and the Study of Literature*. London: Routledge and Kegan Paul, 1975.
Deane, Seamus. *Celtic Revivals*. 1985. Winston-Salem, North Carolina: Wake Forest, 1987.
____. Introduction. *The Field Day Anthology of Irish Writing*. Ed. Deane, et al. Derry: Field Day, 1991. 3 vols. 1: xix-xxvi.
____. "Mary Lavin." *The Irish Short Story*. Ed. Patrick Rafroidi and Terence Brown. Gerrards Cross: Colin Smythe, 1979. 237-47.
Devitt, John. "English for the Irish: Literature and the Post-Primary." *The Crane Bag Book of Studies* 6.1 (1982): 104-10.
Dickinson, A.K., P.J. Lee, and P.J Rogers. *Learning History*. London: Heinemann, 1984.
Donnelly, Mary E. "Mary Lavin." *Studies in Irish Literature*. CD-ROM. Westport CT: Greenwood Electronic Media, 1999.
Donoghue, Emma. "'Out of Order': Kate O'Brien's Lesbian Fictions." *Ordinary People Dancing: Essays on Kate O'Brien*. Ed. Eibhear Walshe. Cork: Cork UP, 1993. 36-58.
Durcan, Thomas Joseph. *History of Irish Education from 1800*. Bala: Dragon, 1972.
Eaglesham, E.J.R. *The Foundations of Twentieth Century Education in England*. London: Routledge, 1967.
"Eamon De Valera Quotations." *Apostles.com*. 4 Apr. 2003 <http://www.apostles.com/devalera.html>.
Ellmann, Richard. *James Joyce*. 1950. Oxford: Oxford UP, 1982.
Fanon, Frantz. "Algeria Unveiled." *A Dying Colonialism*. Trans. Haakon Chevalier. Harmondsworth: Penguin, 1970. 35-64.
____. *The Wretched of the Earth*. London: Penguin, 1990.
Farrell, J.G. *Troubles*. 1970. London: Cape, 1986.
Foster, R. F. "'We are All Revisionists Now.'" *Irish Review* 1.1 (1986): 1-5.
Friedlander, Saul. "Probing the Limits of Representation: The Holocaust Debate." Editor's introduction. Jenkins 384-86.
Gerstenberg, Donna. *Iris Murdoch*. Lewisburg: Bucknell UP, 1975.

Gibbons, Luke. "Challenging the Canon: Revisionism and Cultural Criticism." Deane et al., ed., *Field Day* 3: 561-68.
Goldstorm, J.M. *The Social Content of Education 1808-1870: A Study of the Working Class School Reader in England and Ireland*. Shannon: Irish UP, 1972.
Goodson, Ivor F. *The Making of Curriculum: Collected Essays*. London: Falmer, 1988.
Guillory, John. "Canonical and Non-Canonical: A Critique of the Current Debate." *ELH* 54.3 (1987): 487-527.
Gwynn, Stephen. *The Scholar's Treasury: A Book of Irish Poetry*. Dublin: The Education Company, 1927.
Hammerton, J.A. "The Irish Story-tellers." *The Masterpiece Library of Short Stories: Irish and Overseas*. Ed. Hammerton. 11 vols. Vol. 1 London: The Educational Book, 1923. 9-16.
____, ed. *The Masterpiece Library of Short Stories: Irish and Overseas*. 11 vols London: The Educational Book Company, 1923. Vol. 6.
Harmon, Maurice. "From Conversations with Mary Lavin." *Irish University Review* 27.2 (1997): 287-92.
Holmes, E.G. A. *What Is and What Might Be*. London: Constable 1912.
Horgan, John. "Education in the Republic of Ireland." *Education in Great Britain and Ireland: A Source Book*. Ed. Robert Bell, Gerald Fowler, and Ken Little. London: Routledge & Kegan, 1973. 35-41.
"Humor Offsets Structure Lack of Irish Novel." *Washington Post* 10 June 1945: 13.
Hyde, Douglas. "The Necessity for De-Anglicising Ireland." Deane et al., ed., *Field Day* 2: 527-33.
Igoe, W.J. "Novels Indoors and Outdoors." *Catholic Herald* 7 Dec. 1945: 3.
Inglis, Tom. *Moral Monopoly: The Rise and Fall of the Catholic Church in Modern Ireland*. Dublin: University College Dublin Press, 1998.
"Irish Eyes Unsmiling." *Times Literary Supplement* 13 Aug. 1964: 721.
"Irish Stories." *Catholic Times* 7 July 1944: 9.
Jenkins, Keith, ed. *The Postmodern History Reader*. London and New York: Routledge, 1997. 384-86.
Johnson, Daniel P. "Censorship and Publishing in Ireland in the 1930s and 40s." Diss. U of Ulster, 2001.
Johnston, Denis. "The Call to Arms." *Listener* 17 Mar. 1937. 8.
Joyce, James. "Gas from a Burner." *The Essential James Joyce*. 1948. Ed. Harry Levin. London: Johnathan Cape, 1952. 465-68.
____. *Letters of James Joyce*. 2 vols. Ed. Richard Ellmann. New York: Viking, 1966.
"James Joyce." *Concise Oxford Companion to Irish Literature*.
"Joyce Kilmer: FAQs and Fancies." *Rising Dove Fine Arts and Services*. 5 May 2003 <http:// www.risingdove.com/kilmer/FAQ.asp>.
Kaplan, Laurie. "Imagination and History." *JANSA Newsletter* 7.2 (2001): 24.

Bibliography

Kelly, A.A. Introduction. *Mary Lavin: Quiet Rebel.* Dublin: Wolfhound, 1980. 9-18.

Kermode, Frank. "The Canon." *The Literary Guide to the Bible.* Ed. Robert Alter and Frank Kermode. Cambridge, Mass.: Harvard UP, 1987. 602.

Kiberd, Declan. *Inventing Ireland: The Literature of the Modern Nation.* London: Vintage, 1996.

____. *Synge and the Irish Language.* 1973. 2nd ed. London: Macmillan, 1993.

____. "Story-Telling: The Gaelic Tradition." *The Irish Short Story.* Ed. Patrick Rafroidi and Terence Brown. Buckinghamshire, N. J.: Smythe, 1979.

Kilmer, Joyce. "Easter Week." *Main Street and Other Poems. Representative Poetry Online.* 14 July 2003 <http://eir.library.utoronto.ca/rpo/display/poem1148.html>.

Kilmer, Kenton. *Memories of My Father, Joyce Kilmer.* New Brunswick, NJ: Joyce Kilmer Centennial, 1993.

Laffan, Michael. "Insular Attitudes: The Revisionists and their Critics." *Revising the Rising.* Ed. Máirín Ní Dhonnchadha and Theo Dorgan. Derry: Field Day, 1991.

Langridge, David. *The Development of Geography Teaching in Irish Post-Primary Schools.* Diss. University College, Cork, 1973.

Lampe, David. Introduction. *Five Irish Writers.* Ed. Lampe. Dublin: Dedalus, 1990. 5-9.

Lavin, Mary. "A Fable." *Tales from Bective Bridge.* By Lavin. 1943. Dublin: Poolbeg, 1978.

____. "Conversations with Mary Lavin." Afterword. *Irish University Review: A Journal of Irish Studies* 9.1 (1979): 222-24.

____. "In the Middle of the Fields." Deane et al., ed., *Field Day* 2: 1201-08.

____. *Mary O'Grady.* 1950. London: Penguin, 1986.

____. "My Vocation." *Mary Lavin: Collected Stories.* Boston: Houghton Mifflin, 1971. 269-79.

____. *The House in Clewe Street.* 1945. London: Penguin, 1988.

____. Preface. *Selected Stories.* By Lavin. New York: Penguin, 1981. 3-7.

____. "The Patriot Son." *The Patriot Son and Other Stories.* By Lavin. London: Michael Joseph, 1956. 5-13.

____. "Sunday Brings Sunday." *Mary Lavin: Collected Stories.* By Lavin. Boston: Houghton Mifflin, 1971. 63-90.

Lebow, Richard Ned. *White Britain and Black Ireland: The Influence of Stereotypes on Colonial Policy.* Philadelphia: Institute for Study of Human Issues, 1976.

Lennon, Peter. "Adrift on the Flood." *Guardian* 12 Dec. 1991: 23.

Levenson, Leah. *The Four Seasons of Mary Lavin.* Dublin: Marino, 1998.

Lipking, Lawrence. "Aristotle's Sister: A Poetics of Abandonment." *Critical Inquiry* 10.1 (1983): 61-81.

Livingston, Paisley. "Justifying the Canon." *The Search for a New Alphabet: Literary Studies in a Changing World.* Ed. Herald Hendrix and Joost Kloek. Amsterdam: John Benjamins, 1996. 145-50.

Lloyd, David. Introduction. *Anomalous States: Irish Writing and the Post-Colonial Moment*. Durham: Duke UP, 1993. 1-12.

Lodge, David. *The Novelist at the Crossroads and Other Essays on Fiction and Criticism*. London: Routledge and K. Paul, 1971.

Luddy, Maria, ed. Introduction to "Part II: Education." *Women in Ireland 1800-1918: A Documentary History*. Cork: Cork UP, 1995. 89-92.

Lukács, George. *The Historical Novel*. Trans. Hannah and Stanley Mitchell. London: Merlin, 1962.

Lynch, Rachael Sealy. "'The Fabulous Female Form': The Deadly Erotics of the Male Gaze in Mary Lavin's *The House in Clewe Street*." *Twentieth Century Literature* 43.4 (1997): 326-38.

Lyons, F.S.L. *Culture and Anarchy in Ireland 1890-1939*. Oxford: Oxford UP, 1982.

____. *Ireland Since the Famine*. 1971. London: Fontana, 1973.

MacNamara, John. *Bilingualism and Primary Education: A Study of Irish Experience*. Edinburgh: Edinburgh UP, 1966

Madaus George F., and John Macnamara. *Public Examinations: A Study of the Irish Leaving Certificate*. Dublin: St. Patrick's College, 1970.

Mahon, Derek. "A Disused Shed in Co. Wexford." Deane et al., ed., *Field Day* 3: 1383-84.

McCabe, Edward. "Archbishop McCabe Opposes the Ladies' Land League." 1881. *Women in Ireland, 1800-1918: A Documentary History*. Ed. Maria Luddy. Cork: Cork UP. 262-263.

MacCurtain, Margaret, and Mary O'Dowd. Introduction. *Women in Early Modern Ireland*. Edinburgh: Edinburgh UP. 1991. 2-8.

MacDonagh, Thomas. *Literature in Ireland: Studies Irish and Anglo-Irish*. 1916. Tyone: Relay, 1996.

Meaney, Gerrdine. "Territory and Transgression: History, Nationality and Sexuality in Kate O'Brien's Fiction." *Irish Journal of Feminist Studies* 2.2 (1997): 77-92.

Meenan, James. *Centenary History of the Literary and Historical Society of University College Dublin 1855-1955*. Tralee: Kerryman, 1956.

Mercier, Vivian. "An Irish School of Criticism?" *Studies: An Irish Quarterly Review* 45.1 (1956): 84-87.

____. "Kate O'Brien." *Irish Writing* 1 (1946): 86-100.

McDowell R.B., and D.A. Webb. *Trinity College Dublin 1592-1952: An Academic History*. Cambridge: Cambridge UP, 1982.

McGahern, John. *The Dark*. 1965. London: Quartet, 1977.

Milne, Kenneth. "A Curriculum for Irish Education." *Education in Ireland: Now and the Future*. Cork: Mercier, 1970. 33-50.

McLeod, John. "J.G. Farrell (1935-1979)." *Literary Encyclopedia and Literary Dictionary*. 21 Apr. 2003 <http://www.litencyc.com/php/speople.php?rec=true&UID=1486>.

Bibliography

Moerbeek, Jozien. "Canons in Context." *The Search for a New Alphabet: Literary Studies in a Changing World.* Ed. Herald Hendrix and Joost Kloek. Amsterdam: John Benjamins, 1996. 187-91.

Montgomery, Michael. "The Lexicography of Hiberno-English." *Irish Studies: Working Papers* 93.3 (1993): 20-35.

MacPhail, Fiona. "Major and Majestic: J.G. Farrell's Troubles." Ed. Jacqueline Genet. *The Big House in Ireland: Reality and Representation.* Dingle: Brandon, 1991. 243-52.

Murphy, Catherine. "Mary Lavin: An Interview." *Irish University Review: A Journal of Irish Studies* 9.1 (1979): 207-24.

Mulhern, Francis. "A Nation, Yet Again: *The Field Day Anthology.*" *Radical Philosophy: A Journal of Socialist and Feminist Philosophy* 65.2 (1993): 22-29.

Murdoch, Iris. *The Red and the Green.* London: Penguin, 1965.

____. "The Sublime and the Good." *Chicago Review* 13.2 (1959): 42-55.

Murphy, Christina. *School Report: A Guide for Parents, Teachers and Students.* Dublin: Ward River, 1980.

O'Brien, Edward. Introduction. *The Best British Short Stories of 1930 with an Irish Supplement.* Ed. O'Brien. New York: Dodd, Medd, 1930. ix-xiii.

____. *Modern American Short Stories.* London: Jonathan Cape, 1932.

____. *The Best British Short Stories.* Boston: Houghton Mifflin, 1922.

____. *The Best British Short Stories of 1925: With an Irish Supplement.* Boston: Small, Maynard, 1925.

____. *The Best British Short Stories of 1926: With an Irish Supplement.* New York: Dodd Mead, 1926

____. *The Best British Short Stories of 1927: With an Irish Supplement.* New York: Dodd Mead, 1927.

____. *The Best British Short Stories of 1928: With an Irish and Colonial Supplement.* New York: Dodd Mead. 1928.

____. *The Best British Short Stories of 1930: With an Irish Supplement.* Ed. O'Brien. New York: Dodd, Mead, 1930.

____. *The Best British Short Stories 1933 and the Yearbook of the British, Irish, and Colonial Short Story.* Boston: Houghton Mifflin, 1933.

____. *The Best British Short Stories of 1939 & Yearbook of the British and Irish, and Colonial Short Story.* Boston: Houghton Mifflin, 1939.

____. *The Dance of the Machines.* New York: Macaulay, 1929.

____. *The Guest Book.* London: Arthur Barker, 1935.

____.*White Fountains.* Boston: Small, Maynard, 1917.

O'Brien, Kate. *As Music and Splendour.* London: Heinemann, 1958.

____. *Distinguished Villa: A Play in Three Acts.* London: Ernest Benn, 1926.

____. English Diaries and Journals. *Impressions of English Literature.* Ed. W.J. Turner. London: Collins, 1947.

____. "Irish Writers and Europe." *Hibernia* 29.3 (1965): 15.
____. "Imagination Prose by the Irish 1820-1970." *Myth and Reality in Irish Literature*. Ed. Joseph Ronsley. Ontario: Wilfrid Laurier UP, 1977.
____. *Mary Lavelle*. 1936. London: Virago, 1984.
____. "Memories of a Catholic Education: A Fragment from Kate O'Brien's Last Work." *The Stony Thursday Book* 7 (1981): 28-30.
____. *Pray for the Wanderer*. 1938. London: Penguin, 1951.
____. *The Land of Spices*. 1941. London: Virago, 1988.
O'Brien, Sharon. *Willa Cather: The Emerging Voice*. Oxford: Oxford University, 1987.
O'Connor, Anne V. "The Revolution in Girls' Secondary Education in Ireland 1860-1910." *Girls Don't Do Honours: Irish Women in Education in the 19th and 20th Centuries*. Ed. Mary Cullen. Dublin: Women's Education Bureau, 1987. 31-54.
O'Connor, Frank. *Guests of the Nation*. London: Macmillan, 1931.
____. "The Girl at the Gaol Gate." *A Review of English Literature* 1 (1960): 25-33.
____. *The Lonely Voice: A Study of the Short Story*. London: Macmillan, 1963.
O'Donoghue, Thomas A. *The Catholic Church and the Secondary School Curriculum in Ireland 1922-1962*. New York: Peter Lang, 1999.
Ó Drisceoil, Donal. *Censorship in Ireland: 1939-1945*. Cork: Cork UP, 1996.
O'Flaherty, Liam. *Red Barbara and Other Stories*. London: Dulau, 1928.
Ó Grualaoich, Gearóid. "Responding to the Rising." *Revising the Rising*. Ed. Máirín Ní Dhonnchadha and Theo Dorgan. Derry: Field Day, 1991. 58.
O'Leary, Philip. *The Prose Literature of the Gaelic Revival, 1881-1921*. Pennsylvania: Pennsylvania UP, 1994.
O'Toole, Fintan. "Fodder for an Irish Canon." *Guardian* 21 Nov. 1991: 24.
O'Toole, Michael. "The Art of Writing: Kate O'Brien's Journalism." *Ordinary People Dancing: Essays on Kate O'Brien*. Ed. Eibhear Walshe. Cork: Cork UP, 1993. 128-36.
Paseta, Senia. *Before the Revolution: Nationalism, Social Change, and Ireland's Catholic Elite, 1879-1922*. Cork: Cork UP, 1999.
Pearse, Patrick H. "By Way of Comment." *A Significant Irish Educationalist: The Educational Writings of P. H. Pearse*. Ed. Séamus Ó Buachalla. Dublin: Mercier, 1980. 324.
____. *The Murder Machine*. Dublin: Whelan, 1916.
____. "The Prospectus of Scoil Éanna 1909." *A Significant Irish Educationalist: The Educational Writings of P.H. Pearse*. Ed. Séamas Ó Buachalla. Dublin: Mercier, 1980. 317-47.
____. "St Enda's." *A Significant Irish Educationalist: The Educational Writings of P.H. Pearse*. Ed. Séamas Ó Buachalla. Dublin: Mercier, 1980. 345.
Peterson, Richard F. *Mary Lavin*. Boston: Twayne, 1978.

Bibliography

Prakash, Gyan. Introduction. *After Colonialism: Imperial Histories and Postcolonial Displacements*. Ed. Prakash. Princeton, N.J.: Princeton UP, 1994. 3-5.

Pritchett, V.S. Introduction. *Collected Stories*. By Mary Lavin. Boston: Houghton Mifflin, 1971. ix-xiii.

Plunkett, James. *Strumpet City*. London: Panther, 1969.

Quiller-Couch, Arthur. Introduction. *The Oxford Book of English Verse 1250-1900*. Ed. Quiller-Couch. 1900. Oxford: Clarendon, 1939.

Readings, Bill. "Canon and On: From Concept to Figure." *Journal of the American Academy of Religion* 57.1 (1989): 149-72.

Slattery. J.L. "Christian Brothers of Ireland." *The Catholic Encyclopedia*. 3 May 2003 <http://www.newadvent.org/cathen/03710b.htm>.

"Smalltown Ireland – Victorian Style." *Christian Science Monitor* 1 June 1945: 18.

Smyth, Gerry. *Decolonisation and Criticism: The Construction of Irish Literature*. London: Pluto, 1988.

Spear, Hilda D. "The Romantic Phase." *Iris Murdoch*. By Spear. London: Macmillan, 1995. 51-60.

Spivak, Gayatri Chakravorty. *In Other Worlds*. New York: Methuen, 1987.

Titley, E. Brian. *Church, State, and the Control of Schooling in Ireland 1900-1944*. Montreal: McGill-Queen's UP, 1983.

Thuente, Mary Helen. Foreword. *Representative Irish Tales*. Ed. W.B. Yeats. 1891. Buckinghamshire: Colin Smythe, 1991.

Vance, Norman. *Irish Literature: A Social History*. 1990. Dublin: Four Courts, 1999.

wa Thiong'o, Ngũgĩ. *Decolonising the Mind: The Politics of Language in African Literature*. London: James Currey, 1981.

Waller, A.R, and A.W. Ward, eds. *The Cambridge History of English Literature*. 18 vols. 1908 Cambridge: The UP, 1932.

Walshe, Eibhear. Introduction. *Ordinary People Dancing: Essays on Kate O'Brien*. Ed. Walshe. Cork: Cork UP, 1993.

Walsh, Lorcan. "Images of Women in Nineteenth Century Schoolbooks." *Irish Educational Studies* 4 (1984): 73-83.

Welch, Robert, ed. *Oxford Concise Companion to Irish Literature*. 2nd ed. Oxford: Oxford UP, 2000. 174-76.

White, Hayden. "Historical Emplotment and the Problem of Truth." Jenkins 392-96.

____. "The Politics of Historical Interpretation: Discipline and De-Sublimation." *Critical Inquiry* 9 (1982): 113-38.

Whyte, John H. *Church and State in Modern Ireland 1923-1970*. Dublin: Gill & Macmillan, 1971.

Woolf, Virginia. *A Room of One's Own*. 1928. London: St Albans, 1975.

Yeats, W.B. "Easter 1916." *Selected Poetry*. By Yeats. London Pan, 1974. 93.

____. Introduction. *Stories from Carleton*. By William Carleton. Ed. Yeats. London: Walter Scott, 1889. ix-xvii.

Irish Literary Canon

____. *Fairy and Folk Tales of the Irish Peasantry.* 1888. London: Walter Scott, 1903.
____. Preface. *A Book of Irish Verse: Selected from Modern Writers with an Introduction and Notes.* 1895. Ed. Yeats. 4th ed. London: Methuen, 1920. xiii-xv.
____. *Representative Irish Tales.* Ed. Yeats. 1891. Buckinghamshire: Colin Smythe, 1991.
____. "September 1913." *Selected Poetry.* By Yeats. London Pan, 1974. 55.
____. *The Letters of W. B. Yeats.* Ed. Allan Wade. London: Rupert Hart-Davis, 1954.
____. "The Twisting of the Rope." *The Masterpiece Library of Short Stories: Irish and Overseas.* Ed. J.A. Hammerton. 11 vols. Vol. 11. London: The Educational Book Company, 1923.
____. "The Twisting of the Rope and Hanrahan the Red." *W.B. Yeats: Short Fiction.* By Yeats. Ed. G. J. Watson. London: Penguin, 1995.

Textbooks and Anthologies

Anthology of English Poetry for Leaving Certificate. Ed. J.P. Dunleavy and P.J. Diggin. Dublin: Polens, 1969.
The Cabinet of Irish Literature: Selections from the Works of the Chief Poets, Orators, and Prose Writers of Ireland. Ed. Read, Charles A. Read and T. P. O'Connor. 4 vols. London: Gresham Publishing, 1878-1880.
Emerald Gems: Selected from the Poetry of "The Nation," "The Weekly News," and "Young Ireland." Dublin: T.D. Sullivan, 1885.
Field Day Anthology of Irish Writing. Ed. Seamus Deane. 3 vols. Derry: Field Day, 1991.
Field Day Anthology of Irish Writing: Irish Women's Writing and Tradition. Ed. Angela Burke, et al. 2 vols. Cork: Cork UP, 2002.
Helps for Students: Book Lore. Key to the Primary, Intermediate and Leaving Certificate Courses of the Department of Education, etc. 1936. Ed. William Joseph Maguire. Dublin: Browne & Nolan, 1936.
Intermediate History Notes: Irish and European. Ed. E.J. Hally. Dublin: Educational Company of Ireland, 1957.
Intermediate Irish History. Ed. E.J. Hally. Dublin: Educational Company of Ireland, 1969.
Intermediate Prose: A New Anthology Specially Compiled for the Intermediate Certificate Course. Ed. James J. Carey. Dublin: M.H. Gill and Son, 1941.
Investment in Education: Report of the Survey Team Appointed by the Minister for Education in October, 1962. Dublin: Stationery Office, 1965.
Irish Literature. Ed. Justin McCarthy, et al. Philadelphia: J.D. Morris, 1904.
Irish National Poems by Irish Priests. Ed. T.D. Sullivan. Dublin: M.H. Gill & Son, 1911.

Bibliography

Leaving Certificate Prose. Ed. H.L. Doak. Dublin: The Education Company of Ireland Limited, 1942.

Matriculation and Leaving Certificate Poetry. Ed. Roger J. McHugh. Dublin: Browne and Nolan, 1946.

New Encyclopaedia Britannica. London: Encyclopedia Britannica, 1987.

The New Spirit of the Nation. Ed. Martin MacDermott. London: T. Fisher Unwin, 1894.

Paddy's Resource: Being a Select Collection of Original and Modern Patriotic Songs, Toasts and Sentiments, Compiled for the Use of the People of Ireland. Belfast: Northern Star 1795.

Poems and Ballads of Young Ireland. Ed. W.B. Yeats and T.W. Rolleston. Dublin: M.H. Gill & Son, 1888.

The Queen's University of Belfast Calendars. Belfast: Queen's University at Belfast, 1932-1940.

Reading Book for the Use of Female Schools. Dublin: Commissioners of National Education in Ireland, 1846.

Reliques of Irish Jacobite Poetry. Ed. John O'Day. Dublin: S. Machan, 1844.

"Report of the Council of Education on the Function and the Curriculum of the Primary School, 1954." *Irish Educational Documents: A Selection of Extracts from Documents Relating to the History of Education from 1922 to 1991 in the Irish Free State and the Republic of Ireland.* Vol. 2. Ed. Aine Hyland and Kenneth Milne. Dublin: Church of Ireland College of Education, 1992.

Report of the Council of Education as Presented to the Minister for Education. Dublin: Stationery Office, 1960.

Reviews of National Policies for Education: Ireland. Paris: Organisation for Economic Co-Operation and Development, 1969.

Songs and Ballads of Young Ireland. Ed. Martin MacDermott. London: Downey, 1896.

Soundings: Leaving Certificate Poetry Interim Anthology. Ed. Augustine Martin. Dublin: Gill and Macmillan, 1969.

Story of University College Dublin 1883-1909. Ed. Fathers of the Society of Jesus. Dublin: Talbot, 1930.

The Scholar's Treasury: A Book of Irish Poetry. Ed. Stephen Lucius Gwynn. Dublin: Educational, 1927.

Tears of the Shamrock. Ed. David Marcus. London: Wolfe, 1972.

A Treasury of Irish Poetry in the English Tongue. Ed. S.A. Brooke and T.W. Rolleston. London: Smith, Elder, 1900.

Irish Literary Canon

Examination Papers of Trinity College, Dublin

Trinity College Dublin. The Dublin University Calendar 1930-1931. London: Longmans, 1930.

____. Autumn Entrance Examination Arts and Science: History and Geography. October, 1930.

____. Entrance Examination in Arts: History Geography. January 1930.

____. Entrance Examination in Arts for Medical School: History and Geography, Hilary Term, 1930.

____. Entrance Examination. Midsummer, 1930.

____. Examination for Training College Students: Irish and English Literature. Trinity Term, 1930.

____. Junior and School Exhibitions. Michaelmas Term, 1930.

____. Supplementary Examination for Training College Students: History of Irish and English Literature. Michaelmas Term, 1930.

____. Examination for Training College Students: History of Irish and English Literature. Trinity Term, 1930

____. Special B.A. Degree Examination. Trinity Term, 1934.

____. Supplemental B.A. Degree Examination. Trinity Term, 1934.

____. B.A. Degree Examination: English Literature. Hilary Term, 1936.

____. Special B.A. Degree Examination: History. Trinity Term, 1936.

____. Senior Sophisters Examination: English Literature. Hilary Term, 1936.

____. Entrance Examination: History and Geography. January, 1937.

____. TCD, Senior Sophisters Term Examination, Hilary Term, 1937.

____. Examination for Training College Students: English Literature. Trinity Term 1937.

____. Junior Sophister Term Examination: English. Hilary Term, 1937.

____. Entrance Scholarships and Junior Exhibitions. Trinity Term, 1938.

____. Senior Sophisters and Supplemental B.A. Degree Examination: History. Trinity Term, 1938.

Examination Papers of University College, Dublin

University College Dublin. Calendar for the Session 1931-39.

____. Autumn Examinations: M.A. Degree Examination. 1930.

____. Summer Examinations: English Literature – Honours. 1932.

____. Autumn Examination: MA Degree in English. 1932.

____. B.A. Degree Examination in National Economics of Ireland. 1932.

____. B.A. Degree Examination in Political Economy. 1932.

____. Summer Examinations: B.A. Degree Examination in English Literature – PASS. 1934.

Bibliography

____. Summer Examinations: The Dr. Henry Hutchinson Stewart Literary Scholarship Examination. 1934.

____. Summer Examinations – Honours: B.A. Degree in English Literature. 1934.

____. Summer Examinations – Pass: B.A. Degree Examination in English Literature. 1934.

____. Summer Examinations – Pass: B.A. Degree Examination in Modern Irish History. 1934.

____. Summer Examinations – Honours: First University Examination in Arts and Commerce. 1936.

____. Summer Examinations – Honours: First University Examination in Arts and Commerce, English. 1938.

Series Subscription

Please enter my subscription to the series **Studies in English Literatures**, ISSN 1614-4651, as follows:

- ❏ complete series   OR   ❏ English-language titles
-   ❏ German-language titles

starting with
- ❏ volume # 1
- ❏ volume # ___
  - ❏ please also include the following volumes: #___, ___, ___, ___, ___, ___,

___
- ❏ the next volume being published
  - ❏ please also include the following volumes: #___, ___, ___, ___, ___, ___,

___

- ❏ 1 copy per volume   OR   ❏ ___ copies per volume

Subscription within Germany:
You will receive every title on 1st publication at the regular bookseller's price incl. s & h and VAT.

Payment:
❏ Please bill me for every volume.
❏ Lastschriftverfahren: Ich/wir ermächtige(n) Sie hiermit widerruflich, den Rechnungsbetrag je Band von meinem/unserem folgendem Konto einzuziehen.

Kontoinhaber: _____ Kreditinstitut: _____
Kontonummer: _____ Bankleitzahl: _____

International Subscription:
Payment (incl. s & h and VAT) in advance for
- ❏ 10 volumes/copies (€ 319.80)   ❏ 20 volumes/copies (€ 599.80)
- ❏ 40 volumes/copies (€ 1,099.80)

Please send my books to:

NAME_____ DEPARTMENT_____
ADDRESS _____
POST/ZIP CODE_____ COUNTRY _____
TELEPHONE _____ EMAIL_____

date/signature_____

Please fax to: **0511 / 262 2201 (+49 511 262 2201)**
or mail to: *ibidem*-Verlag, Julius-Leber-Weg 11, D-30457 Hannover, Germany
or send an e-mail: ibidem@ibidem-verlag.de

ibidem-Verlag
Melchiorstr. 15
D-70439 Stuttgart

info@ibidem-verlag.de

www.ibidem-verlag.de
www.edition-noema.de
www.autorenbetreuung.de